Learn Linux in a Month of Lunches

STEVEN OVADIA

MANNING

SHELTER ISLAND

For online information and ordering of this and other Manning books, please visit
www.manning.com. The publisher offers discounts on this book when ordered in quantity.
For more information, please contact

>   Special Sales Department
>   Manning Publications Co.
>   20 Baldwin Road
>   PO Box 761
>   Shelter Island, NY 11964
>   Email: orders@manning.com

Manning Publications Co.   Development editor: Frances Lefkowitz
20 Baldwin Road   Technical development editor: Gary Park
PO Box 761   Copyeditor: Benjamin Berg
Shelter Island, NY 11964   Proofreader: Elizabeth Martin
                              Technical proofreader: Mayur Patil
                                         Typesetter: Marija Tudor
                                     Cover designer: Leslie Haimes

ISBN: 9781617293283
Printed in the United States of America
1 2 3 4 5 6 7 8 9 10 – EBM – 21 20 19 18 17 16

brief contents

contents

foreword

When I began tinkering with Linux and Fedora years ago, I needed more than a month to get my bearings. I didn't have a resource like this book by Steven Ovadia. Steve guides readers through Linux basics in a clear, systematic way, demystifying it for new users (and teaching experienced ones a thing or two as well). The book is thorough while remaining concise. It's clear, but never oversimplified. And it really stresses what makes open source such a powerful force. Linux isn't just for seasoned system administrators. It's for everyone. And Steve's book reminds us of that.

JIM WHITEHURST,
PRESIDENT AND CEO
RED HAT

preface

I first came to Linux through my father, who was very interested in Windows freeware and shareware in the 1990s. This was in the days before the internet, when everything happened through the postal mail. My dad would request catalogs and my sister and I would order games, most of which were free. In conversations about how and why people would make games available for free, my dad came to tell me about Linux, a cost-free operating system. Nothing came of the discussion, but a seed was planted.

When I was in college, I had a roommate who was also a Linux fan. It put Linux on my radar once again. After I became interested in using Linux myself, although in those days, I had to order installation CDs from an online store, because my dial-up connection was too slow to grab the installation files off the internet. Once the CDs came in the mail, it took me days to get things working.

Years later, I once again became interested in the state of Linux. I tried Ubuntu, which I had read was a very strong distribution. This time, the installation was much easier. The interface was much better; so much so I found I liked Ubuntu better than Windows. Linux let me choose how my desktop looked. Linux had lots of free software I could use. Linux was faster than Windows and worked better on my aging computer.

I dual-booted my laptop because I needed Windows for graduate school, but once I graduated, I replaced Windows with Ubuntu and never looked back.

This book is my way of sharing what I love about Linux. I enjoy using Linux and think it's a lot of fun, but beyond that, I think Linux is important. Linux gives us a level of control over our computers that isn't possible with other operating systems.

Linux lets us customize our workspaces in ways that make sense for us, rather than forcing us to use workspaces customized by Linux. And I believe that's the way things should be. Our computers work for us—we don't work for them.

As you read this book, I want you to learn to use Linux, but I also want you to become empowered by it. Linux is more than a tool. It's a way of thinking about your tools.

I hope by the end of *Learn Linux in a Month of Lunches*, you love and appreciate Linux as much as I do.

acknowledgments

This book, like Linux itself, was a collaboration among amazing people.

I can't thank Frances Lefkowitz, my editor, enough. She constantly pushed me to improve and clarify, but also to find my own voice. Working with her was like taking a writing seminar and I'm incredibly grateful I had the chance to work with her.

Greg Wild, also of Manning, saw (and sees) the potential of Linux for a wider audience. He worked with me to organize and conceptualize the book and those early meetings were very important in terms of shaping this book.

Of course, I'm grateful to everyone else at Manning who worked to get this book out. I extend my appreciation to the following reviewers whose suggestions were always welcome: Aditya Sharma, Arnaldo Ayala, Fabrizio Cucci, Gavin Baumanis, Jean-François Morin, László Hegedüs, Luke Greenleaf, Mayur Patil, Michel Klomp, Nick McGinness, Robert Walsh, Sau Fai Fong, Selcuk Beydilli, Shawn Bolan, and Terry Rickman. Thank you to the entire production team including copyeditor, Ben Berg; proofreader, Elizabeth Martin; my wonderfully calming production editor, David Novak; and all those operating behind the scenes. Everyone I worked with had only one goal—to create the best book possible.

This book began with a month-long professional leave from my academic librarian position to develop a book about Linux. I'm grateful to my union, the Professional Staff Congress, for negotiating that wonderful benefit.

I also owe a huge debt of thanks to Jim Whitehurst, who took time out of his busy schedule as President and CEO of Red Hat, to write a lovely foreword. I'm also grateful to Jim's colleague Bryan Behrenshausen, who was incredibly helpful in connecting Jim to this project.

ACKNOWLEDGMENTS xvii

This book might not have been published without the inspiration and support of Jennifer Poggiali. Her enthusiasm for this project, before I had a contract, was contagious. I think it also helped that I was trying to impress her by getting a book contract (and I suppose it worked—we're now dating).

Last, but not least, I'd like to thank the wonderful Linux community. It's amazing to think of all of the people who are collaborating across the globe to create robust, cost-free tools I used to write this book. And while technical people often have a reputation for being impatient, all of the people I reached out to for help with this project were gracious and kind.

For instance, I had Linux certification questions for chapter 23 and got wonderful, thoughtful responses from Niels Kobschaetzki, Aaron Toponce, Charles Profitt, and Peter Green.

Linux is a culture with a lot of traits, but the predominant one is generosity. This book is a product of that generosity.

about this book

This book came about because I saw that while there were lots of technical Linux books for people who work with servers, there was nothing to help people learn Linux for desktop work.

My goal is that by the end of this book, you'll be able to use Linux for your day-to-day system. Linux has gotten much better to work with as a desktop operating system. The interfaces are easier to work with and hardware is much more cooperative.

In fact, Linux gets better and better every year. But it's still not an easy thing to learn. And while there's lots of great help online, it varies in quality and in the level of technical ability required to understand and execute.

As you work through this book, I want you to feel as if I'm right there with you, explaining concepts and showing you how to do different things, from using the command line to customizing the look and feel of your entire system. I want to build up your technical skills, as well as your confidence in your ability to manage your own Linux system.

Part I of the book shows you how to get Linux up and running. You'll learn:

- What Linux is and how it works
- How to install Linux (it's not as hard as you think!)
- How to get to know your system
- How desktop environments work as well as how to use these new interfaces

Part II prepares you to use Linux for your home office. There you'll learn:

- How to install software, using both the command line and the GUI

- How to work with Linux productivity software to do things such as word processing and editing photos
- The beauty and convenience of text editors
- What the command line is and how to use it
- How to run Windows programs in Linux
- Tips to work effectively in Linux

Part III shows you how to be a home system admin. In that final section, you'll learn about:

- Package management
- Updating your operating system
- Linux security, including how to keep your system safe.
- Connecting to other computers
- Printing (a surprisingly interesting chapter!)
- Collaboration using version control

There are numerous "try-it-nows" throughout the book and labs at the end of some chapters. I encourage you to do them. The difference between reading about Linux and using it is huge. The hands-on work is what allows you to test yourself and to identify the potential challenges. The answers to the labs appear at the end of the book and online at www.manning.com/books/learn-linux-in-a-month-of-lunches. The only way to learn Linux is to use Linux.

Along the way, you'll also be asked to think about what you want out of your Linux system in terms of software, interfaces, and stability. Linux isn't only about learning commands and terminology. A big part of it is learning what you want out of your desktop computer. I'll help you to figure that out.

By the end of this book, you'll not only know how to use Linux, you'll also have a strong sense of how you want to use it. Linux seems intimidating, but as you'll learn over the next month, broken down into steps, it's a very manageable technology to learn and implement.

Author Online

Purchase of *Learn Linux in a Month of Lunches* includes free access to a private web forum run by Manning Publications where you can make comments about the book, ask technical questions, and receive help from the author and from other users. To access the forum and subscribe to it, point your web browser to www.manning.com/books/learn-linux-in-a-month-of-lunches. This page provides information on how to get on the forum once you are registered, what kind of help is available, and the rules of conduct on the forum.

Manning's commitment to our readers is to provide a venue where a meaningful dialog between individual readers and between readers and the author can take place. It is not a commitment to any specific amount of participation on the part of the author, whose contribution to the AO remains voluntary (and unpaid). We suggest you try asking the author some challenging questions lest his interest stray! The Author Online forum and the archives of previous discussions will be accessible from the publisher's website as long as the book is in print.

About the author

 Steven Ovadia is a professor and librarian at LaGuardia Community College, CUNY. He curates The Linux Setup (www.mylinuxrig.com), a large collection of interviews with desktop Linux users, and writes for assorted library science journals. He lives in Queens, NY. (Author photo by Michael Massenzio, © 2016 Ammerican Photography.)

Part 1

Getting Linux up and running

These first six chapters of *Learn Linux in a Month of Lunches* get you started using Linux. This section is designed to get you up to speed on what Linux is and get it running for you. Think of this section as your introduction to Linux, with an emphasis on getting you using it as quickly and as easily as possible. You'll learn

- What Linux is and how it works
- How to install Linux
- How to get to know your system
- How desktop environments work as well as how to use these new interfaces

Before you begin

1

When asked to name an operating system, most people probably come up with Windows and OS X. These are the two most commonly used desktop operating systems at home and at work. But Linux has always been around, less viewable than other operating systems. Linux powers many of the internet's servers and the Android mobile operating system. Linux is viable for desktop work as well, with people around the world using it for everything from word processing, to audio editing, to plain old web surfing.

While the common picture is of a systems administrator sitting in front of hundreds of terminal screens, typing feverishly into a command line, the reality is that most people can learn to use it for their day-to-day work. This book is designed for those interested in Linux. Some readers might walk away from this book with the skills and desire to move into something technical, like systems administration. Others might choose only to use Linux for their daily work. Both outcomes are great and both outcomes are possible because of the flexibility of Linux.

1.1 Why Linux matters

Our relationship with our computers is intimate. It's where many of us spend most of our time. You might consume content on a tablet, but if you're doing serious work, from editing photos to writing articles, you're probably doing it on a laptop or desktop. OS X and Windows are moving in a mobile direction, letting users interact with apps and icons via touch screens, but not necessarily supporting serious work or customizations. The ability to customize and to craft a personalized experience is where Linux shines.

Linux was developed by Linus Torvalds in the early 1990s. Torvalds, then a computer science graduate student, wanted the UNIX operating system on his computer and developed the Linux kernel (more about the kernel in chapter 2) as an alternative form of UNIX. There are different versions of UNIX—OS X is built on it, too. When Torvalds made Linux available, he did so with a permissive license, allowing anyone to download the underlying code and to change it.

Torvalds also allowed anyone to contribute code to the kernel, which is what makes Linux so flexible and customizable. People and corporations around the globe contribute to the project. This allows for all kinds of software development for Linux, since the underlying codebase is available to anyone, as opposed to Windows and OS X, which are distributed by corporations that only give access to the codebase to their employees.

Linux is an open ecosystem, and that openness allows for all kinds of software projects to emerge. For that reason, many choose to use it because it allows them to customize their workflow in a way that isn't possible with other operating systems. In fact, most Windows and OS X programs have some sort of Linux equivalent. And with the rise of cloud-based software (software that you interact with through a web browser), the underlying operating system is less and less important, in terms of software.

With Linux, you have a level of control over your system that is not technically possible with other operating systems. It's like the difference between driving a car with an automatic transmission versus a manual one. Users have a choice in terms of how their system looks, which programs they use for each task, and even how they interact with their system. Instead of conforming to the interface, Linux lets users choose their own path, which is why many people use it for their day-to-day desktop work. Linux allows users access to different desktop interfaces and lots of software, with much of it free.

I came to Linux out of frustration with Windows. Windows never did what I needed it to do, in terms of speed and in terms of moving around my computer. I had heard of Linux from a college roommate, and had played with it, but had never gone further than brief experimentation. Finally I reached a tipping point and decided to install Linux on my laptop next to Windows, giving me access to both operating systems. Suddenly my world made sense. I had a fast responsive system that worked the way I wanted it to. I could choose how my operating system behaved and I had access to a whole new world of software. This is a fairly typical Linux story and it might even be (or become) your story.

Linux isn't only about customizability, though. Some use Linux because it's free and because it runs well on older hardware. Others use it because they relate to the free and open software aesthetic.

1.2   Is this book for you?

Many people who are interested in Linux are seeking a career as a system administrator, working with servers. They're highly technical jobs and require a sophisticated skill set. This book is not designed for that audience, although if you are interested in a career as a system administrator, this book is certainly a solid first step. Instead, *Learn Linux in a Month of Lunches* is designed for users interested in transitioning to Linux. Maybe there's a small web server you'd like to run for yourself. Or maybe you'd like to run Linux on your home computer. Or maybe you're running it and you're not sure what to do next.

I believe that Linux is for everyone. Although it requires a certain degree of technical expertise, anyone who is interested in it can learn how to use it effectively as their day-to-day operating system. This opens up a world of software and workflow opportunities that make life a whole lot easier than it sometimes is with closed-source operating systems. Linux is used by everyone from artists to journalists to musicians to educators. In other words, it's useful for anyone who needs to use a computer to do their job. This book is for anyone looking to learn how to use Linux, whether it's to get more done at work, or as a path into system administration.

This book will show you, step-by-step, how to take advantage of Linux without requiring extensive technical or programming chops. It will explain the concepts and terminology of Linux and how to use the GUI, which is how most people use it. It will also show you how to use the command line, which is not as hard as it sounds. Linux can seem intimidating but working through this book should make you comfortable enough to use it full-time.

Also, this book isn't exhaustive. Linux is a huge topic that takes more than a month to master. My goal is to have you up and running with it at the end of the month. My hope is by the end of the month, you'll be primed to explore Linux even deeper.

1.3 Using this book

The idea behind *Learn Linux in a Month of Lunches* is that you read one chapter a day. You don't *have* to read it during lunch (I have no way to determine when you're reading it), but each chapter should take you around 40 minutes to read, with the remaining 20 minutes for either scarfing down your lunch or practicing what the chapter showed you. Try to work on just one chapter a day. Focus on it. Let your brain absorb it. Then, the next day, you'll be prepared for the next chapter, refreshed and ready to learn more.

1.3.1 The main chapters

The bulk of this book, chapters 2 through 23, represents most of the content that will help you to learn Linux. That means you should be able to get through this book in about a month, by working through a chapter a day. Try to stick to that schedule, really learning just one chapter a day and practicing what you learned. Try not to rush through multiple chapters in a day. And remember that not every chapter requires a full hour, which means some days you'll have extra time for practice (and eating), before going back to work.

The chapters comprise three parts:

- Part 1 teaches you how to get Linux running and how to interact with it
- Part 2 teaches you how to work with Linux as a user
- Part 3 teaches you how to maintain and administer your Linux system

1.3.2 Hands-on labs

Most of the main content chapters include a short lab for you to complete. You'll be given instructions, and perhaps a hint or two to guide you in the right direction. The answers may be found in the back of the book and online, at www.manning.com/books/learn-linux-in-a-month-of-lunches, but try your best to complete each lab without looking at them.

1.3.3   *Further exploration*

A few chapters in this book only skim some of the cool potential of Linux, and I'll end them with suggestions for how you might explore those parts of Linux on your own. I'll point out additional resources, including free stuff that you can use to expand your skill set as the need arises.

1.4   *Setting up your lab environment*

I'm going to talk about installing Linux in chapter 3 so for now, you don't have to do anything.

There are many different versions of Linux called *distributions*. Each distribution can use different desktop environments. This means that there's not a consistent look across Linux. Even two people using two different versions of Ubuntu might not see the same things on their screens. For the purposes of this book, I'm using Ubuntu 14.04. If you're very new to Linux, I recommend you use it, too. It's a long-term support release, meaning it will be updated until 2019. This means you won't have to worry about security updates for quite some time. Figure 1.1 shows what Ubuntu looks like by default.

If you prefer another distribution, or if you want to use a different version of Ubuntu, it's no problem for this book! Just be aware that some of my screenshots might look different than yours. Things might be in slightly different places. Some

Figure 1.1   The default Ubuntu 14.04 desktop. A good place to start if you haven't tried Linux before.

commands and programs might also be different on a different distribution. The beauty of Linux is the freedom it provides to its users, but the price is that people might experience it differently. As you work through the upcoming chapters, you'll see it's a small price to pay for a wonderfully powerful tool.

1.5 Online resources

I hope you'll find time to visit www.manning.com/books/learn-linux-in-a-month-of-lunches. It offers supplementary resources for this book:

- Example answers for each end-of-chapter lab
- Links to discussion forums, where you can ask questions or submit feedback about this book

I'm passionate about Linux and I love hearing about other people's passion for it. You're always welcome to reach out to me through Twitter (@steven_ovadia). I'd love to hear your feedback about what we might add to the book's website (www.manning.com/books/learn-linux-in-a-month-of-lunches) and perhaps even to future editions of this book. Also, if you're reading this book, you'll probably enjoy my site, My Linux Rig (www.mylinuxrig.com), which features weekly interviews with people about their Linux setups. Maybe you'll even submit yours!

1.6 Being immediately effective with Linux

My goal for the book is to make you immediately effective. As much as possible, I'll try to focus each chapter on something that you could use in your real Linux environment, right away. That means I'll sometimes gloss over some details in the beginning, but when necessary, I'll circle back and cover them at the right time. In many cases, I had to choose between hitting you with 20 pages of theory, or diving right in and accomplishing something without explaining all the nuances, caveats, and details. When those choices came along, I almost always chose to dive right in, with the goal of making you immediately effective. But all of those important details and nuances will still be explained at a different time in the book.

That's enough background. It's time to start being immediately effective. Your first lunch lesson awaits.

Getting to know Linux

The previous chapter was an introduction to this book, and now that introductions are out of the way we get to have fun learning Linux! This chapter will walk you through the concept of distributions and repositories. We talk about Linux as this monolithic concept, but it's actually several different types of structures built on one common core, the Linux kernel. At the end of today's lunch you'll understand all of that, allowing us to spend the rest of the book working with our specific systems.

2.1 Distributions

Distributions, or *distros*, are flavors of Linux. Distributions take the Linux kernel (I'll talk about the kernel in a minute) and build upon it, crafting an experience for the user, selecting certain software and making certain technical choices. This includes

- What software is included in that distribution's repositories (the equivalent of the Windows App Store or the iTunes store for Mac)
- The software versions available within those repositories
- How that software might be implemented on the user's system

What this means is that even though Linux is Linux, not all distributions are interchangeable. If you're using one distribution and want to switch to another, you can't simply flip a switch. Instead, you would need to completely install the new distribution. If you're running one distribution and want a piece of software that's in the repositories of another, you can't connect to another repository. And if you find a software package for one distribution online, you can't necessarily install it on your system.

Different distributions might look the same, but there are technical differences between them that prevent them from being interchangeable with each other. Distributions are ecosystems. The big advantage of Linux is that it's not a closed ecosystem. There's a lot of choice and flexibility in it, so if you don't like the default music player chosen by your distribution, removing it and replacing it with the one you like is trivial. If a piece of software you want isn't in the repositories, there's usually a way to install it.

Distributions also have personalities. Some distributions prefer to have the newest versions of software while others privilege stability. Some distributions strive to create a deliberate journey for the user, selecting certain software and implementing certain designs, with the goal of having users interact with the software in a certain way. Other distributions prefer to leave everything relatively stock, so that users can make their own choices about their systems. Choosing a distribution is a personal choice and most people find the one that's right for them by *distro-hopping*, the process of trying out different distributions, until, like Goldilocks, you find the one that's just right.

Free and open source software

You'll often hear the terms *free and open source software* used with Linux. This term means that anyone has access to the underlying code of Linux and that's what allows projects to grow quickly and efficiently. Instead of starting from scratch, free and open source projects use existing code and enhance it and change it in new ways. There are lots of other projects besides Linux that use a similar philosophy, which is often indicated with some kind of open license. For instance, Firefox is free and open source software. Anyone can download the code and change it, or make their own version of Firefox.

You'll often hear the term *free* with Linux. Within the community, members talk about "free as in beer," meaning cost-free, and "free as in freedom," meaning open source software. Not all cost-free software is open source and not all open source software is cost-free. Some companies make money by adding value to open source tools. For instance, WordPress, the blogging tool, is free and open source, but they offer paid hosting of the free software. Some people who use Linux for political reasons don't want to interact with closed, non-free formats. Other people want the ability to do things like watch YouTube videos, which can require proprietary software.

Not all Linux software is free and open source, though. Some companies make proprietary software for Linux, meaning that while the software runs on Linux systems, and is even found in repositories, the underlying code is not available nor visible. The most common example of this around Linux is Flash, software sometimes used to view videos within websites. But there are many more examples. Google's Chrome browser is not open source, but there is an open source version of the project called Chromium.

> **(continued)**
>
> If you came to Linux to support free and open source software and projects, these kinds of distinctions are important. But many people use Linux because it's customizable (in part because of the open source nature of so many of its components) and works well. And of course, many people come for practical reasons and wind up staying for political ones.

2.2   *Ubuntu*

Since we're working with Ubuntu (figure 2.1) in this book, let's spend a few moments talking about it as a distribution. Ubuntu's reputation is as a user-friendly distribution. It has a straightforward installation process, as you'll see in chapter 3, and it aims to make things easy for the user. However, the price for that ease is that Ubuntu makes a lot of decisions for the user, which some appreciate but some do not. As part of the ease-of-use, Ubuntu tends to have older, more stable versions of software but not necessarily the latest versions, which can sometimes be unstable and even break things within your system. Ubuntu has a concept called *long-term stable* release, LTS for short:

- LTS releases are supported for five years.
- Non-LTS releases are supported for nine months.

If you're looking to keep your desktop for a while, without needing to upgrade to a new version of Ubuntu, the LTS release, which we're using here, is the way to go.

Figure 2.1   The Ubuntu logo. Ubuntu is the distribution we'll be using for this book.

Ubuntu is based upon the Debian distribution. This is something else you'll notice with Linux distributions—they're often built upon other distributions. In the case of Ubuntu, the developers use Debian as the base and then add their own software and design decisions on top of it. Because no one owns Linux, this kind of collaboration is possible without complicated negotiations or contracts.

2.2.1   *Debian*

Debian (figure 2.2) is the distribution upon which Ubuntu is based. Debian strives for stability, with a philosophy of "release when ready." What this means is that new releases aren't tied to a specific calendar. Instead, the community will hold onto releases until they are considered to be stable enough to be live. A Debian desktop is shown in figure 2.3.

Figure 2.2   Image of the Debian logo. Ubuntu is based upon Debian.

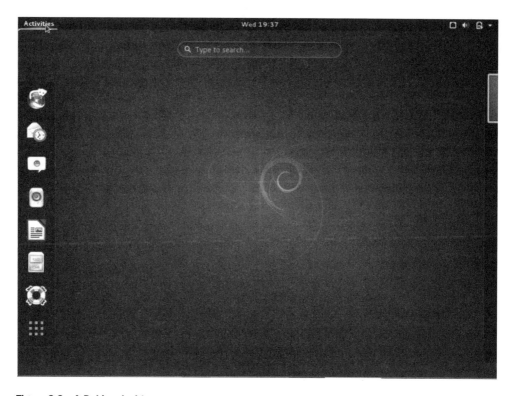

Figure 2.3 A Debian desktop.

Within the Linux world, you hear a lot of talk about stability. Stability is another word for predictability. It indicates software that is expected to run without any issues. Often, this means using older software, which has been more extensively tested than newer software. Because Linux is often used on servers, which are used for myriad important applications, stability is an important quality—often considered to be more important than newer versions of software. Stability is also an important quality for desktop Linux. You always want to be able to access and use your desktop system.

There are three versions of Debian:

- *Stable*—The current release
- *Testing*—Software versions being considered for Stable
- *Unstable*—Where developers work on Debian, testing software before placing it in the repositories of Testing and eventually Stable

Stable, as the name implies, is stable, but many people use Testing for their day-to-day work without incident. Debian also has more of a free and open source ethos, and while there are packages to help users view closed-source formats like Flash, it's not as baked into the installation process as it is in other distributions. It is for that reason that many people who use Linux for political reasons gravitate toward Debian.

2.2.2 *Fedora*

Fedora (figure 2.4) is the community version of Red Hat Enterprise Linux. Red Hat is a publicly traded company that sells its own version of Linux to corporations. Fedora is the cost-free version that allows it to test ideas and concepts. However, the Fedora project is led by a council, some of whom are elected by the community. This governance model exists in many free and open source projects and is particularly effective with Fedora, in that it maintains a balance in the project, preventing it from becoming another version of Red Hat.

Figure 2.4   The Fedora logo. Fedora is related to Red Hat Linux, but is a community-driven project.

Fedora tends to have more recent versions of software, and for that reason can sometimes be more challenging for new users to manage. Fedora comes out with a new version about once every 6 months, and supports each release for 13 months, meaning (in theory) you'll need to update your Fedora installation around once a year, although in practice, many people keep theirs longer. The Fedora desktop is shown in figure 2.5.

Figure 2.5   The Fedora desktop, which looks a lot like the Debian one (they use the same desktop manager)

2.2.3 *Linux Mint*

Linux Mint (figure 2.6) is another distribution that's considered friendly for beginners. Linux Mint is built upon Ubuntu, so if you're following along at home, it's two steps removed from Debian. There is a version of Linux Mint based upon Debian, Linux Mint Debian Edition, but for the most part, it's considered an Ubuntu variant.

Figure 2.6 The Linux Mint logo. Linux Mint is based on Ubuntu, which is based on Debian. Many distributions are connected like this.

Linux Mint is a great example of how distributions can vary based upon curatorial choices more than technical ones. Linux Mint has its own look, part of which is based upon desktop environment choices (see figure 2.7), some of which are based upon things like its color palette. It includes easy-to-install, non-free multimedia support, unlike Debian, but users get to decide if they want that kind of support. Non-free multimedia means proprietary formats, like Adobe Flash and MP3.

One final note about Linux Mint. While most distributions encourage users to update to the latest release, Linux Mint tells users to stay on a release that's working for them.

Figure 2.7 A Linux Mint desktop—one of its two default desktop environments

2.2.4   *Arch*

Arch (figure 2.8) is among the least user-friendly distributions, although people within the Arch community wouldn't describe it that way. The Arch philosophy is to give users complete control over their Linux desktop, from the software that's installed to how often it's updated. The price for that flexibility is that since the distribution isn't thinking about these things, the end-user needs to (figure 2.9).

Figure 2.8   The archlinux logo. Arch always has the latest versions of software, making it sometimes challenging to manage.

Arch is complex to install. It doesn't use the graphical installer seen in distributions like Fedora, Ubuntu, and Mint. Everything about Arch is well documented, but updates have been known to break systems. Within the Arch community, breakage is considered a good thing, as it helps users to learn about their system by figuring out how to fix them. But not everyone wants to know their system in that kind of detail. One of the things that makes Arch more volatile than other distri-

Figure 2.9   Arch doesn't have a default anything, so it can look like whatever the user wants it to.

butions is that it uses the latest versions of software. So just as Debian is valued for its stability, at a cost of using older but tried and trusted versions of software, Arch is valued for having the latest software, at a cost of stability.

2.2.5   *Other distributions*

There are lots of other distributions. Some are completely original projects, such as OpenSUSE. Others are variants built upon existing projects. For instance, you just read about how Ubuntu and Mint are variants of Debian. Manjaro Linux is a variant of Arch. Understanding variants is helpful in terms of finding a distribution that works for you. Table 2.1 compares the five distros we've mentioned here for stability and their open source ethos—the two points of comparison we've mentioned so far. You may like to keep a list of comparison points as you go through the book and expand this table for your own reference.

Table 2.1   Comparing distros for stability and open source ethos

Distribution	Stability	Open source ethos
Arch	Cutting-edge software	Completely up to the user
Debian	Debian Stable is stable; Testing has newer software.	Up to the user, but privileges free and open source ethos

Table 2.1   Comparing distros for stability and open source ethos

Distribution	Stability	Open source ethos
Fedora	Newer software, but relatively stable	No proprietary software by default
Mint	Established software	Includes some proprietary software
Ubuntu	Established software	Includes some proprietary software

Some people know they like Debian-based distributions, and knowing that helps you to find potential distributions. You'll also see variations of distributions based upon the desktop environment (I'll talk more about desktop environments in chapter 5). But for now, just be aware that when you see something like Lubuntu, it's a version of Ubuntu with a different interface on top.

2.3   *Choosing a distribution*

For the purposes of this book, we're using Ubuntu 14.04, so you haven't had much choice in terms of choosing your own distribution. But in a month you'll be finished with this book and you might want to try something other than Ubuntu. Choosing a distribution is personal, but there are some general things to think about. It's still early in learning about Linux to commit to a distribution, but it's not too early to think about what might work for you and your workflow. We'll explore a lot of the ideas discussed here in further detail, but for now, here are some things to consider about distributions:

- *Does the interface makes sense to you?* We'll talk about desktop environments in chapter 5 but for the most part, you can use the desktop environment you want with just about any distribution.
- *Think about software.* Do you want the most up-to-date versions of things or are you more concerned with keeping your system up and running? Arch will give you the most up-to-date software. Debian Stable uses older software, providing a more stable system. But for some, Debian Testing is a good compromise.
- *Consider your politics.* Are you coming to Linux to support free and open source software? Are you trying to avoid proprietary software? Distributions like Debian and Arch are, broadly, more supportive of that kind of usage, with no assumption that the user would want to work with proprietary software. Your politics could influence the distribution you choose.
- *Consider the community.* Every distribution has its own community. Which one feels right in terms of support and documentation? Arch is challenging but the documentation is spectacular. And because Ubuntu is such a common distribution, there is lots of help in the support forums.

Choosing a distribution isn't a lifetime commitment but it can be something of a time commitment—especially to someone new to Linux. Ubuntu 14.04 will serve you quite well for the next month but as we work through this book, I'll periodically ask you to reflect upon what parts of Linux will work best for you.

2.4   Repositories

Since we're talking about software, let's move into a quick overview of how software works with Linux. For the most part, you're downloading software out of a *repository* maintained by your distribution. You're rarely navigating to a website, downloading a program, and then installing it. A repository is a software collection. It's a single place where all of a distribution's software is kept. Think of it as an app store with a additional rules. If fact, one of the ways you can access the Ubuntu repositories is through an app store interface called the Ubuntu Software Center as shown in figure 2.10.

Figure 2.10   Ubuntu's app store looks like the one you might access on your phone.

In general, repositories have different versions of software. Some repositories tend to have newer versions of software; others might have older versions. Because software is always changing, there's no canonical version. Instead, the version of software you're using depends upon what's available in the repositories.

- Repositories are distribution-specific, so if something is in one distribution's repositories, it might not be in another's.
- Repositories are also version-specific, so if a piece of software is in the Ubuntu 12.04 repositories it might not be in the newer Ubuntu 14.04 one. This is what separates releases of the same distribution from each other.

Repositories are part of what make distributions different from each other. Software is added to repositories by people who work or volunteer for distributions. Most distributions try to do some kind of testing on software before it's added to or updated within repositories.

> **NOTE** When I say software, I'm not talking about programs only for humans, like Firefox. Repositories also handle security updates as well as updates to the Linux kernel.

We'll discuss repositories in more detail in chapter 17.

2.5 *The Linux kernel*

Linux is an operating system just like Windows, OS X, iOS, Android, and others. An operating system is what controls an entire device, from the hardware to the software, and at the heart of the operating system is the *kernel.* This controls the operating system, handling things like processes and memory. If an operating system were a person, then the kernel would be the brain.

Kernels are quite small—it's the graphical desktops and apps that take up all the space—and can be used on lots of devices besides desktops, laptops, and tablets. It's the same way you have an engine in your car, lawn mower, and scooter, but they're very different sizes—although they all work in the same way.

Operating systems and kernels aren't just the visible processes we see on our laptops and devices. They also operate in ways we can't see, controlling everything from appliances to medical devices. Many of these devices use the Linux kernel to run. We can't see how our TV is using the Linux kernel but it is.

The Linux we'll be working with is built upon the Linux kernel, but has lots of software added on top to make it useful for humans to interact with. The Linux kernel is the most basic level of our Linux operating systems. It's what makes Linux Linux. But lots of software is added to the basic kernel to make it something we can use for our day-to-day work, as shown in figure 2.11.

In the same way, a car is made up of lots of other parts besides the engine. However, just like a car won't work without an engine, your Linux desktop wouldn't work without the kernel. If we had a car engine in our garage, we couldn't do much with it. For it to be useful, we need to add things, like wheels, a

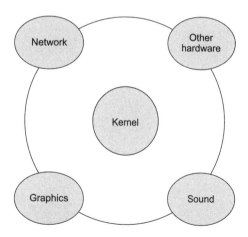

Figure 2.11 **The Linux kernel is at the heart of the operating system, coordinating how it looks, sounds, operates hardware, and communicates with other devices over a network and the internet.**

transmission, and a steering wheel. The Linux kernal is key, but it's not enough to write a document or play a game. You need to add other software to make it a desktop operating system.

> **NOTE** If you move into more technical fields, Linux might mean just the kernel. For the rest of this book, when I discuss Linux, I mean the kernel and the software added to the kernel that allows us, as humans, to interact with our machines.

2.6   *Wrapping up*

This lunchtime was spent learning about Linux in a conceptual way. Now that you understand distributions and repositories, you're beginning to get a sense of how your Linux system works. With that knowledge, you're ready to delve deeper into your system, which is what we'll do next time.

GLOSSARY OF TERMS

In this chapter I explained:

> *Distributions*—Flavors of Linux that take the Linux kernel and build upon it, crafting an experience for the user, selecting certain software and making certain technical choices.
> *Free and open source software*—Software that anyone has access to the underlying code.
> *Kernel*—The part of an operating system handling things like processes and memory.

2.7   *Lab*

We spent the bulk of this chapter talking about different distributions.

1 Which distributions would you choose if you wanted the most up-to-date versions of software?
2 Which distributions would you choose if you wanted proprietary software, like Flash, preinstalled?
3 Which version of Debian would you recommend to someone looking for something that's been well-tested?

Now I'm asking you to do your own research. Choose one of the distributions we discussed here and visit its website. Read up on one of the non-Ubuntu ones that sounds interesting to you. Then, go to DistroWatch (www.distrowatch.com), a website that tracks Linux distributions. Go to the Page Hit Rankings, which ranks distributions based upon visits to the DistroWatch page for each distribution. Explore one of the popular (according to DistroWatch) distributions that wasn't discussed here.

Installing Linux

Now that you have some background on Linux and distributions, you're ready to move on to the fun (and most intimidating) part—*installing it*! One thing that makes this less scary is that the installers have gotten much better each year. People who tried to install Linux years ago are often amazed at how much easier the process has gotten.

As I mentioned in chapter 1, we're going to be working with Ubuntu 14.04. Ubuntu is the distribution and 14.04 is the version. That means 14.04 has its own repository of software. As I mentioned before, 14.04 is a long-term support release, meaning the software in the repositories will be updated for five years.

I'm using a loose definition of the term "installation" here, too. I'm actually going to discuss three different ways to get Ubuntu running:

1 Write Linux to your local computer.
2 Run a *live image* that runs off of a DVD or USB drive without touching your local hard drive.
3 Run Linux in a virtual machine, which is like installing it in a computer within your computer. I'll discuss it more in the Lab section at the end.

The goal of this chapter is to get Ubuntu on your machine in some way. Don't worry if you install it and there are issues. Problems are chances to learn! As you work through the book, you'll learn how to address any imperfections you come across in this initial installation. So really, at the end of this chapter, you should be able to boot into Ubuntu. Nothing more and nothing less.

3.1   *Live vs. installation*

Which method should you choose? It's a personal choice.

The lab of this section is going to walk you through installing Ubuntu into a virtual machine. We'll talk more about virtualization in chapter 15. Installing Ubuntu into a virtual machine is a great option for learning Linux. You have your own Linux machine running within your existing operating system. It's the best of both worlds, in that you have convenient access to two operating systems.

The live image method is probably the safest installation option. It doesn't change your computer at all. However, depending upon how you set up your live environment, you might not be able to save files and settings, starting with a brand-new Ubuntu environment each time you boot up. It's not always convenient, but it should be fine for the purposes of this book.

Virtualization and live sessions are good options if you have only one computer, or if you have a computer you share with other people (and those other people aren't working through this book with you). They're both also great options if the computer you use isn't your own. For instance, if your employer provides you with a computer, it might not be well-received if you return it with a new operating system. Ubuntu can also be tricky to install on Apple hardware, so if you have an Apple machine you were considering wiping, you might want to work with a live image or virtual installation for now and move to a permanent installation after you've finished this book.

Installing over your existing operating system is a great option if you have a spare computer lying around. It's low-risk and it gives you easy access to a Linux computer. But then the question becomes whether to install Ubuntu over everything or to dual-boot your computer, leaving two operating systems. That too is a personal choice. If you have convenient access to another Windows machine and feel fairly confident about using Ubuntu regularly, I'd say to go for it and install Ubuntu over Windows, removing Windows from your system. It'll leave you with a machine with lots of space. Depending upon the size of your hard drive, having Ubuntu and another operating system together might not leave you with much space for other files. And it goes without saying that if you rely on operating system-specific software for certain tasks, and you're not aware of any Linux equivalents, you probably want to maintain a partition—a part of your hard drive that runs the other operating system, whatever it is.

3.2   *Creating a Linux boot image*

Installing Ubuntu begins by downloading the image from the Ubuntu website (www.ubuntu.com). An image is the full version of an operating system. You're looking to download the Ubuntu Desktop and not the Cloud or Server versions, which are not designed for desktop work. We're working with 14.04, even though there are newer versions. The 14.04 release is the best-supported one as I write this. You'll also have a choice of downloading the 32-bit version or the 64-bit version. If you're not sure which one your computer is, you can look at the system information of your computer within Windows via the Control Panel and within OS X under About This Mac.

After selecting the correct architecture, you'll be prompted to donate to Ubuntu, but you can skip that screen and download it free of charge (many distributions use the download areas to encourage donations to projects). Ubuntu will be a large .iso file. An .iso file is an image. Until now, when you've burned DVD and CDs, you've probably only worked with media files, meaning pictures and sounds, or both. But .iso files are different, so you can't burn them the way you burn a CD.

3.3   *Burn the image to DVD*

Once the file downloads, you'll need to burn it as an image. You'll need to do this whether you want to have a live Ubuntu session or you want to install it onto your hard drive. You'll either be burning it to a DVD or to a USB drive. If you're using a DVD, there should be a burn image option in whatever burning software you're using (OS X and some versions of Windows have a built-in image burner). If your Windows installation doesn't have a tool, ImgBurn (www.imgburn.com/) is a free option.

3.4   *Install the image to USB*

If you're going to use a USB drive, you'll need to download one more piece of software called Universal USB Installer. Download it from www.pendrivelinux.com and install it on your Windows computer. Once you've done that, insert your USB drive into your computer. It'll need to be at least 2 GB. Also, whatever you have on your USB drive will be erased, so make sure you don't have anything important on it. Universal USB Installer will basically ask you three questions: what distribution are you using (Ubuntu), where is the .iso file, and where is your USB drive? Figure 3.1 shows you

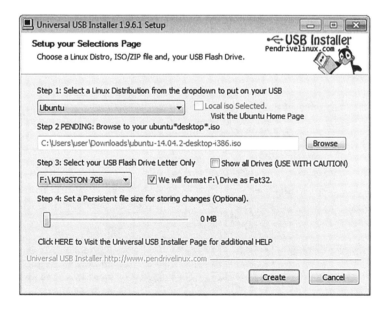

Figure 3.1
The interface of the
Universal USB installer

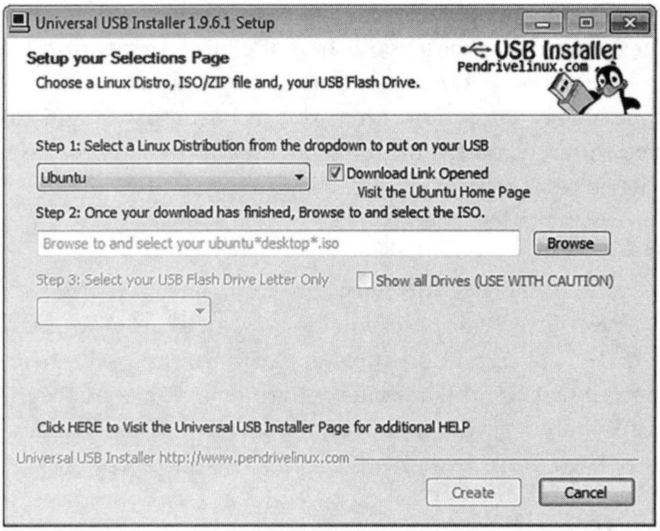

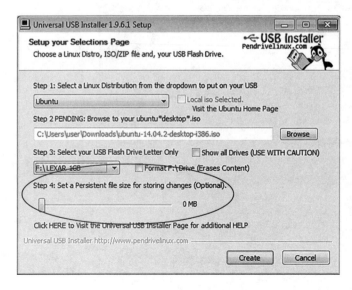

Figure 3.2   Universal USB Installer can download the Ubuntu image for you.

how it should look configured. You can also have it download the Ubuntu image for you automatically by clicking the Download Link Opened option (see figure 3.2).

You'll notice a Step 4 asking about a persistent file size for storage (figure 3.3). This option allows you to save changes you make to your installation (including files you save), so you're not always starting with a clean, unconfigured version. This is a good option, but there are some caveats:

- It doesn't work for every distribution (but it does work for Ubuntu).
- It requires a lot of USB space. I'd go with the maximum 4 GB, just to be sure.
- Not all settings are saved, but it's hard to predict which ones might not work.

Figure 3.3   Persistent storage allows you to save most of your customizations between logins.

Despite those potential issues, it's still a good option if you have a huge USB drive.

Once you've decided what you're doing and answered the questions, click the Create button and wait for the job to finish. Images are different than regular files, which is why they can't be dragged over to the USB drive the way you might do with an MP3 file. You need Universal USB Installer to format your USB drive in a way that your computer will recognize the file as an image.

After this, you're ready to go. Insert the USB or DVD and reboot your computer. Your computer should see the image and boot into whichever one you've inserted. If it doesn't, just reboot again, hitting F12 or Esc as your computer starts. That should give you a boot menu where you can manually select your boot drive. Your DVD drive will usually have the word DVD in its name and your USB drive will have whatever it was named. Manually choose that and you should boot into Ubuntu. Sometimes, for whatever reason, the boot doesn't take right away, so you might have to try it more than once.

Installing is much easier than it used to be, but it still requires some mental bandwidth. Make sure you give yourself time the first time you try it. Don't do it five minutes before your lunch break ends. Instead, give yourself a time buffer, so if anything does go wrong, you'll be better equipped to deal with the issue.

Give it a few moments and wait for the Welcome screen.

3.5 Boot from the image

Once Ubuntu boots, you have two choices: try Ubuntu or install Ubuntu, as shown in figure 3.4. If you just want to run a live session, click the Try button and you'll have full access to Ubuntu. However, anything you save won't be there next time, so don't

Figure 3.4   The opening Ubuntu screen. Here is where you choose to run it as a Live session or to install it.

spend too much time tweaking or configuring (unless you set up persistent storage). The nice thing about a live session is you can't break it. Whatever you do will be undone the next time you boot up. It's kind of like *Groundhog Day.* Try the live session for a while. It'll let you see how Ubuntu works with your hardware, although, in general, older hardware works better than newer hardware, since older hardware drivers are in the kernel, whereas newer ones often are not.

I understand that installing is a huge psychological barrier for many users. If you're not comfortable yet, it's fine to stick with a live session. Things will be a little slower, but it'll be the same experience. I want you to be relaxed and comfortable about moving to Linux, not scared and edgy. Trust takes time. We'll get there.

3.5.1 *Installation preparation*

If you're going to install Ubuntu, you'll click Install and see the preparation screen in figure 3.5. Ubuntu will make sure you have enough disk space. It'll also remind you to have your computer plugged in while it's installing, since a sudden power loss could wreck the installation. It'll also ask you if you want third-party software installed. We'll talk more about this in chapter 4, but for now, check the box unless you're opposed to proprietary software. Keep in mind that not having this installed could make it harder to do things like watch movies and listen to music, simply because you're not given a choice about this kind of software with Windows and OS X.

If you have an internet connection, you can have Ubuntu download updates while it installs, but it's not a big deal if you don't have a connection yet. Then, click Next.

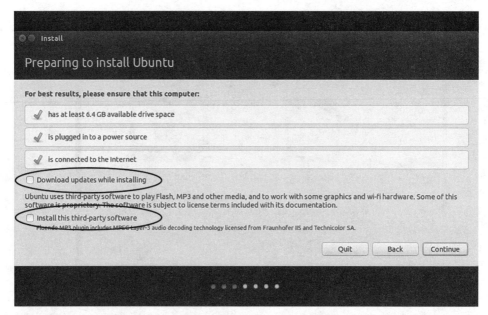

Figure 3.5   The installation preparation screen. Here is where Ubuntu recommends the best way to install it on your hard drive.

3.5.2   *Installation type*

On the next screen, Installation Type (figure 3.6), Ubuntu will ask you where you want to install it if you have more than one hard drive or more than one partition on a hard drive.

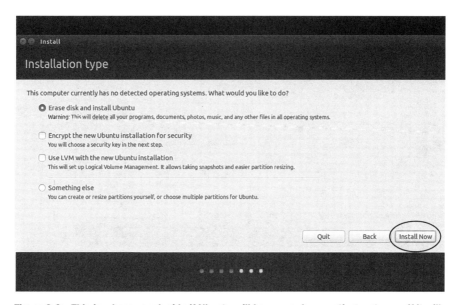

Figure 3.6   This is where you decide if Ubuntu will be your only operating system or if it will share space with another operating system.

You'll have to choose if you want to install it alongside your current operating system or to replace your current operating system.

If you're going to install it next to another operating system, it'll ask you to specify how big you want both systems to be. Ubuntu needs around 5 GB just to run. Windows takes up a lot of space, so don't make it too small—especially if you're going to keep using it. If you're just going to surf and write on your Ubuntu partition at first, I'd go for a 10 GB installation and leave the rest for the other operating system.

You can always resize the partitions later, or maybe even go back and remove your other operating system. Of course, if you're paving over that other operating system, you don't need to allocate space.

Also note on this screen that you can customize the installation if you do want to play with directory sizes. If you're reading this book, you probably don't want to do that right now, but eventually you might, so it's a nice option to remember.

This screen also has some questions about encrypting the installation and using LVM (logical volume management). We'll discuss these later, but the reality is that your first Linux installation isn't a long-term thing. You'll want to upgrade and explore other distributions, so while you may want to consider these options when you make more of a long-term commitment to a Linux distribution, I would ignore them for now and click Install Now.

3.5.3 *Where are you?*

The next screen (figure 3.7), Where Are You, will ask you to select your time zone.

Figure 3.7   One of the easier parts of the installation process—choosing your location.

3.5.4 *Keyboard layout*

The next screen (figure 3.8) asks you to choose your keyboard layout. There's a little typing area to make sure you select the right keyboard. You can also see if Ubuntu can detect it for you.

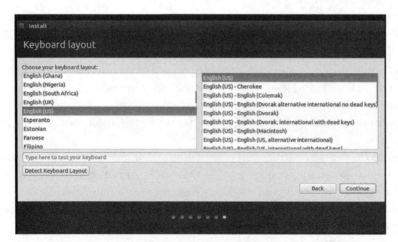

Figure 3.8   This is where you choose your keyboard layout, which generally depends upon where you're from or where you live.

3.5.5   *Who are you?*

The Who Are You? screen is next (figure 3.9). Enter your name (just a first name is fine), choose a name for your computer, give yourself a login name, and choose a password (and don't forget it!). I always require a password at login, so no one can access my files, but feel free to do what feels right for you. Encrypting your home folder, which is your personal folder with all of your personal files and configurations, is always a nice idea but you don't need to do that now for the reasons I discussed earlier. We'll talk more about security in chapter 19.

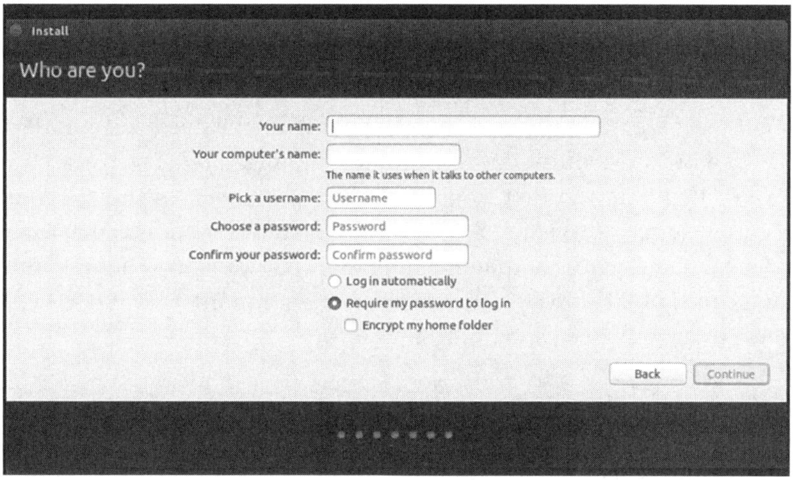

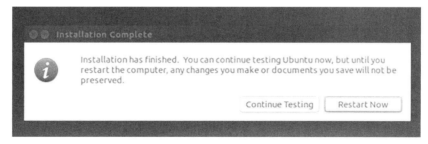

Figure 3.9   The screen where you tell Ubuntu who you are. Don't forget your password!

Click continue and you're done! Just wait for it to finish installing. You'll be prompted to restart the computer (see figure 3.10) and when it boots up again, it'll either boot into Ubuntu or into a screen giving you the option of booting into Ubuntu. Congratulations!

Figure 3.10   The final message you get before you boot into your newly installed Ubuntu system.

3.6   *Common issues*

The most common installation issue is a corrupt image. The corruption can take place at two stages—coming down from the Ubuntu site or getting moved onto your media (DVD or USB drive). To make sure your download isn't corrupted, you can use a checksum to verify the integrity of the file. You use a program to pull a letter/number combination out of the image. You then look up the number on the Ubuntu site. If the numbers match, you have the entire image. WinMD5Free (http://winmd5.com/) is one free Windows program that does this. Download it, install it, and direct it to your Ubuntu image. It will give you a hash, or code, which you can then look up on the Ubuntu site (just do a search for Ubuntu hashes). If the numbers match, there's no issue with your download, meaning the issue is probably with your DVD/USB and you should try burning the image again. And as I mentioned before, sometimes you just have to try the boot a few times before it "catches."

Another issue is getting the computer to boot from the correct drive. If your image isn't corrupt and you've burned it a few times, you might need to research your computer. I once had a laptop that would only boot from one of the USB ports, which never occurred to me as an issue! So there are tiny hardware quirks that can cause you to learn more about your computer than you might want to. The nice thing is that once you fix an issue like this, you never forget the solution! To this day, I check to see which USB ports my device can boot from.

For advanced users: Unified Extensible Firmware Interface

Another common issue is that some newer Windows computers use the Unified Extensible Firmware Interface (UEFI), which replaces BIOS, the software used to start your computer. If we go back to our car metaphor, BIOS (and now UEFI) are the keys turned to start everything up. If you run into this issue, the solution is usually to go into UEFI and disable any quick start/fast boot options. Windows has an advanced startup setting that gives you the option of booting into UEFI and disabling the option.

3.7   *Purchasing hardware with Linux installed*

Before this chapter concludes, I want to provide one other option for installing Linux: buying a computer with Linux already installed. Companies like Dell sell computers with Ubuntu already installed. There are also computer vendors who sell machines with Linux already installed. Most Linux users like these machines because it helps to support Linux and the Linux community, but also because it means the machines have hardware that works well with Linux (we'll get into this in the next chapter).

If you're interested in Linux, you're probably interested in tinkering with your machine—both hardware and software. But if that holds no appeal for you, consider purchasing something with Linux already installed. System76 (www.system76.com)

and ZaReason (www.zareason.com) are two of the more famous vendors in the Linux community.

3.8 *Wrapping up*

Now you know the difference between installing Linux and running it via live media. The following lab will walk you through installing Ubuntu into a virtual machine. And now you get to figure out which option is best for you!

If you depend upon a single machine, you might stick with the Live or virtual methods for now. But if you have an older computer lying around, or have multiple machines lying around (especially Windows ones, which are easier to install Linux on), then why not commit to a true installation? You can dual-boot, so you have a partition or you can put Ubuntu on your entire hard drive, which forces you—in a good way—to commit to using Linux.

GLOSSARY OF TERMS

In this chapter I explained:

Image—The full version of an operating system

Live session—Running an operating system off of media, like DVD or USB, rather than installing to a hard drive

NOTE These steps are very specific to Ubuntu 14.04, but they apply to most other distributions with a graphical installer. Basically, the installer is always asking you questions and you're answering. So even if these screens look different on Ubuntu 16.04 or 18.04, you should be able to use these steps to get it installed.

Some distributions, like Fedora and Debian, have a graphical installer that, though not identical to Ubuntu's, is conceptually similar. Others, like Arch, have a much more complicated installation process that's not as user-friendly. As you use Linux more, you'll get a sense of which kind of installation process works best for you.

3.9 *Lab*

You've read about the different ways to get Linux on your computer. Now choose one and do it! If you're installing Ubuntu onto your hard drive, you might not want to cram it into your lunch hour (this is the only lab where I'll say that), but otherwise, download Ubuntu, burn it, and you're all set to go. In order to practice installing it now, you're going to install Ubuntu in a virtual machine:

1 Download a virtualization tool. VirtualBox is free and available for Windows and OS X: https://www.virtualbox.org. Download and install it.

2 Download the Ubuntu .iso file, too. Make sure it's the 32-bit version.

3 Once you have VirtualBox installed, create a new machine by clicking the New button. A wizard will open. Name it Linux Lunches. Choose Linux for the Operating System and Ubuntu for the version and click Next.

4   VirtualBox will ask you for base memory size. The default is 512 MB. That should be fine for our purposes, although you can go higher if you have a machine with a lot of RAM.

5   For the virtual hard disk, create a new one and leave Start-up Disk checked. Then click Next.

6   For file type choose VDI and click next.

7   For storage details, choose Dynamically allocated and click Next.

8   For the size, VirtualBox should default to 8GB. That should be plenty for now. Click Next.

9   Review the summary, make sure it's correct, and then click Create. You now have a virtual computer on your computer.

10 To install Ubuntu, double click on the Linux Lunches virtual machine. A wizard will open.

11 Click Next.

12 For the media source, choose the Ubuntu .iso file you just downloaded.

13 Click Next and Start and install Ubuntu. When you're done, you'll have a virtual computer with Ubuntu on it.

Getting to know your system 4

Part of the fun of Linux is that you get to learn how your computer *really* works. After a while, you'll feel the same pleasure fixing your computer that you might feel completing a puzzle or finishing a big Lego project. It's much like the difference between driving a vehicle with a stick shift or one with automatic transmission. With the stick, you really feel like you know your vehicle. And after some time with Linux, you'll really feel like you know your computer.

It's tough when you bring your car to a mechanic and can only vaguely describe the problem, maybe making a sound or using imprecise terms to tell the mechanic what the issue might be. Linux is self-supported, in the sense that you—the user— are responsible for fixing any issues with the system. There's no support desk to call or email.

One of the tougher things for new Linux users to learn is that the better they can understand and describe their issue, the better the chances the issue will be fixed. This isn't to say that you need to learn to code to use Linux. It just means you need to learn a few basic processes that will help you understand where the problems with your system may lie.

Now that you've got Linux running, either live or installed, it's time to get to know your system, learning how the hardware and software work together to do your bidding! This chapter will help you with that process, teaching you how to identify all of the hardware your computer is using. I'll also talk about drivers, which help your operating system communicate with your hardware and codecs, which are used to make music and video playable on our computers. One way to think about it is that *drivers unlock hardware and codecs unlock audio and video*. If your drivers are working, then you know you just need to find the codec that will unlock that particular file.

31

Finally, I'll move into logs, which track what's happening with your system. By the end of this chapter, you'll have a clear picture of what's going on with your system, allowing you to find help if things aren't working exactly as you need them to.

4.1 Identifying hardware

When something isn't right with your system, it's a hardware issue, a software issue, or a combination of the two. If your Ubuntu laptop can't connect to your WiFi network, and the issue isn't with your network itself (please make sure the issue isn't something like your router is turned off!), then you need to figure out where the problem is.

- If the issue is with software, maybe it's not configured properly.
  - Or maybe the correct wireless software isn't installed.
- If the issue is with the hardware, maybe your laptop's wireless card is broken.
  - Or maybe it's not turned on.

But the most common issue, especially with a fresh Linux installation, is that your distribution is having trouble talking to your wireless card. Before we can fix it, we need to know what kind of wireless card your laptop has. While this might be in the manual for your laptop, or on the support website for your laptop's manufacturer, the reality is that laptops are often made up of different parts. Two of the same kinds of laptop might have different wireless cards, depending on when and where they were made.

Linux gives a relatively straightforward way to get this information. It involves our first trip into the command line, which we'll access via the terminal. We'll talk about this extensively in chapter 10. For now, just know the command line is another way to interact with your computer. Rather than using your mouse to click and open a program to give you system information, you're going to open your terminal, which will allow you to type commands directly to your computer. You're cutting out the graphical middle man.

To access the terminal, click the Ubuntu icon in the top left corner of your screen. A search bar will open and you can type the word `terminal` (see figure 4.1). You'll see the word Terminal open under Applications. Click the word or icon and the terminal will open.

Once in the terminal, type the command `lspci -v`. This command (see figure 4.2) will show you all of the hardware used in your system, from wireless cards to memory to graphics cards.

It's *not* easy to read, but if you scroll through the list, you can look for words like *network* or *802.1*, which usually denotes a wireless protocol. Reading through that section of the output, you can get the make and model of your wireless card. If you're having problems with it, you now have a more specific way to search for solutions. Rather than doing a search like *"wireless won't work in Ubuntu,"* which will bring up myriad issues across models, you can now search on your wireless card, which will only pull up information that will help your particular issue.

Figure 4.1   Typing the word `terminal` **will open up a terminal in Ubuntu.**

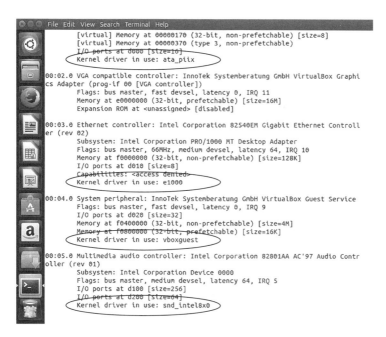

Figure 4.2   The `lspci` **command in your terminal**

You'll also see a line that says *Kernel driver in use*. We talked about the kernel in chapter 2 and how it's the most basic part of your system—the thing upon which everything else is built. But what's a driver? We'll cover that next.

4.2   *Drivers*

A driver is a piece of software that allows the Linux kernel to talk to your hardware. I pointed out the kernel driver line in the output of the lspci command. Drivers exist in all operating systems, but they're usually installed by the hardware manufacturer. In the case of Ubuntu, it automatically handles the installation of drivers, looking at what you have and installing what you need. But sometimes, the wrong drivers are installed, which is what causes technical issues.

Another issue with drivers is that not every hardware manufacturer makes drivers for Linux, which means the drivers sometimes need to be reverse-engineered. Companies that provide their own drivers tend to produce better results. This is why you sometimes see people advising against things like certain graphics cards for Linux systems—if the drivers aren't good, it's harder for the operating system to communicate with the hardware.

In a perfect world, you have your kernel in the middle of your system, trying to communicate with the various pieces of hardware around your computer—things like the graphics cards, the wireless card, and even your computer's motherboard. The drivers are the bridge between the kernel and these different pieces of hardware, as figure 4.3 illustrates. And again, this is how *all* computers work. But with Linux, the driver issue is more transparent, which makes it easier to fix any issues that emerge. One of the nice things about Linux is that it isn't just a way to run your computer—it also teaches about how your computer works.

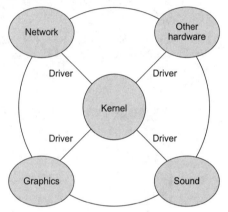

Figure 4.3   Drivers help the kernel communicate with your hardware.

If there are any issues with drivers, you already know how to see which drivers are controlling what hardware: use the lspci -v command, which includes not only the hardware, but also the driver interacting with the hardware. This is helpful for troubleshooting, in that you can research if there are known issues with certain drivers and certain pieces of hardware. Interestingly, but perhaps unsurprisingly, Linux tends to work better with older hardware, since the driver issues have already been worked out either with the distribution or with the kernel. Newer devices are more untested and can pose more complications.

One complication with drivers is that not all of them are open source. Some drivers are contributed to the kernel by the manufacturer, but the source code remains closed, making it harder to tweak them if there's a communication issue somewhere in the chain that's going from kernel to driver to hardware. As a result, you'll sometimes see a reference to *proprietary drivers*, meaning they are closed source and provided by the hardware manufacturer, and *open source drivers*, which are either reverse engineered by developers to interact with hardware or provided by the manufacturer with the underlying code available for anyone to modify and view. Depending upon the level of commitment to free and open source software, some users try to avoid proprietary drivers, while others choose the driver that works best for their software.

If your system doesn't have the best driver installed by default, there are a few options to install the correct one.

One is to research any issues with your current drivers and hardware. I give some places to begin your research at the end of this chapter. Fixing a driver is as simple as installing the correct one. It usually takes a minute or two. The `lspci -v` command gives you all of the information you need—your hardware and the driver associated with it. Then, some quick online searching should reveal the issue and the correct driver, which you'll learn how to install in chapter 7.

Most times the right driver is in the distribution's software repository and you can install it from there yourself. Sometimes you need to get the correct driver from a manufacturer's site. This is often the case with printer drivers, because there are so many different kinds of printers that it's hard for any operating system to keep track of all of the drivers. Printing on Linux will be discussed later in the book.

Some distributions offer automated driver management. For instance, you can ask Ubuntu to help you with your drivers.

Try it now: letting Ubuntu check your drivers

1 Click the top left icon and type `Software & Updates`
2 Click on the Additional Drivers tab

This will cause Ubuntu to look at the drivers on your machine and see if there are others that might be better. If your system is working fine, you can ignore this area. But if you are experiencing a challenge, this is a helpful area to explore. Often Ubuntu can find the drivers you need for you.

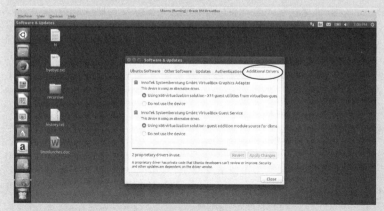

Ubuntu will look at your drivers and see if there's another one that might do the job for you.

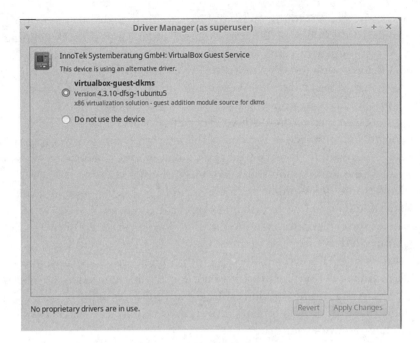

Figure 4.4   Linux Mint, which is based upon Ubuntu, will also automatically check your drivers for you.

Other distributions, like Linux Mint, also have a driver management component (see figure 4.4).

> **LINUX SOFTWARE AND FEATURES**   Different distributions have different features. Distributions like Ubuntu and Mint have a more automated driver management component, others do not. Different distributions have common elements and unique elements. To return to our car metaphor, if you learned how to drive on a 1995 Honda Civic, you should have no trouble driving a 2012 BMW Series 5. They're different cars, with different features, but conceptually they're the same. So if you're not using Ubuntu for this book, don't worry if you see software in Ubuntu that's not on your computer. With Linux, there are always multiple ways to approach a challenge.

This is all you need to know about drivers, though. They're like keys that unlock different pieces of hardware around your computer. Windows and OS X can handle drivers efficiently because they put their operating systems on specific hardware, so they know just which drivers to include. With Linux, you could be installing the operating system on just about any hardware, so the system needs to figure out which drivers to use.

The driver issue is serious enough that many people research hardware issues before installing Linux. This gives you a sense of potential driver challenges. The live installation method is also good for sussing out these kinds of driver issues. If your graphics card doesn't work in a live session, there's a good chance you have a driver issue.

4.3 Codecs

Codecs are another technology that operate in the background with most other operating systems but can become visible with Linux. Part of this is the role codecs perform—they encode and decode (hence the name codec—*enCODe\DECode*) audio and video. Most distributions install standard codecs by default. These are the codecs allowing you to do things like listen to MP3s and watch movies. Some distributions avoid installing codecs because of international software patent issues (different countries have different patent rules). Debian used to be one such distribution but it now includes a variety of multimedia codecs by default. But codecs still are not a straightforward process with Linux.

For example, you'll often hear about a multimedia framework called *GStreamer*. Most distributions have this installed by default. Some multimedia still won't work, despite GStreamer being installed. In certain cases, you'll need to install a collection of codecs called something like *gstreamer-ugly*. For instance, on Ubuntu, they're called *gstreamer1.0-plugins-ugly*, but on Arch, they're called *gst-plugins-ugly*. Different distributions call the codecs by slightly different names. You can install them via the package manager. You'll learn how to use that in chapter 7.

There are codecs that could present legal issues for the distribution, so the distributions make it available in a "don't ask, don't tell" kind of way, but don't install them by default.

The only time you have to think about codecs is if you're trying to do something with audio and/or visual content, and it's not working for you. If your drivers are working, then you know you just need to find the codec that will unlock the file format. Remember: Drivers unlock hardware and codecs unlock audio and video. Both work in the background—until they don't work, which is why it's useful to have a basic understanding of what they are.

4.4 Using log files

Think about when a plane crashes (not a pleasant thought, I know). What's one of the first things people ask about the crash? They always ask about the black box. The black box is a piece of equipment that records everything going on with the plane. The black box allows investigators to figure out what went wrong with a plane and why it crashed. Log files serve the same purpose. They record everything happening in the different systems on your computer, allowing you to see errors that might have gone unreported to you.

Log files aren't easy to read, but they often provide useful clues, in the form of error messages, when something isn't working on your system. A lot of times, if something is broken, you get a nice, useful error message which you can then go ahead and research online. What's tough is when something doesn't work and there's no error message to guide you. Log files are another way to get an error message you can research.

Log files aren't just a Linux feature. They exist on Windows and OS X and even on your phone. The issue is that they're not always accessible, or easily accessible, to the end-user. Sometimes they're buried deep within systems, almost impossible to find. They're also not the kind of thing most people know to look for. But once you're in the habit of looking at log files, you'll find it terribly frustrating to troubleshoot in systems that don't have them.

Ubuntu has a built-in tool to help you view logs. It's called *System Log*. To access it, click the Ubuntu icon in the top left corner and then type System Log. System Log will show you certain log files in a single interface (figure 4.5). The left navigation of System Log shows you the different log files you have access to. For example, syslog are messages from your system. Xorg.0.log are messages about your display software. These aren't necessarily failures—instead they record everything going on in a given system.

Event date and time   Event

Figure 4.5   The Ubuntu System Log tool makes logs *slightly* easier to work with.

The logs are a running list of everything that's happened. As you scroll down the list, events will get more recent. When you're in the logs, you're looking for a clue about what might have gone wrong. For instance, if your system suddenly rebooted on its own 10 minutes ago, you can go into the system log and look for any events that occurred around the time of the error. It's hard to say exactly what you're looking for, but you'll often know it when you see it (especially if you look for words like *failure* and *warning*). System Log is also searchable, via the magnifying glass icon. So if you have a suspect in what caused an error, you can search the log file for that term.

Log file names may change as systems and protocols change, but the concept remains the same: The log file is where your operating system reports what's going on. So even if the syslog disappears, which it could, there will be another log you can look at which will give you the same information. So don't worry too much about the names of the log files. Instead, think only about their role and their use.

System Log doesn't show you all of the logs you have available to you, but it lets you easily add more. To do that, click the sprocket icon on the top right and select Open. The file navigator will open in the directory where all of your log files are stored. You can add any and all into System Log. You can usually get a sense of what the log file monitors from its name. For example, kern.log contains messages related to the kernel.

As I mentioned, all of your log files are in a single directory. We'll talk more about the Linux directory structure in chapter 14, but for now, just know that if you navigate to the /var/log directory, you can see all of your log files and then open them with any text editor—they're just text files that can be read by a wide variety of programs. System Log is convenient, but it's not a universal piece of software, so if you migrate off of Ubuntu, you might want to be familiar with this method of seeing the various log files.

4.5 *Finding help*

Linux, for the most part, doesn't come with support. Especially not for just a single person (some companies, like Canonical, the company behind Ubuntu, offer support subscriptions, but they're targeted at small businesses and not individuals—home users). This can be scary to some users, but if you think about it, have you ever called Microsoft or Apple for support? Did they help you? Or did you search online until you either found your answer or learned to live with the problem?

As we've seen in this chapter, Linux gives us a lot of tools to understand why our system doesn't work. But of course, knowing the problem and knowing the answer are two very different things.

In terms of tracking down the answer, there are specific sites you can visit. Unix and Linux Stack Exchange is a great resource: http://unix.stackexchange.com/. It's a cost-free site where registered users can post questions and answers, with users voting on the quality of the responses. In order to vote on answers, you have to have a certain reputation within the Linux and Unix Stack Exchange community, with points earned for things like answering questions and making edits. But you don't even need an account to search it to see if your question has been asked before.

The Manning forums (https://forums.manning.com/) are also a great place to go for help.

Other distributions have their own on-site documentation and forums. It's usually prominent on the distribution home page, under something like community or support or help. However, because Ubuntu is so commonly used in the Linux community, there is lots of online support for it. Linux Mint is also popular, but because it's based upon Ubuntu, a lot of the Mint answers will apply to Ubuntu questions (and vice versa). Ubuntu's help area can be found at https://help.ubuntu.com/. You can also get help within Ubuntu by clicking the top left Ubuntu icon and searching on help.

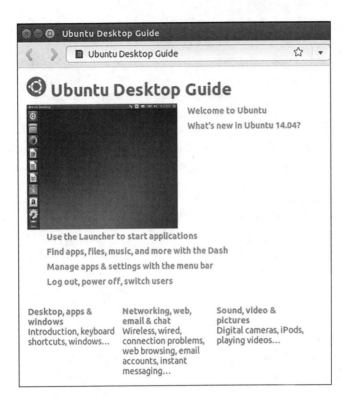

Figure 4.6   The Ubuntu Desktop Guide is a nice overview of your system but isn't great for detailed technical help.

This will bring up the Ubuntu Desktop Guide (see figure 4.6), which is a decent overview of Ubuntu, but it isn't going to get into the more technical issues you might be having with your system.

Ubuntu has its own official forums at http://ubuntuforums.org/ but it seems like more and more people go to Ask Ubuntu (http://askubuntu.com/), which is on the same platform as Unix and Linux Stack Exchange and works exactly the same way.

But before reading through sites and documentation, you might want to take a few minutes to do an internet search on your problem. If you're getting an error with your sound card, try a search on the sound card model and Ubuntu 14.04, which is our specific Ubuntu edition. If that doesn't work, broaden your search by dropping the 14.04 and if that doesn't work, replace Ubuntu with Linux. Go from the specific to the general. These searches will turn up information from places like Ask Ubuntu, but also will reveal blog posts and the forums of other distributions. Often, the distribution doesn't matter, so much as the answer. A configuration that will fix an issue on Fedora might also fix it on Ubuntu.

In general, the answers on the forums are well-intentioned, but be careful about running commands you don't understand. The wrong command can completely erase your system. I would hold off on that kind of troubleshooting until after you've completed this book. But in just a few chapters, you'll be able to look up commands, what they do, and how they work. Sites like Ask Ubuntu and Unix and Linux Stack

Exchange, which privilege more experienced users' advice, are also helpful in terms of evaluating the quality of the answer.

4.6 *Wrapping up*

The goal of this chapter was to familiarize you with the various components of your Linux system that are most likely to work (or not work) in unexpected ways for you. Now, you should feel ready to identify issues and then go and find your own solution online. The reality is that though there are plenty of Linux users who can read a log file and know exactly what the problem is and how to fix it, it's probably just as common to be a Linux user who finds the problem in the log and then needs to look online for answers. It doesn't matter how you get to the answer—just as long as you find it.

GLOSSARY OF TERMS

In this chapter I explained:

Codec—Software that encodes and decodes audio and video
Driver—A piece of software that allows the Linux kernel to talk to your hardware
Log files—Files that document everything happening in the different systems on your computer, allowing you to see errors that might have otherwise gone unreported to the end-user

4.7 *Lab*

Now it's time to get to know *your* hardware:

1 How would you find out what kind of wireless card you have on your computer?
2 Where do you find your computer's log files?
3 Go into your Additional Drivers area and see if there are any additional drivers for your system. If everything is working, leave the drivers alone, but if there are any problems with your system, see if the new drivers help.
4 Take a look at your syslog file. What's the last thing that it reported?
5 Using System Log, can you identify what the different log files are for in /var/log?

Desktop environments 5

The *desktop environment* (also sometimes called a *desktop manager*) concept is one of the more challenging parts of Linux to understand. Most users are familiar with Windows and OS X. Those operating systems only have one desktop interface. The user can tweak those desktops to a certain extent, but essentially you're stuck with whatever Apple or Microsoft has decided to do. Menus are always going to be in certain places and key combinations are going to be tied to specific tasks and programs. The user doesn't have a say in the design of their work environment, nor can they change it very much. And for the most part, users of these systems are conditioned to accept this limitation. This is often why you see people who haven't updated their systems in years—they like the existing interface and don't want to move onto something different. This could be the reason Windows XP managed to survive for 12 years (and why it's still seen out in the wild).

This freedom and flexibility to choose the interface is especially important to serious desktop users, who spend a fair amount of time in front of computers, doing serious work, from writing, to research, to communicating. Users of OS X and Windows have probably noticed those interfaces becoming more tablet-like, with icons and touch screens and apps. These are wonderful tools for users who are on tablets or phones, or for users who are using a laptop or desktop to consume content. But for those of us doing more than consuming content, these interfaces can feel overly simple and frustrating. Lots of Linux desktop environments, when mastered, will allow you to work more efficiently than is possible on a generic Windows or OS X interface. There is a learning curve with these desktops, but many find that the initial time investment at the beginning yields considerable productivity down the road.

Also, because many of us spend so much time in front of our computers, we want a certain degree of customizability, because our personal relationship with our computer becomes almost intimate. Just as most of us customize our offices or work space, whether with photos or furniture or paper placement, we also want the ability to create a computing environment that reflects our personal work style, from our menu locations to how programs are launched and displayed.

This chapter will explore GNOME, KDE, and Xfce, three of the most popular desktop environments. It will also discuss Unity, Ubuntu's default desktop environment (not to be confused with the Unity gaming engine, which is used to make video games; the two projects are unrelated). There are many other desktop environments, but those four are enough to get you started.

5.1 Desktop environments

The desktop environment is the look and feel of the GUI of an operating system. It has no equivalent in the worlds of OS X and Windows, since those operating systems have just one desktop environment each. It's fair to say that different versions of OS X and Windows might have different looks and different interfaces, but there's no way to get the Windows 7 interface on Windows 10.

As mentioned earlier, Linux is a kernel. It controls the operating system but the desktop environment is the look and feel of your system. In addition to smaller things like where the date and time are located on the interface, it controls things like how windows are presented. Other desktop environment elements include:

- *How windows are closed.* Is the close button on the top right? Or the top left? The desktop environment determines that.
- *Navigation elements.* Is there a dock? A taskbar? Where are they located?
- *How you move between applications.* What happens when you use Alt-Tab? Is it animated? Are there flat images?

Designers make choices about how they want the desktop environment to look and feel. The desktop environment is your experience on your computer. In the case of Windows and OS X, there is just the one desktop environment. Linux does not have this limitation.

No only do Linux interfaces tend to be more customizable, but users can even choose different desktop paradigms. For example, GNOME and Unity, which we'll discuss in a few minutes, don't rely on traditional navigation menus. Instead, they use launchers, which allow the user to type the name of the program they wish to launch. For many users, this is a new desktop model. With Linux, you can toggle between interfaces when you log in to your computer, meaning if you can't choose between two desktops, you can alternate between them, without having to reinstall software or copy files between two parts of your computer. Instead, it's simply a matter of logging out of one desktop environment and logging into a different one (see figure 5.1).

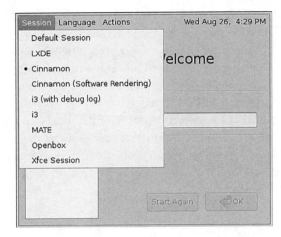

Figure 5.1   You can choose your desktop manager when you first log in to your computer.

Most distributions support multiple desktop environments so if you don't like the default, you can install a new one. For example, Debian gives users a choice of desktop environments upon installation, whereas Ubuntu installs Unity by default. If you want to install Ubuntu with a desktop environment other than Unity, you need to either choose a different flavor, like Xubuntu, which comes with the Xfce desktop environment, or install a new desktop environment from the software repositories. We'll cover installing a new desktop environment in chapter 7.

All Linux programs are usable with all Linux desktops, so you never have to worry about a program not working with a certain desktop environment. It's not like how Windows programs don't run within OS X. Your favorite program in Unity will be right there for you in Xfce. Different desktop environments have different default software choices, but with Linux, the end-user can always change those defaults, so they're really more recommendations than orders.

Now, we're going to talk about some specific desktop environments that are available for Linux.

5.2   GNOME

GNOME is a popular desktop environment, serving as the default for many distributions. The current version is known as GNOME 3, which distinguishes it from GNOME 2, which looked and operated very much like Windows XP.

5.2.1   Interface

GNOME 3 has a more contemporary look, using a launcher concept to open programs and file. Rather than using a menu to open a program, you type what you want to open in a launcher area, just like we do with Unity, which is what we've been using with Ubuntu. Conceptually, the GNOME interface will remind some of the OS X Spotlight utility or the Windows Start menu search, both of which can be used to find and launch files and applications. It will also probably remind you of Unity.

GNOME does not rely on menus the way you might be used to. For instance, with Windows, most users interact with the interface by using the bottom left-hand dock to navigate to the file they wish to open or the program they wish to launch (so much so, that the beloved Start menu was made more prominent in Windows 10). GNOME has a menu concept but mostly you're expected to open a launcher and type whatever it is you're looking for, or to choose an icon from the menu on the left, as seen in figure 5.2. You can also launch the menu with the Windows key, without having to click anything (the Windows key is also referred to as the *Meta key* or the *Super key*). Some users find this launcher wildly convenient, as programs and files can easily be opened without fingers needing to come off of the keyboard. But some users find it tremendously frustrating, preferring to navigate menus to find and launch files.

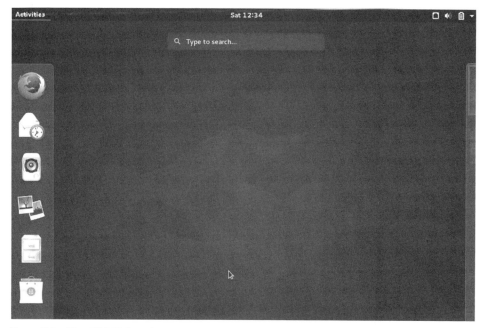

Figure 5.2   The GNOME launcher area is sparse. You type what you're looking for and the desktop environment finds it for you.

GNOME, like most Linux desktop environments and OS X, has a multiple desktop concept, where users can have different programs open in different desktops, almost as if they're working on multiple machines, but within the confines of a single monitor. This kind of functionality is especially suited to desktop work, which often has users toggling between graphical programs. Some use Alt-Tab to toggle between windows and programs, but for users trying to keep things separate, multiple desktops allow a word processor to be open in one desktop and a web browser and PDF reader to be open in another, with the user toggling between desktops instead of programs. This workflow allows some programs to display full-screen in one workspace and a group of programs to share the same window in another.

Many computer users make considerable use of their desktop, using it to hold files and icons. GNOME has a desktop file path but the desktop itself doesn't display files by default. Some users find this confusing. Others appreciate the clean look it gives their computer. Files saved on the desktop are always available through the file manager, but users accustomed to navigating to their desktop to open files and folders might need to tweak this particular default by installing *GNOME Tweak Tool*, a program that lets you easily change certain GNOME settings from a GUI.

5.2.2 *Customizing*

GNOME is also interesting in that, despite this chapter's introductory statements, it's not very configurable on its own. However, there are many extensions that can customize the GNOME interface. Interestingly, these are accessed via a web browser, rather than a settings menu as many might expect. The list of extensions available is at https://extensions.gnome.org/. Users find the extension they want and activate it from the browser and the change is made within GNOME (see figure 5.3). This allows you to customize everything, like adding a more traditional menu to launch applications, or changing GNOME's default Alt-Tab behavior, which doesn't cycle between windows the same way most other operating systems and desktop environments do. The extensions are sorted by popularity, letting new GNOME users get a sense of what can be done to tweak the interface.

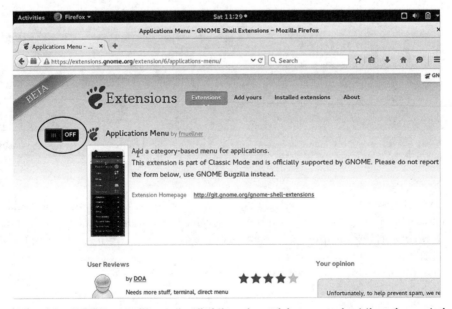

Figure 5.3   GNOME extensions are handled through a web browser and not through a control panel, as in most other desktop environments.

5.2.3 Software

While GNOME is a desktop environment, the developers behind the project are also developing software to go along with the desktop. These projects include gedit, the text editor; Epiphany, the web browser; and Notes, a note-writing application. These programs work across desktop environments but are designed to integrate with the GNOME look and feel.

GNOME feels different than a traditional desktop, but once you adapt to the concept behind it—that you're not searching through menus so much as you're summoning programs and files—you might find it hard to go back to a more traditional desktop.

5.3 KDE

KDE, originally short for the K Desktop Environment, is the other popular Linux desktop environment. Technically, the desktop is KDE Plasma, with KDE the larger project that creates applications in addition to Plasma. But colloquially, most people refer to KDE Plasma as KDE.

5.3.1 Interface

KDE uses traditional menus but also has a launcher. The interface should feel fairly familiar to most users. What makes KDE notable, and popular, is that just about every part of it can be customized, so it can look however you want it to.

Because KDE is a bit complicated, the distribution you choose is more significant than with other desktop environments. The better pre-configured KDE is, the easier it is to work with—especially for a newer user. OpenSUSE, for example, is known as a KDE-friendly distribution. Netrunner is also considered to be a strong KDE implementation. Ubuntu has a version using the KDE desktop called Kubuntu. Linux Mint also has a KDE version.

Beginning with a more curated version of KDE, with pre-configured options and functionality, will allow a new user to get a sense of what is possible with it, which makes things easier for new users. Working with a stock KDE environment, as one might in something like Arch, can be challenging for even experienced KDE users, since users don't have a strong sense of everything that is possible with the desktop environment.

5.3.2 Customizing

Power desktop users would probably be most interested in KDE's *Activities* functionality, which allows you to configure different desktops for different kinds of tasks. So you might have a writing activity that includes desktop shortcuts to a word processor and a citation manager. There might also be a research activity with shortcuts to a web browser and a PDF reader. Someone working with data might have a data activity that has an open data folder and a shortcut to the R statistical tool.

Activities are like virtual desktops, but with software and folders pre-selected based on how the desktop is used. For most users, especially less technical ones, who probably spend most of their computer time in a web browser, and perhaps, in an email client, the concept seems to be overkill. But for anyone looking to really tweak their desktop experience, especially if their desktop work is complicated, activities have major potential.

Let's say I want to set up an activity for writing. The activity will give me a desktop with my writing folder open and a shortcut to my word processor.

1   First, I'll click New Activity in the top-right corner, and then I'll click Activities (see figure 5.4).
2   Then, click on the wrench to name the activity (see figure 5.5).

Figure 5.4   KDE allows you to set up your desktop in different ways for different types of work.

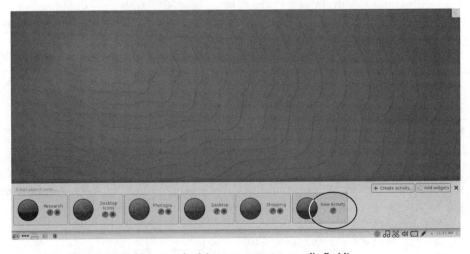

Figure 5.5   Give your activity a meaningful name so you can easily find it.

3 Finally, set up your desktop. Figure 5.6 shows my KDE writing activity.

4 To switch to another activity, click on the top-right corner again and click Activities again (see figure 5.7).

5 Finally, click on the new activity you wish to launch (see figure 5.8).

You'll now see a new desktop, configured for your new task (see figure 5.9).

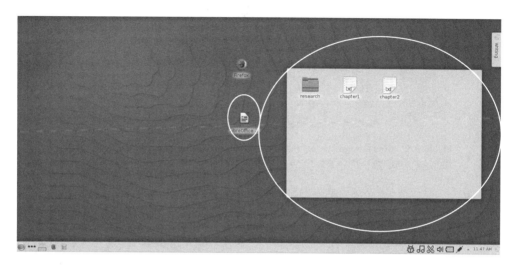

Figure 5.6   This activity has a folder open and a shortcut to a word processor.

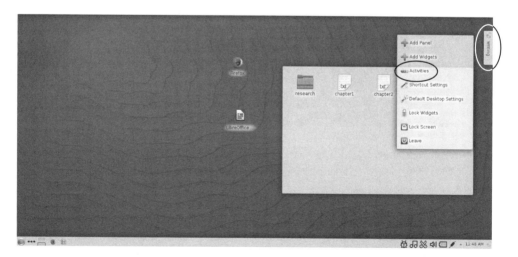

Figure 5.7   Click on your activity name to return to the Activities menu.

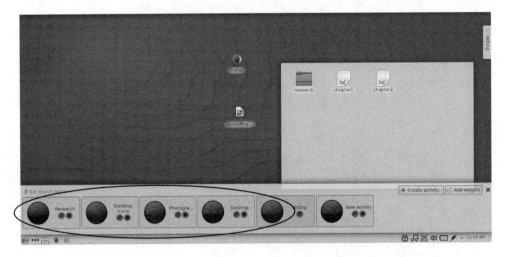

Figure 5.8   Group programs and folders together as Activities and then move between activities rather than opening and closing programs.

Figure 5.9   Switching to a new activity gives you a whole new desktop with different folders and shortcuts.

Most Linux desktop projects undergo major redesigns at some point. KDE has had some serious overhauls over its lifetime and not all users have appreciated the new direction. (I'm not sure there's ever been a desktop environment redesign that's been universally loved by all users.) Luckily for those unhappy KDE users, there are projects designed to capture earlier versions of KDE. KDE is currently at version 5 but the

Trinity Desktop is based upon KDE 3. Most new Linux users probably would not be interested in Trinity, but it serves as a reminder that Linux desktops never truly disappear. Instead they often live on in the form of smaller, niche projects.

5.3.3   *Software*

As mentioned previously, Linux applications run across all desktop environments. But KDE has its own set of applications, which tend to start with the letter K. So Kate is the default KDE text editor and KRunner is the default KDE application launcher. KDE even has its own web browser, called Konqueror (see figure 5.10). This is not to say any of those programs won't successfully work for GNOME. It just means KDE has its own software ecosystems.

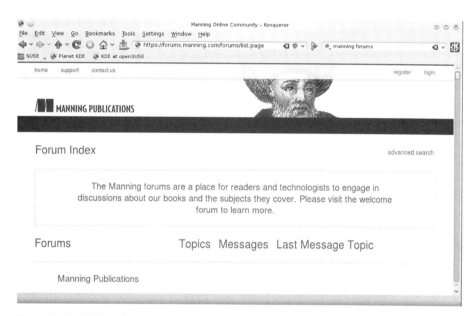

Figure 5.10   KDE has its own web browser called Konqueror.

KDE, more than any of the desktops discussed in this chapter, simply clicks for some people and not for others. Some users, even new ones, try KDE and instantly become enamored of all of the configuration options and are happy to spend time and energy getting their desktop just right. Others find the process frustrating, wishing that so many decisions were not left up to the user. It is sort of the flip side of GNOME, which is customizable, but not in an obvious way. KDE is, perhaps to some, overly customizable. But for users who want to have a very personal, focused desktop experience, there is perhaps no better desktop environment.

5.4   Unity

Unity is specific to Ubuntu, serving as that distribution's default desktop environment. It is based upon GNOME 3 and in truth, looks and behaves remarkably similar. When Unity was first launched, it was a little buggy, as early software often is. Many in the Linux community resented Canonical, the company behind Ubuntu, for not working with GNOME directly, as Ubuntu previously had with other releases. However, Unity has steadily improved over time, although there is still some resentment in the Linux community.

Unity is most closely associated with Ubuntu but some distributions have ways to install it. Arch Linux, for instance, has Unity within its repositories.

5.4.1   Interface

The main thing that separates Unity from GNOME is the Lens/Scope concept. *Lenses* are similar to the GNOME application launcher, but can be restricted to search certain kinds of content, from music, to Google Books, to the web, to shopping sites, to text. Lenses are ways to restrict your search within the Unity dashboard area, or Dash, in the parlance of Unity. The *scopes* are the content being searched by the lens. This kind of functionality has implications for focused users, who might wish to search files and collections without necessarily navigating into folders or to web sites.

You can see what scopes and lenses are available by using the Filter Results button on the Unity Dash (see figure 5.11). This lets you choose sources to search when you

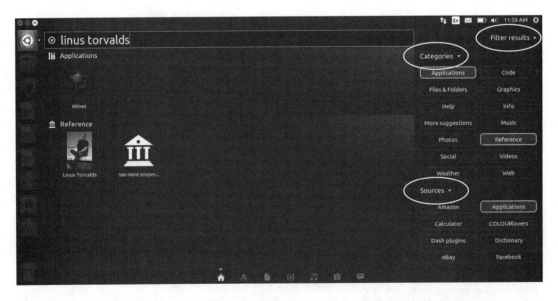

Figure 5.11   The Dash area lets you choose what exactly you're searching from it. You can go beyond files on your local machine.

type something into the Dash. For instance, you can use it to search eBay without having to visit eBay.

5.4.2 *Customizing*

The Unity interface is not very configurable. This has to to do with Canonical wanting to have a consistent user experience across devices, so that Unity looks the same on phones, desktops, and tablets. This is not an issue if you like the Unity interface but does present a challenge to users who only like certain aspects of it. However, Unity, which began in 2010, has slowly but consistently improved over the years. Many of the users who take exception to Unity were early adopters who used the desktop environment while it was still being defined and developed. And there have been some speed bumps, most notably a Unity setting that automatically opted users into Amazon results being shown in their Dash search results. However, that setting has since been changed to an opt-in.

It is also worth mentioning that there is a *Unity Tweak Tool* which provides a graphical front-end to make changes to certain aspects of Unity. The Tweak Tool is not installed by default but is available within the Ubuntu repositories. We'll discuss how to install something like this in chapter 7.

5.4.3 *Software*

Unlike GNOME and KDE, there is no software associated with Unity, although it tends to use GNOME default software for its own defaults. Most people use Unity because it's the default for Ubuntu but it actually is a strong desktop option. It's very similar to GNOME, separated mostly by the Lens/Scope concept. If you're using Ubuntu already, it's worth spending some time with Unity.

5.5 *Xfce*

Xfce might be considered the Rodney Dangerfield of desktop environments in that it gets little respect. It occupies an interesting place within Linux desktop environments.

5.5.1 *Interface*

Xfce is more lightweight than KDE, GNOME, and Unity in terms of system resource consumption. However, at the same time, it is not especially innovative or fully featured. It's simply a rock solid desktop environment using a familiar computing paradigm of menus to launch programs, although Xfce also allows multiple workspaces, so you're not limited by what fits in a single window.

To many, Xfce's lack of innovation is a feature. You don't need to learn to use it because you already know how to use it. There's a menu you can use to open programs. There's also a built-in launcher/application finder for those who want an interface more like GNOME or Unity. It also has a nice dock, or bottom panel with software icons. This will remind many of OS X and for users who like clicking on icons to open programs, the Xfce dock is an excellent and visually engaging option (see

Figure 5.12   Xfce isn't terribly innovative but it has a lot of nice features, including an OS X-like dock at the bottom of the screen.

figure 5.12). Using Xfce is straightforward. It won't challenge you or make you rethink your workflow, but it will allow just about any user to work quickly and effectively without a lot of tweaking.

5.5.2   *Customizing*

For those interested in tweaking, Xfce is very customizable. You can choose where taskbars appear and how programs are grouped. Taskbars can also be customized with applications that do everything from showing battery power to the weather. Xfce also makes it easy to create keybindings, so that a certain key combination will open a certain program.

Despite Xfce's dull-yet-sturdy reputation, it's a common option across distributions. Linux Mint has an Xfce version, as does Ubuntu (Xubuntu). Debian briefly used Xfce as its default desktop environment before switching back to GNOME. Most major distributions have some kind of Xfce implementation and the ones that don't will have it in their repositories.

5.5.3   *Software*

Like Unity, Xfce lacks its own software ecosystem. Because Xfce works well on older hardware, some distributions will put lighter versions of programs on by default. For instance, you might see AbiWord as the default word processor rather than the more system-intensive LibreOffice. Luckily, the default programs don't matter much, as you'll see in the next chapter, which will show you how to install and remove programs.

Without biasing you, I feel compelled to reveal that I use Xfce for my desktop environment on my main laptop. It runs well and stays out of my way, which is what I look for in a desktop environment. It's not particularly flashy or innovative but it lets you tweak it just enough to make using it feel like someone designed a desktop just for you.

5.6   *Choosing a desktop environment*

So how exactly do you choose a desktop environment? The first thing to remember is that a desktop environment doesn't need to be a long-term commitment. As mentioned in the previous chapter, desktop environments can coexist without requiring files to be moved. So if a desktop doesn't work for you, you can easily install another one, either keeping the previous one or removing it. This will have no impact on work files.

But before even getting to that stage, it might be useful to spend some time with the desktop that sounds or looks most interesting. If KDE seems intriguing, spend a few weeks with it, forcing yourself to use it. And as you encounter issues, research them and see if there's a way to change them.

The strength and beauty of Linux is that, at its core, it's changeable. Most users have been conditioned to accept the limitations of their operating system. Buttons can't be moved and behaviors can't be changed. But with Linux, this is often less of an issue. So while you probably can't make every change to a desktop environment—at least not without some serious programming—you might be able to change a desktop enough to make it workable for your personal style. Depending upon the desktop, these changes might be made through a graphical menu, through commands, or through file editing.

In terms of choosing a desktop, it's also important to focus on your work process, rather than on the desktop environment you're using. Conceptually, this is a huge switch from Windows and OS X, which require the user to work with the desktop paradigm chosen by the designers of those operating systems. Because of the locked-down nature of those desktops, the end-user can tweak to a certain extent, but really must work within specific constraints. Linux desktops often have similar constraints, but because of the variety of desktop environments, users can usually find *something* that conforms more to their personal preferences. So when it comes time to choose a Linux desktop, experiment with a few and then figure out which aspects are most appealing.

Hardware might also play a part in your desktop selection. Older hardware might not handle more sophisticated desktop environments, like KDE or Unity. If you're looking to get the most out of an older machine, you might think in terms of a less resource intensive desktop, like Xfce.

As mentioned previously, software is completely interchangeable across desktop environments. KDE-associated programs will work in Unity or any other desktop environment. However, if you find yourself using many KDE programs, it might be worth using KDE, in terms of saving disk space and system resources.

As desktop interfaces become more reminiscent of mobile ones, the freedom to choose how a desktop looks and behaves becomes more important for users who are doing more than checking email on their computer.

Table 5.1 looks at the desktop environments we discussed here and breaks them down into board topics.

Table 5.1   An overview of desktop environments

Desktop environment	Interface	Customization	Software ecosystem	Learning curve
GNOME	Launcher	Via third-party tool and extensions	Own ecosystem	Average
KDE	Launcher and menus	Built-in	Own ecosystem	Complex
Unity	Launcher	Via third-party tool	Tends to use GNOME programs	Average
Xfce	Launcher, menu, and/or dock	Built-in	Tends to use light programs, but lacks own ecosystem	Simple

Everything changes…?

It's worth repeating that some desktop environments mentioned in this chapter have a bit of a learning curve. Even the more simple, straightforward desktops, like Xfce, will require some work in getting up to speed in terms of features and functionality. The more time spent learning a desktop environment, the more (presumably) the user will get out of it, but for the average user, who might not wish to tweak every aspect of the desktop experience, simple online searching will reveal the answers to certain customization questions.

As mentioned elsewhere within this book, Linux is a dynamic environment. Software is always changing and being updated. Desktop environments are no exception—they sometimes change dramatically. This doesn't mean that someone running KDE will one day wake up to a completely new desktop experience. However, someone moving to a new distribution or new release of a distribution might find KDE has changed since their previous install.

This is where choice again becomes an important variable. You can choose a desktop that is more reminiscent of the previous desktop version, or you can find a new environment that does what you need it to, or you might find that the new version of their desktop environment is just what you needed. This is why understanding your own workflow is so important with Linux—by knowing what you need, you know if your desktop is doing what you need it to. So the work you do in understanding desktops and workflow is not a one-time experience. The information learned from this process will be helpful throughout your time on Linux, and throughout your time with other operating systems and interfaces.

5.7   *Wrapping up*

The desktop environment is an important part of the Linux experience. While the distribution controls things like what software is available, the desktop environment is how you will interact with your computer.

There is nothing wrong with using the default desktop that ships with whatever your chosen distribution is. In fact, there's a certain logic to it, because the default desktop environment is usually given the most attention within projects. You should also remember that you are not trapped with the default desktop environment. Even if you decide to stay with whatever the default is, there are still lots of ideas and tweaks to be gathered from trying different desktop environments and different implementations of desktop environments. Many times these ideas can be implemented, in some way, within another desktop.

Serious work requires a serious desktop. The average user might only need a web browser to do everything they need to, but many of us require much more from our computers. Linux is a way to create an experience that bends to our will, rather than us bending to the will of the interface.

GLOSSARY OF TERMS

In this chapter I explained:

Desktop environment—The look and feel of the GUI of an operating system

5.8   *Lab*

Now, you're going to try *another* desktop environment, either as a live image or as a second virtual machine on your computer. *Don't install these over your existing Ubuntu installation!* We're going to keep working with Ubuntu for the rest of the book.

Think about this chapter and which desktop environment, other than Unity, sounds interesting.

- Which one do you want to try?
- If you're interested in Xfce, download and install Xubuntu (http://xubuntu.org/).
- If you're interested in KDE, download and install Kubuntu (http://www.kubuntu.org/).
- If you're interested in GNOME, download and install Ubuntu GNOME (http://ubuntugnome.org/)—see the sidebar.

Install the other desktop environment either virtually or as a live image (the process will be just like chapter 3) and use it for 10 minutes.

- How do you close windows?
- How do you launch programs?
- Can you save files to the desktop?
- How does it compare to Unity?
- How does it compare to your current operating system?

Installing GNOME virtually

If you're having trouble installing GNOME virtually, you might need to disable 3D acceleration. To do that:

1 Right click on your virtual machine and click Settings.
2 Click on Display.
3 Uncheck Enable 3D Acceleration.
4 Click OK and try the installation again.

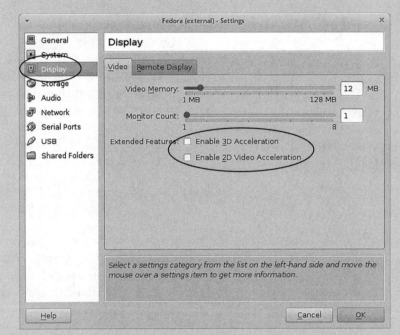

If you're having trouble getting GNOME to run in your virtual machine, try disabling the 3D acceleration.

Navigating your desktop 6

Now it's time to start exploring your desktop! We discussed a few desktop environments in the previous chapter, and today we're going to focus on using your Linux desktop for basic tasks. I'm going to use Unity, Ubuntu's default desktop environment, for many of the examples, but I'll also show you how things work with some other desktops. Also, most of what we discuss here should seem pretty familiar to you, as a regular computer user. What I'm going to do is take basic, everyday things you do in your current operating system and show you how to do them with Linux.

6.1 Working with programs

In this section I'm going to show you how to find, launch, and close programs on your Ubuntu system. I think most readers will find this process familiar. It's not that different from using other operating systems, but it's different enough to merit a walkthrough. This way, we're all on the same page.

6.1.1 Finding programs

We've talked about this a bit already, but to find programs in Unity, you use the navigation dock on the left (or Windows/Super key) and type the name of the program you wish to launch into Dash, Unity's launcher (see figure 6.1).

But what if you don't know the name of the program you wish to use? The first thing to remember is that Unity does some aliasing with program names so unlike the command line, where you need to be precise, with Unity (and most other desktop application launchers) you don't necessarily need to type the exact name of a program. Instead, you can just type a category of program. For instance, if you want to launch the Firefox web browser, you can enter Firefox and click the Firefox icon, or press Enter from the search bar once it comes up on the list.

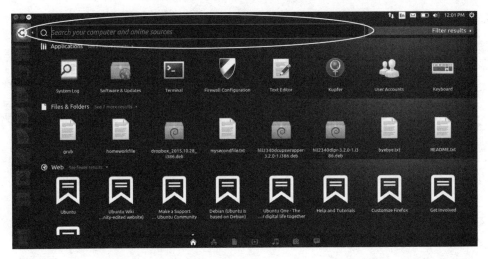

Figure 6.1   This is Unity's Dash area. The circled area is where you type the name of the program or file you wish to launch.

But what if you weren't sure which browser, or browsers, ship with your distribution? In that case, you can type web browser and you'll see Firefox come up. If you go on to install another web browser, that one will come up, too (see figure 6.2).

Figure 6.2   Typing web browser into Dash will bring up *all* of the web browsers installed on your computer.

But what if you can't find the program you need? Unity will let you see all of the programs installed on your computer, although unlike other desktop environments, they won't be in any particular order.

To browse all of these programs:

1   Open the Dash (either by clicking the top-left icon on the task bar or using your Windows/Super key).
2   Toggle to the application scope at the bottom of the screen.

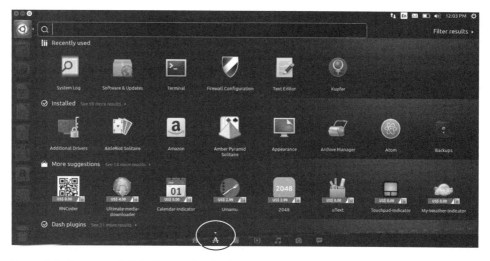

Figure 6.3 You can ask Unity to search only through programs on your computer using the Application scope on the Dash screen.

This scope has Unity search through only your applications, rather than your programs and files and whatever scopes you have activated (see figure 6.3).

Other desktop environments, specifically more menu-driven ones, make it easier to find programs by sorting them into a rough subject order using menu headings. For instance, in KDE if you wanted to find your web browser:

1 Open the KDE menu in the bottom left corner
2 Click Applications
3 Click Internet
4 Click Web Browser

KDE will then show you all of the web browsers installed on the machine (see figure 6.4). You would click the one you want to launch.

As you can see, finding programs in the various desktop environments is as simple as typing or using menus—which is probably what you're already used to.

In the next section, we're going to delve further into working with programs in Linux, starting with Nautilus, the default Ubuntu/GNOME file manager.

Figure 6.4 KDE sorts applications by their function.

6.1.2 *Launching programs*

To open Nautilus, launch the Dash and then type *file*. Interestingly, you'll notice that if you type file manager, it doesn't get picked up. That's because Ubuntu calls its file manager *Files*. Files' "real" name is Nautilus. Files is an alias for Nautilus. So you're fine if you type file or files, but if you type more than that, the application won't be found. You could also find it via the Dash by typing Nautilus.

You'll also see a Nautilus icon below the text in the Dash area. If you look at the left navigation dock, you'll see that same icon (see figure 6.5). Programs can also be launched from the dock. GNOME has a similar navigation dock on the left side of its screen and Xfce has one at the bottom (see figure 6.6). The trick with these docks is often just a matter of recognizing the icons.

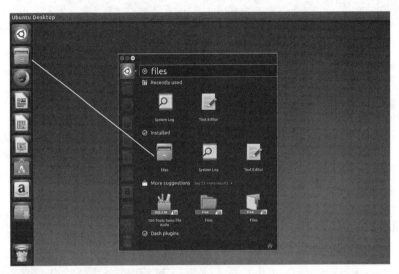

Figure 6.5   If you're unsure of what an icon means, the Unity Dash will show you.

Figure 6.6   Other desktop environments, including Xfce, also define icons.

6.1.3   Closing programs

In Unity, the close application button is on the top-left side of the screen (see figure 6.7). KDE, GNOME, and Xfce all have top-right corner close buttons.

Figure 6.7   Unity's window controls are on the top left, like OS X. Other desktop environments use the top right.

6.1.4   Top menu bars

You might have noticed that programs lack the top menu bar seen in other operating systems (see figure 6.8).

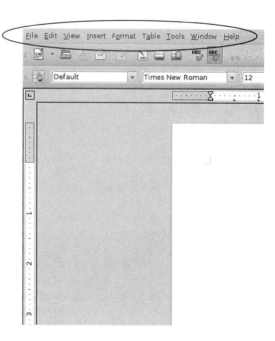

This is another Unity design choice—menus are integrated into that top panel. It's sometimes confusing to users who don't think to look that far up their screen. To get top menus to appear, bring your cursor to the top panel (it's the panel that has the clock). See figure 6.9.

Figure 6.8   Unity doesn't show top menus like this by default.

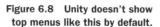

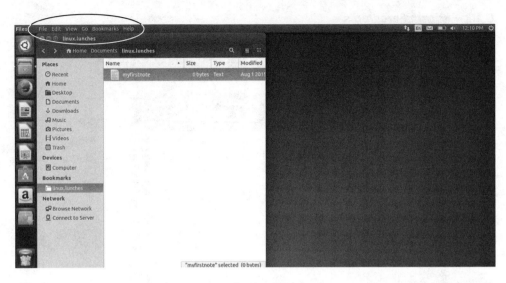

Figure 6.9   **With Unity, bringing your cursor to the top of the screen causes the top menu bar to appear.**

Once your cursor touches that panel, you'll notice that menus appear.

6.1.5   *Customizing your dock*

Every distribution with a dock concept allows it to be customized, in terms of adding and removing programs.

    With Unity, whenever you open a program, its icon appears on the left dock, with small triangles indicating it's the active program (see figure 6.10).

Figure 6.10   **Unity shows you which program is active on its left dock with two small triangles on either side of the program icon.**

Figure 6.11   Programs can be added and removed from the Unity dock.

To add or remove a program from the dock:

1 Right-click on the dock icon (see figure 6.11)
2 Click Unlock from Launcher

The icon will remain visible while the program is open but disappear when the program is closed. This is good for programs you don't use often.

To add a program to the dock:

1 Right-click the dock icon
2 Click Lock to Launcher

Then the icon will always be present. This is good for programs you use frequently.

This process is essentially the same for GNOME, except GNOME uses a light blue underline to indicate an active program (see figure 6.12) and calls its dock Favorites rather than Launcher like Unity does (figure 6.13).

Different distributions and desktop environments will have different processes for adding and removing programs to and from docks, taskbars, and panels, but more often than not, you're using a right click on an icon to accomplish this.

Figure 6.12   GNOME uses a subtle blue underline to indicate the active program on its dock.

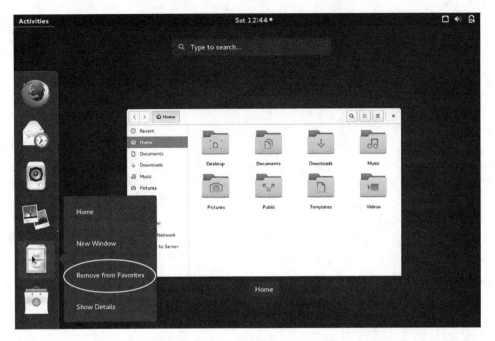

Figure 6.13   GNOME calls its dock Favorites and like Unity allows you to add and remove programs.

Now, open up Nautilus, however you choose, and we'll move forward into working with files on your Linux desktop.

6.2   *Working with files and folders*

As in other operating systems, just about every Linux desktop environment has three ways to open a file:

1   Double-click a file to open it.
2   Open the file via an application.
3   Open the file via a launcher.

Files are in folders, so let's start by working with folders for a moment.

6.2.1   *Creating folders*

First, we need a folder to work with.

> **Try it now: creating folders**
>
> 1 Go into Nautilus and double-click your Documents folder.
> 2 You are now within that folder. This should feel familiar to you. The Linux desktop is quite similar to other operating systems.

3 Now, right-click in the empty, white area of the Documents folder and click *New Folder*.

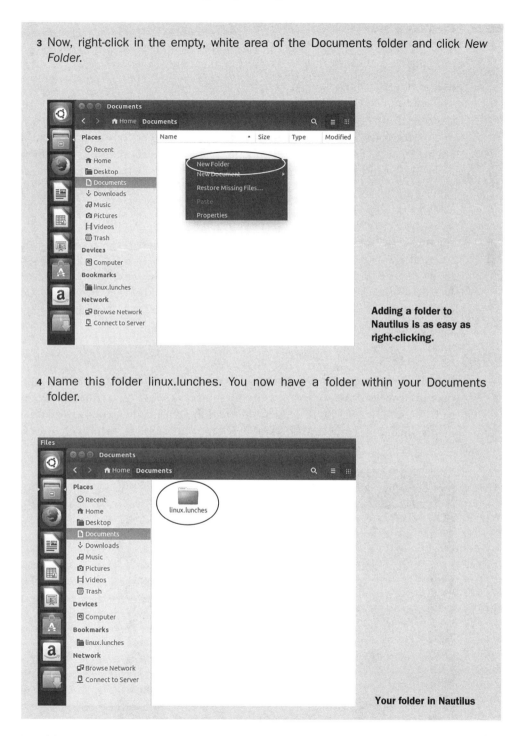

Adding a folder to Nautilus is as easy as right-clicking.

4 Name this folder linux.lunches. You now have a folder within your Documents folder.

Your folder in Nautilus

Double-click into this new folder, placing you within the linux.lunches folder.

6.2.2   *Creating files*

Now we're going to place a file in this folder. Right-click again, like we did to create the folder, but this time click New Document and then Empty Document. A new file will be created, which you can call myfirstnote.

You'll notice I didn't include a file extension. Some users are probably used to saving everything with a file extension (and if you don't, some operating systems will put one on for you). The file extension is the two-, three- or four-letter suffix that comes after the period at the end of a file name. The file extension helps some operating systems understand what kind of file it's dealing with and what is needed to open it. So when it sees a .docx file extension, the system assumes it's working with a Word file. Without the file extension, some operating systems will ask you to choose a program to use for opening that file. But Linux doesn't require extensions in that same way. It can make the association without the file extension.

So if it's your habit and preference, you can save the file as myfirstnote.txt. But Linux systems will assume the empty file is a text file—even without the extension. Because of that, you can save the file as myfirstnote. Either way, the file will be opened with whatever your default text editor is. And note that you've created a text file without opening a text editor, which is kind of impressive!

6.2.3   *Opening files*

Now let's practice opening the file. Double-click myfirstnote to open it, as on any operating system. As you expect, the file opens. The program that opens it is called gedit (see figure 6.14). It's a text editor that's a default in many desktop environments, including Unity and GNOME. We'll talk more about gedit in chapter 9.

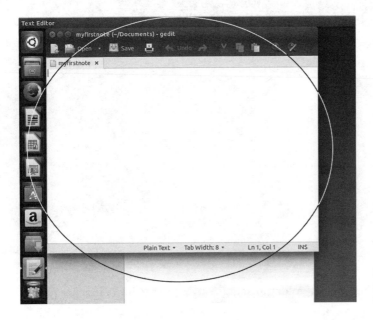

Figure 6.14   gedit is a simple text editor common to Unity and GNOME.

Now close gedit.

Now open gedit. To open gedit this time, you'll use the Unity launcher and type `gedit` or `text editor`. Another way to open the file is by using the Open dialog in `gedit` and navigating to the file. This is common across operating systems. gedit conveniently has an Open button right along its top navigation menu. Use that top navigation to open myfirstnote (see figure 6.15). Then, close gedit again.

The final way of opening a file uses Dash. Instead of typing the name of an application, you can type the name of a file (see figure 6.16). Type `myfirstnote` and the file

Figure 6.15   Files can be opened via applications. This is universal across desktop environments and operating systems.

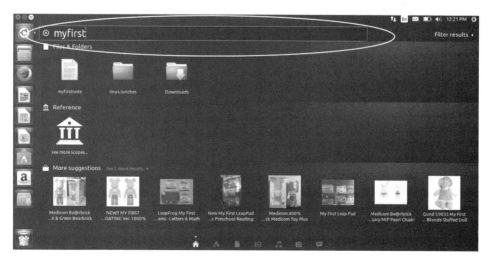

Figure 6.16   The Unity Dash searches for files.

will appear in the Dash (although it wouldn't if you were using the Application scope, which only searches programs and not files). GNOME and KDE both have this functionality (see figures 6.17 and 6.18).

Figure 6.17   KDE is another desktop environment that provides easy access to files without having to navigate through folders.

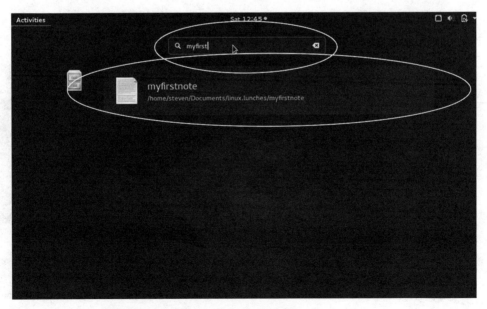

Figure 6.18   GNOME can search for files as well as applications.

However, many people prefer to navigate to the file via a file manager or application. Once you're in the habit of opening files by typing their names, you'll find it's a much quicker and more efficient way to work—across distributions and operating systems.

6.2.4 *Moving folders and files*

Moving folders and files is standard across distributions. Just click once on a file to select it and then drag it to the directory where you want it to appear. Nautilus allows you to bookmark directories, much like other file managers. The advantage to bookmarking a directory is that it makes it easier to move files into frequently used directories. Let's bookmark our linux.lunches directory, and then drag a file into it.

First, open the Nautilus file manager as we did earlier in this chapter. Then, navigate into the linux.lunches directory, which we made earlier (it's in Documents). To access the Nautilus bookmark area, you're going to need to bring your cursor all the way to the top of the screen, to the top panel, which has the clock (see figure 6.19).

Figure 6.19 To access the Nautilus bookmark menu, you need to activate it using the top Unity panel.

Once your mouse is up top, you can click the Bookmark menu and then Bookmark this Location. You'll now see linux.lunches under Bookmarks in Nautlius's left navigation area (see figure 6.20).

Figure 6.20   Most file managers, including Nautilus, allow you to bookmark frequently used directories.

Now, using Nautilus, navigate into the Desktop folder and create an empty document called mysecondnote. Click it once and drag it into linux.lunches (see figure 6.21).

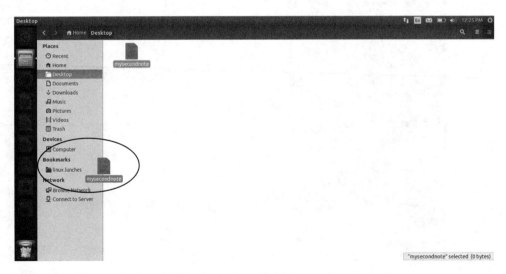

Figure 6.21   Files can be dragged into directories, which helps you to organize them.

6.2.5 Copying folders and files

To copy a folder or file:

1 Right-click it to get a context menu (see figure 6.22).
2 Select Copy To if you want to copy it to another directory using the file manager, which will open after you select this option (figure 6.23).

Figure 6.22   Right-click on a file to get its context menu.

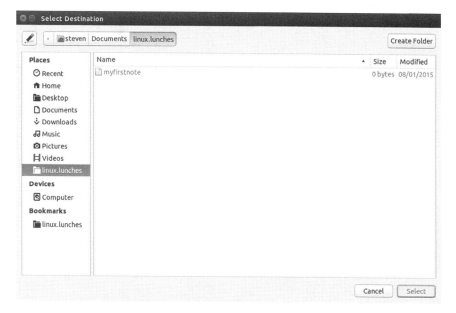

Figure 6.23   Copy To calls up a file manager.

3 Select Copy if you want to manually paste it into a folder.

4 To paste it into a folder, navigate to the destination folder and then right-click in the folder. A Paste option will show up on the context menu (figure 6.24)

Figure 6.24   Right-click in the destination folder to paste a copied file.

6.2.6 *Deleting folders and files*

Perhaps unsurprisingly by this point, deleting folders and files is also similar to other operating systems. You can click a folder or file and press the Delete key on your keyboard, or you can right-click and move it to the trash using the context menu (figure 6.25).

Figure 6.25   Right-click on a file to move it to the trash.

6.2.7 *Changing the look of the folders and files*

You might have noticed the Nautilus file icons are big and take up a lot of space.

If you prefer a more streamlined view, you can easily change that in Nautilus. First, go to the top panel, which will make the Nautilus panels appear. Then, go to the Edit menu and select Preferences. From there, you can customize some of Nautilus's behaviors. For instance, if you don't like files and folders represented as chunky icons, you can switch to a list view, which is found under the Views tab (see figure 6.26). The Preferences area allows you to change quite a few things, such as if you want to open folders with a single click instead of a double-click. The changes take effect the next time you open Nautilus. Figure 6.27 shows our folders in the more compact List view.

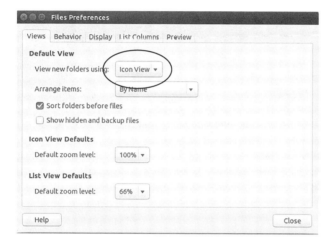

Figure 6.26 You can streamline the Nautilus interface by switching to the List view.

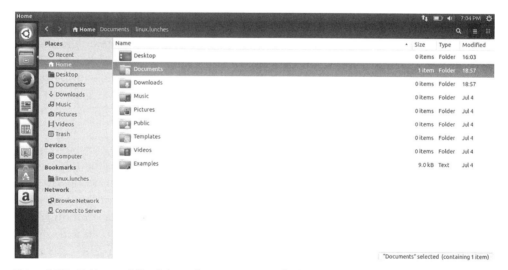

Figure 6.27 Folders and files take up less screen space in the Nautlius List View.

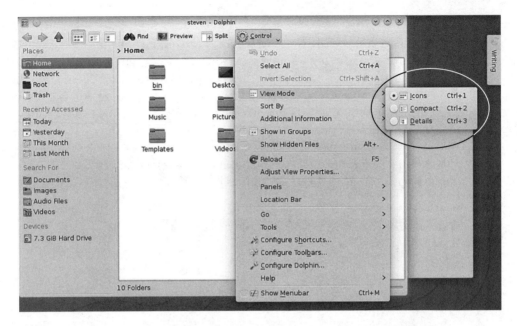

Figure 6.28   Most Linux file managers offer different view options, including KDE's Dolphin.

This type of configuring is standard across file managers. For instance, you can do something similar with Dolphin, the default KDE file manager (see figure 6.28).

6.3   *Wrapping up*

Now you should have a good sense of how to navigate your desktop. This book assumes you are using Unity on Ubuntu. If you are using a different environment on a different distribution, or a different desktop environment within Ubuntu, all of the concepts we reviewed here will apply—things might look a little different within your desktop environment or distribution.

I hope you'll focus on the ability to launch files via launchers, either in the menu area, like with KDE, or via a Dash/launcher area, like with Unity and GNOME. Opening files without having to navigate down into folders is a huge time-saver. Though not every desktop environment supports that ability, the major ones, like GNOME and KDE, do. And desktops without this ability can be made to by installing a launcher, which we'll talk about in chapter 16. Users who have intricate file folder hierarchies will love the ability to instantly call up the file they need. However, users who prefer traditional click-and-open file access always have that option with Linux.

But in general, I hope you now see that Linux isn't all that different from other operating systems. Linux is amazingly customizable, as we've seen with the different ways to open files in different desktop environments, but at its core, the GUI should feel quite familiar.

GLOSSARY OF TERMS

In this chapter I explained:

Context menu—Menus presenting additional options. They are often found by right-clicking a file or folder.

Super key—The Windows logo key on a keyboard.

6.4   *Lab*

This chapter focused on Ubuntu and Unity, but as you saw, navigation and file manipulation is essentially the same between different desktop environments. For your homework:

1   Create a folder within your Documents folder and call it homework.
2   In the homework folder, create a document called homeworkfile.
3   Bookmark the homework folder.
4   Move homework into linux.lunches.
5   What happens when you go to the homework bookmark? Did homeworkfile move with it?

There are multiple ways to do all of this. There's no right way or wrong way as long as the folders gets made and the file and folder get moved.

Extra credit

1   How would you see the properties of a file?
2   How would you see the properties of a folder?
3   How do you make a shortcut to a file or folder?

Part 2

A home office in Linux

The chapters in this second part of *Learn Linux in a Month of Lunches* prepare you to use Linux for your home office, how you'll work with Linux in your day-to-day life. You'll learn about the vast world of software available to you, how to install it, and how to work with it. You'll also learn the mysterious-and-seemingly-intimidating-but-it's-really-not-that-bad-you'll-see command line. You'll also learn:

- How to work with Linux productivity software to do things like word processing and editing photos
- The beauty and convenience of text editors
- What the command line is and how to use it
- How to run Windows programs in Linux
- Tips to work effectively in Linux

Installing software

7

Welcome to part 2 of our journey! Now that you've got Linux running and understand how it works, in terms of things like distributions and desktop environments, we're going to spend time getting it ready for you to work with. The next 10 chapters are going to teach you to work with and customize your Linux environment so you can work efficiently. For instance, once you learn the command line, you might not ever want to go back to graphical programs. For now, let's talk about a basic level of customization—installing new software on your system.

Every distribution comes with software preinstalled. In the last chapter we saw that GNOME and Unity each come with the Nautilus file manager and gedit text editor. But what if you don't like those tools? The beauty of Linux is that you're rarely stuck with software. In this chapter, you're going to learn how to install and remove software with Linux. More specifically:

- I'll discuss package managers, which are used to install and remove software.
- We'll open and use the Ubuntu Software Manager to install Synaptic, *another* package manager.
- We'll open and use Synaptic to install Vim.

I'm also going to discuss some of the basic concepts of how software installation works with Linux. However, this chapter is going to focus on the mechanics of installing software. I'll explore more of the "how everything works" in an upcoming chapter. For now, I'm guessing you might have some favorite software you might want to get on your computer, so I want to show you how to do that first.

7.1   *Package managers*

Linux software installation, removal, and updating is handled by package managers. A *package manager* is what operates between us, the users, and the distribution software repositories. It's where you look for software to install.

The package manager is also what keeps software up-to-date on your computer. As I mentioned previously, some distributions have more up-to-date versions of software than others. Some distributions might be using version 3.17 of gedit while another might be using 3.4 (the higher the version number, the more recent the software). The version used depends on what's available in the repositories.

If software isn't available in a repository, it can't be installed with a package manager. The package manager is also what you'll use if you want to install a new desktop environment. You find it and install it, and you have another desktop.

Also, for the most part, you're going to install, remove, and update software using a package manager and not by downloading software from websites. As I mentioned before, think in terms of how your phone works. Most of us probably install software on our phones using the phone's app store and not by downloading from different websites. This process is familiar to anyone used to an app store, but most likely feels strange to Windows users (although Windows uses a package manager-like concept for removing software from the computer via the Add/Remove software area). However, once you get used to it, you'll be thrilled with the ease of removing and installing software.

Your computer has only one package manager, but there are different interfaces for it. Despite the different looks, you're always interacting with the one package manager. Later on, we'll use commands to install and remove software.

In this chapter, we'll look at Synaptic (figure 7.1), which is a graphical package manager used by Debian-based systems. We'll also look at the Ubuntu Software Store, which is another graphical package manager. You can install software with one or both, with no repercussions to your system.

Even though they're different interfaces, they're using the same backend. In the case of Debian-based distributions, the backend is *Apt*, which stands for *Advanced Packaging Tool*. Different distributions use different package managers, but the concept behind them remains the same. For instance, Fedora and OpenSUSE share a backend called *RPM*, which stands for *RPM Package Manager* (yet another charmingly infuriating recursive Linux acronym). The graphical interface for RPM on Fedora is called *Software* and is the GNOME software installer (see figure 7.2). This is also the default software installer for Ubuntu 16.04, which no longer uses Ubuntu Software Center.

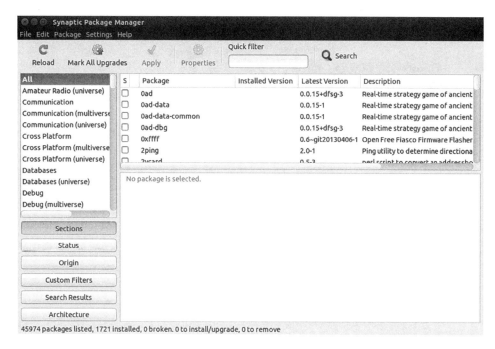

Figure 7.1   Synaptic is available for every Debian-based system making it very useful to know.

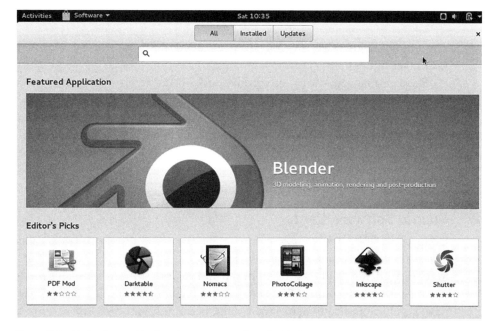

Figure 7.2   Fedora's graphical package manager is called Software. It uses the RPM package manager. Note how it looks like an app store.

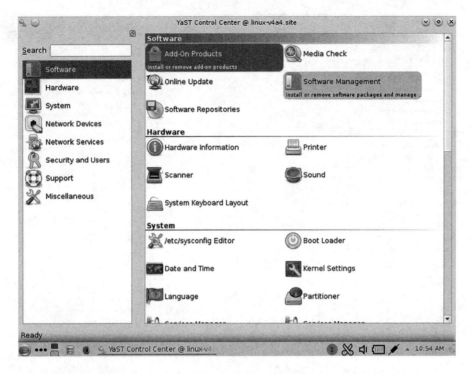

Figure 7.3   OpenSUSE's graphical package manager is called YaST. Like Fedora, it uses the RPM package manager. Notice how it looks more like Synaptic.

The graphical interface for OpenSUSE is called *YaST (Yet Another Setup Tool) Control Center* (see figure 7.3).

Package managers work much like desktop managers—the technical underpinnings are the same but the GUIs can be different. The key difference is that the interfaces are distribution-specific, so if you like the look and feel of YaST, you can't use it on Fedora. However, the behavior, in terms of how you'll interact with it, is pretty much identical across distributions. Ubuntu no longer comes with Synaptic installed so before we look at it, we'll need to install it. Let's start with Ubuntu's graphical package manager, which is what we'll use to install Synaptic.

7.2   Ubuntu Software Center

Ubuntu's default package manager in 14.04, the version we're using, is called *Ubuntu Software Center.* It's not a true package manager in that it doesn't handle updating software. Instead, it only allows you to install and remove software. Also, it's modeled on a store, so it includes things like reviews and recommendations that you don't see in most graphical package managers. Finally, because it's modeled on a store, not everything in it is free. This is unusual in terms of Linux but is fairly standard in terms of mobile app stores.

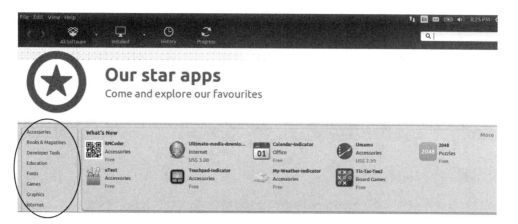

Figure 7.4 The Ubuntu Software Center looks like a standard app store.

Though the Ubuntu Software Center looks nice, I find it to be slower than a pure graphical package manager, like Synaptic. Also, though there is plenty of great, purchase-worthy content in the Software Center, I rarely have a need for it. So the first thing we're going to do is install a *different* package manager.

To launch Ubuntu Software Center, go into the Dash and type Ubuntu Software Center and then click into the application. You'll see something like figure 7.4.

This is pretty standard across graphical package managers. If you wanted to see all of the Office programs, you could click the Office link and see a list.

The Software Center also lets you see what programs you have installed as well as a history of programs you've installed, removed, and updated (figure 7.5). This list is sorted by date, which is helpful if you're trying to find something you accidentally removed or installed.

Figure 7.5 The Ubuntu Software Center provides a list of all software you have installed and tracks software added, removed, and updated.

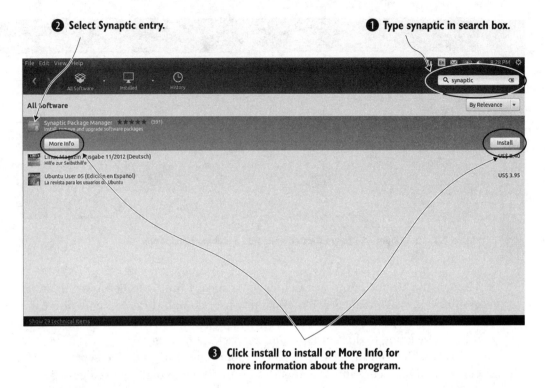

2 Select Synaptic entry.

1 Type synaptic in search box.

3 Click install to install or More Info for more information about the program.

Figure 7.6   Once you find the software you want, you can either install it or get more information about it.

Since we know the name of the software we want to install, Synaptic, we can search on it using the search box.

The Software Center will match as you type so eventually you'll see a list of results with Synaptic at the top of the list. Click it and you'll have the option to either install it or get more information about the program (see figure 7.6).

The More Information screen (figure 7.7) has interesting information. In addition to the description of the software, which is fairly standard for graphical package managers, the Ubuntu Software Center offers user reviews and links to related software. This isn't common to graphical package managers, but could be helpful to new users. The More Information screen also has a link to install the software, allowing you to read a bit about software before installing it. Click Install to put Synaptic on your system.

You'll be asked to authenticate by inputting your password (see figure 7.8). This is also a Linux concept. Some operating systems, mobile and desktop, allow anyone to install software unless otherwise specified. However, Linux systems have an *administrator* concept, meaning only certain people have the rights to install new software. We'll talk about this more in chapter 19.

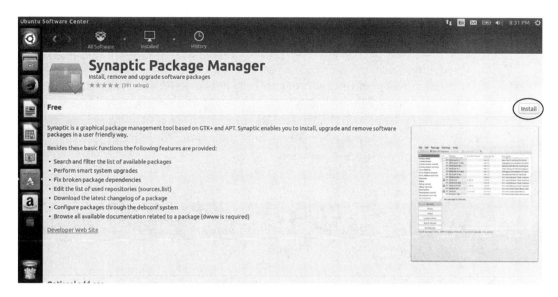

Figure 7.7   Software can be installed via the More Information area of the Ubuntu Software Center.

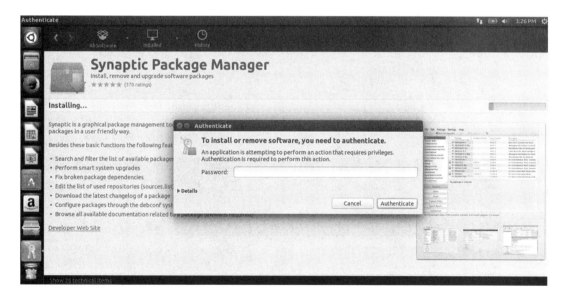

Figure 7.8   All Linux systems require a password to install software.

After your password is entered, the software is installed. When it's done you'll see a green circle with a white check in the middle as well as the date of installation. You'll also now see a Remove button, in case you've changed your mind about the installation (see figure 7.9).

To remove Synaptic, or any other software, click Remove. If you click the back arrow in the Software Center, you'll go back to the list of programs you just searched. If you click on Synaptic, you'll now see a Remove link instead of an Install one (see figure 7.10). Removing software in general means searching for it in the Software Center and then removing it from your system.

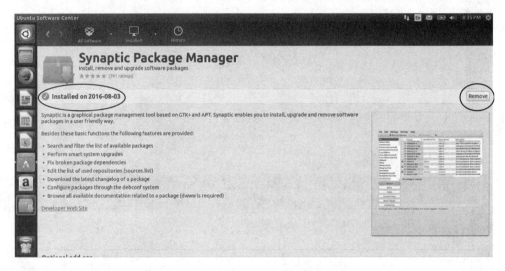

Figure 7.9   Once software is installed, you have the option to see when you installed it and to uninstall it.

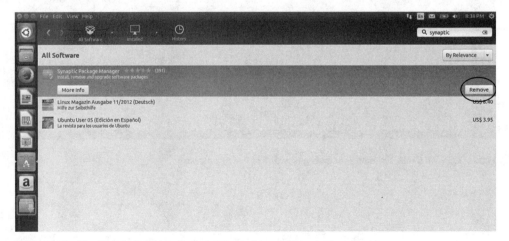

Figure 7.10   The Ubuntu Software Center can also be used to remove software.

I know this seems very Ubuntu-specific, but the process is the same across distributions. Figure 7.11 shows the Mint Software Manager, which has a similar look to the Ubuntu Software Center. You'll see I'm doing a search for Synaptic there.

In figure 7.12 you see the results list, which has a look similar to the Ubuntu Software result list. You see Synaptic with a white check in a green circle, meaning it's installed. You also see stars and reviews, like you saw in the Ubuntu Software Center. However you can't remove it from this screen as you can with the Software Center.

Figure 7.11   Mint's Software Manager has a similar look to the Ubuntu Software Center.

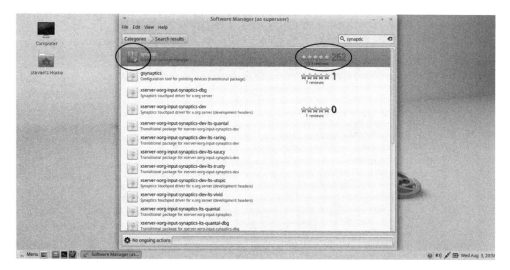

Figure 7.12   The Mint Software Manager results screen also looks like the Ubuntu Software Center.

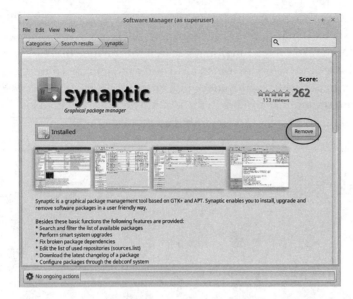

**Figure 7.13   You can
remove software once you
double-click into the Mint
Software Manager entry.**

When you double-click on the Synaptic entry, you're taken to a screen that's also similar to the Ubuntu Software Center (see figure 7.13). From that screen you can remove
Synaptic (or add it, if it wasn't already installed).

As you can see, it's essentially the same process, no matter what package manager
you're using. Now, as long as you have Synaptic installed, let's look at installing software using that.

Ubuntu Software in 16.04

The software client in Ubuntu 16.04 is called Ubuntu Software.

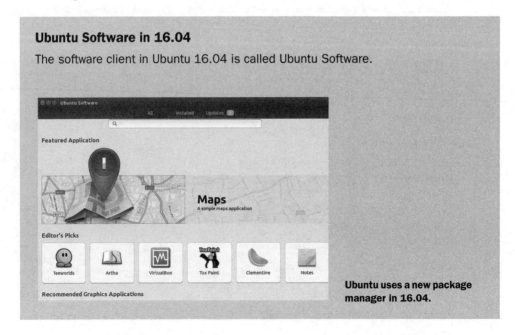

**Ubuntu uses a new package
manager in 16.04.**

The interface is very similar to Ubuntu Software Center. Software is arranged by category or can be searched.

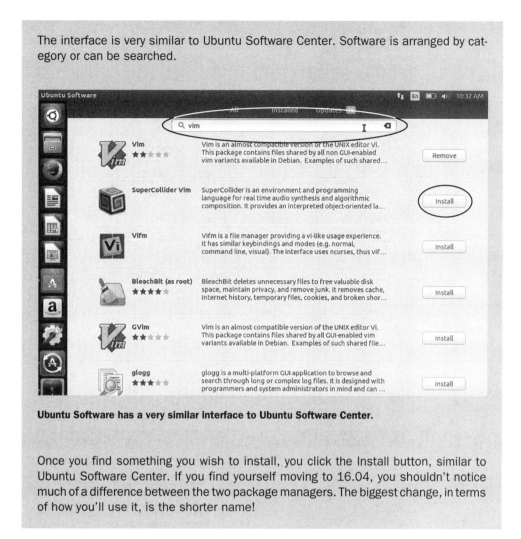

Ubuntu Software has a very similar interface to Ubuntu Software Center.

Once you find something you wish to install, you click the Install button, similar to Ubuntu Software Center. If you find yourself moving to 16.04, you shouldn't notice much of a difference between the two package managers. The biggest change, in terms of how you'll use it, is the shorter name!

7.3   *Synaptic*

Synaptic is available for *all* Debian-based distributions, which means it's an option on quite a few distributions. Synaptic also allows you to update software, or get newer versions, which we'll talk about in chapter 17. Close the Ubuntu Software Center if you still have it open and open Synaptic (you can only have one package manager open at a time). When you open Synaptic, it'll ask for your password *before* you try to do anything. The first time it opens it'll give you a brief explanation of how it works

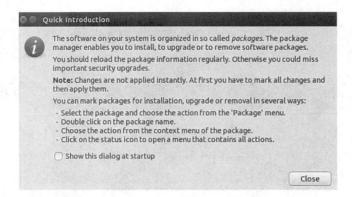

Figure 7.14 The first time you open Synaptic, it gives you a brief explanation of how it works.

(see figure 7.14). We're going to cover that in this section, so feel free to close the notification.

The layout of Synaptic is similar to what we saw in the Ubuntu Software Center and Mint's Software Manager (see figure 7.15). There's a rough sort of the software

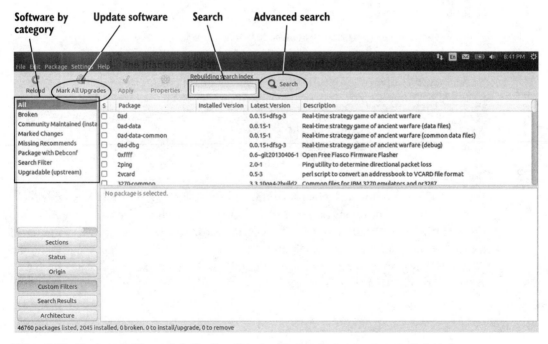

Figure 7.15 The layout of Synaptic is like the other graphical package managers we looked at.

available by typing the software and a search option. You'll notice some of the subjects have *multiverse* and *universe* in their titles. *Multiverse* refers to non-free, proprietary software (there is no way to purchase software through Synaptic so it doesn't refer to cost). *Universe* refers to software contributed by the community but not officially supported by Ubuntu.

For now, do a filter search for Vim, which is a text editor we'll talk about later in the book. Type vim in the quick filter box and then click Enter. The quick filter search is usually fine for searching for software, although Synaptic has an advanced search option that allows you to do things like search by *dependency* (I'll talk about that term in just a moment) or software version.

The software we want is right at the top of the list. If it were installed on the system, there would be a green box instead of a white one. Each of the column settings are sortable, so if you wanted to sort the list by the name of the package, or software, you could click on Package and the sort will change to alphabetical by package name (see figure 7.16). The S column lets you sort by what you already have installed on your computer. But since we see the package we want, just leave the sort as is for now.

If you click the vim entry, you'll get a brief description of the software. You don't get as much information and feedback as you would in the Ubuntu Software Center, but most of the time, you know what you want to install and don't need additional information.

Figure 7.16 Synaptic lets you sort by a few parameters.

Click the empty box next to vim and you'll get a little pop-up box (see figure 7.17). Click Mark for Installation and you'll be asked to install additional software (see figure 7.18). This is software Vim needs to run. It's called a *dependency*, meaning it's a program another program needs to run. We'll talk about this in chapter 17. For now, click Mark to indicate you want this installed also. You'll now notice a check in the box next to vim. This means it's ready to be installed.

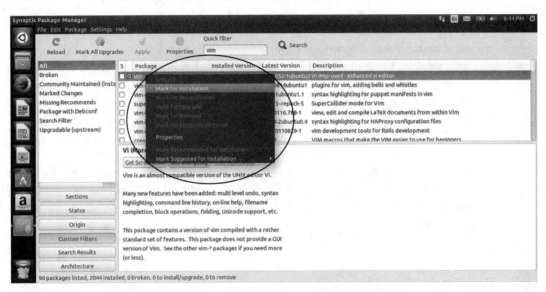

Figure 7.17   Use Mark for Installation to indicate you want the software installed.

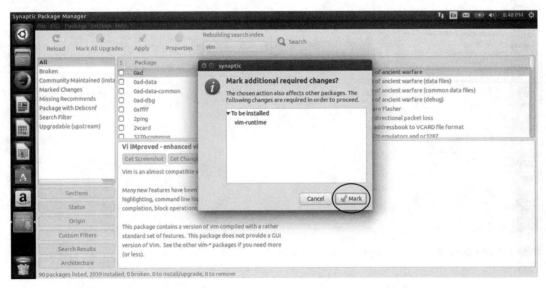

Figure 7.18   Package managers automatically install software needed by other software.

At this point, you could keep going, marking software to install and remove. You don't need to do one thing at a time. But since we're only installing Vim, you can click Apply (see figure 7.19). Synaptic will give a pop-up summarizing what you're doing and asking you to confirm by clicking another Apply. Click it and Vim will be installed.

When Synaptic is done, you'll get a message telling you the changes have been applied. You can then close the dialog box. You'll notice the box next to vim is now green, indicating the software is installed on your computer (see figure 7.20).

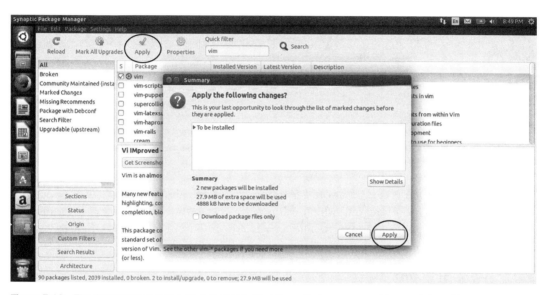

Figure 7.19   The Apply button is the final step in telling Synaptic to remove, add, or update software.

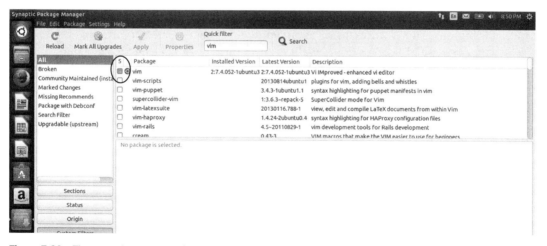

Figure 7.20   The green box next to vim means the software has been installed.

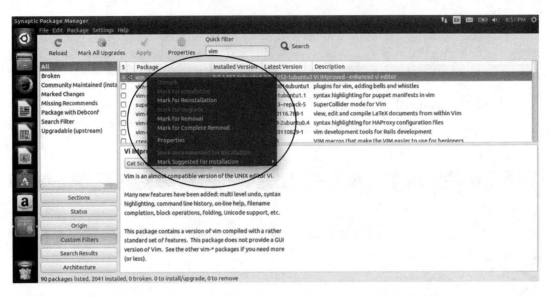

Figure 7.21   Clicking the green box next to the program allows it to be reinstalled or removed.

If you click the green box, you'll see options to reinstall the software, if it's not working correctly to remove it, which will remove the software; or to *completely* remove it, which will remove the software and associated configuration files (see figure 7.21).

Let's leave Vim installed for now.

7.4   *Wrapping up*

As you can see, even if the tools for installing and removing software are different across distributions, the process is similar. We focused on Ubuntu, but as you saw the Ubuntu Software Center is similar to Synaptic, which is common across Debian-based distributions. Other graphical package managers work in the same way for other distributions. There's more to say about package management, but for now, I want you to have a sense of how it's done. We'll get into the why of package management in a few more lunches.

GLOSSARY OF TERMS

In this chapter I explained:

Package manager—Allows you to install and update software from repositories and keeps software up-to-date on your computer

Repository—Distributions' collections of software

7.5   *Lab*

Go into Synaptic and remove Vim. Then, go into the Ubuntu Software Center and install it again.

1 How do you initiate a search in Synaptic?

2 How do you initiate a search in the Ubuntu Software Center?

3 If you needed to update your software, which tool would you use?

Browse for office software in both tools (we're discussing office software in the next chapter).

- Which interface do you prefer to search?
- Which interface is easier for discovering software?
- Why do you prefer that interface?

An introduction to Linux home/office software

Once you can install software, which you learned how to do in the previous chapter, Linux really opens up for you. Because software is how you customize your desktop and make it your own. This chapter is going to cover the typical software most users work with daily. Some of this software is installed in Ubuntu (or your distribution of choice) by default, and some of it will need to be installed, which you now know how to do! I'm going to walk you through

- Office productivity software, so you can use spreadsheets, word process, and handle email.
- Image editors, so you can crop and resize your photos.
- Multimedia players, so you can watch movies and listen to music.

This is going to be a brief overview of the various tools available to you. For the most part, they're similar to their Windows/OS X counterparts, so you should be able to get around these programs pretty easily (the GIMP image editor is a bit more complex and could probably benefit from its own book). I'm going to cover a lot of software so you can see some of what's available and decide which tools work best for you and the work you do. A lot of the programs discussed in this chapter also have Windows/OS X versions, so if you find something you like, you might be able to use it across operating systems.

WEB BROWSERS I'm not going to get into web browsers here because they're pretty much the same across operating systems. Though you don't have Internet Explorer, Edge, or Safari for Linux, you have Chrome and Firefox and they're exactly the same.

Most repositories have a browser called Chromium, which is the open source version of Chrome. The browsers are very similar, but Chromium has some proprietary code excluded from it. Part of the excluded code is support for Adobe Flash.

Some people will notice a difference between Chrome and Chromium but most won't. However, if you do notice the difference and you wish to use Chrome instead, you can download and install it from Google. We'll talk about how to install software from outside of repositories in chapter 17.

8.1 Office/productivity

I can pretend I'm talking about a genre of software when I say "office/productivity" but I think everyone knows I mean Microsoft Office. Microsoft Office is a suite of programs:

- Word (word processor)
- Excel (spreadsheet)
- PowerPoint (presentations)
- Outlook (email)
- Access (database)
- OneNote (note-taking)
- Publisher (desktop publishing)

8.1.1 LibreOffice

The closest Linux equivalent to Microsoft Office is LibreOffice (see figure 8.1), which is a bundled suite of similar programs (you have to install the entire suite—you can't pick only one application).

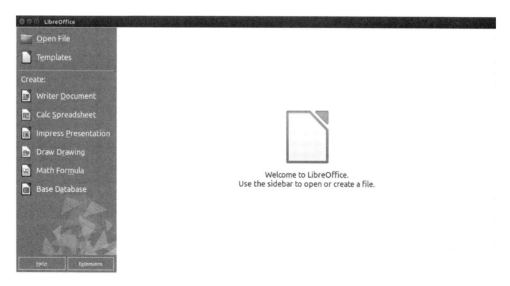

Figure 8.1 LibreOffice is a suite of office programs, comparable to Microsoft Office.

LibreOffice offers:

- Writer (word processor)
- Calc (spreadsheet)
- Impress (presentations)
- Draw (drawing)
- Math (mathematical formulas)
- Base (database)

Though the overlap isn't perfect, you can see LibreOffice covers a lot of the same ground. You should have LibreOffice already installed on your system. Let's look at Calc, the spreadsheet application, in action.

1 Open Calc.
2 Create a column with the heading Chapter.
3 Create another column with the heading Date.
4 Enter the chapters we've covered and the dates you completed them.

WHAT ABOUT OPENOFFICE? You might have heard about OpenOffice as an open source productivity suite. Many people know it as a free, popular, cross-platform alternative to Microsoft Office. In fact, it might have broader name recognition than LibreOffice.

OpenOffice has gone through many name changes, from OpenOffice.org to Apache OpenOffice.org to Apache OpenOffice. LibreOffice is a *fork* of Open-Office, meaning the LibreOffice team used the OpenOffice code to develop their suite. The LibreOffice team took the OpenOffice code in a different direction (thus the term fork) and while the two suites are similar, Libre-Office is more actively developed and is widely considered to be superior to Apache OpenOffice.

Apache OpenOffice is still developed, albeit slower than LibreOffice, and is still available in most repositories, so if you prefer it, for whatever reason, you still have access to it.

LibreOffice is not identical to Office. The interface is similar (see figure 8.2), but power Office users might need to spend time getting used to it. Users working with complex files might find it hard going between both programs, but for most users, doing simple things like creating budgets and writing reports, LibreOffice should work just fine. LibreOffice is also available for Windows and OS X.

Figure 8.2 **LibreOffice Writer looks similar to Word, but is not identical.**

8.1.2 *Calligra*

Of course, you're not limited to LibreOffice in terms of an office suite. Calligra is another example. While it's associated with the KDE desktop, it is usable on any desktop environment. It offers:

- Words (word processor)
- Stage (presentations)
- Sheets (spreadsheet)
- Flow (flow charts)
- Kexi (database)

Like LibreOffice, the interface is slightly different, but should seem familiar to most users (see figure 8.3).

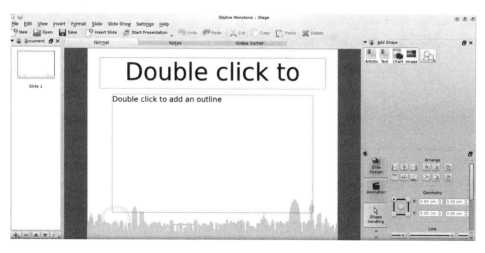

Figure 8.3 **Calligra Stage is the Linux equivalent of Microsoft PowerPoint.**

There are also standalone office programs available in most repositories. For instance, AbiWord is a simple word processor that doesn't come bundled with any other programs. Gnumeric is a simple spreadsheet that comes by itself. These are good options if you don't need everything that comes with something like Calligra or LibreOffice.

8.1.3   Email clients

In terms of Outlook, the Microsoft email client, Linux users have quite a few alternatives. There are lots of email clients for Linux. Two of the most popular are Evolution, and Thunderbird. Evolution is developed by the GNOME project, and because of that, it integrates with the GNOME desktop environment. When you click the time along the GNOME top navigation, it pulls in information from your Evolution calendar (see figure 8.4).

Figure 8.4   Evolution data is readily available via the GNOME desktop environment.

Evolution supports the Exchange email protocol via a free plugin, whereas Thunderbird requires the ExQuilla add-on, which requires an annual subscription. Evolution has built-in calendar support and is more directly comparable to Outlook, in that it feels like a comprehensive corporate email tool (see figure 8.5). Thunderbird feels more appropriate to home users who don't want a lot of bells and whistles (see figure 8.6). Both support IMAP and POP3, which are used in non-commercial email services like Gmail and Yahoo!, without any plugins or add-ons.

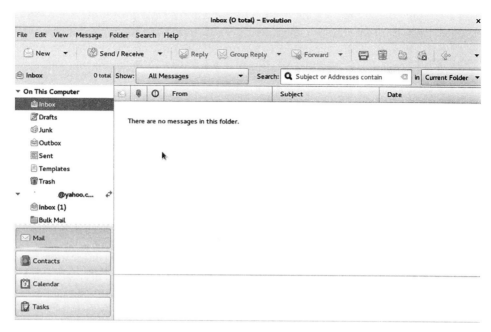

Figure 8.5   Evolution is a powerful email program that includes its own calendar application.

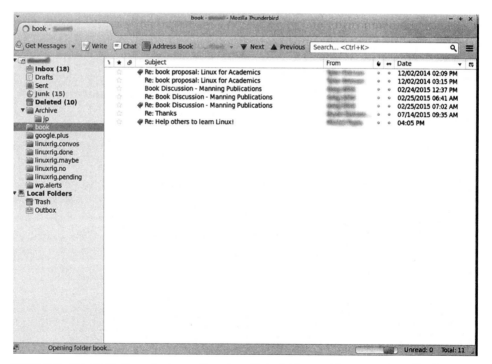

Figure 8.6   Thunderbird is a simple email program that might appeal to users not working in corporate environments.

Thunderbird is also available for Windows and OS X. Evolution is Linux-only. Thunderbird is already installed on your system. Open it and see if you can get your mail working with it. It's designed to automatically import the settings from most major email providers, so you'll put in your name, email address, and password, and Thunderbird will do the rest.

8.1.4 Choosing your office program(s)

So which program is best? LibreOffice is probably the most commonly used, meaning there's the most help and documentation available. But in terms of choosing a program, you probably want to think about two things:

1. Interface
2. File rendering

When I say interface, I mean ease of use:

1. Which program makes the most sense to you, in terms of layout?
2. Which program makes the most sense to you, in terms of navigation?
3. Which program makes the most sense to you, in terms of behavior?

Open LibreOffice Writer, the word processor:

1. Write down five things for which you use word processors.
2. Make the list bold and double-space it.
3. Change the font.
4. Look at the question above and think about how Writer is working for you (and keep the file open).

All of the programs discussed here behave like their Office equivalents, but there are subtle things, like the organization of the menus, that can mean the difference between a program that's easy to use and hard to use.

File rendering means how well the program handles your files. For example, if LibreOffice is having trouble with a template used in your workplace, another word processor, like AbiWord, might be a better choice.

Because Microsoft uses proprietary file formats, other programs sometimes have trouble working with them, which is why something might look OK in one word processor, but different in another. In general, you'll find it easier to work with files when they're saved in an OpenDocument format, because those are designed to be shared and don't have proprietary code in them. OpenDocument is usually an option in your Save As menu across programs and operating system. OpenDocument file formats include:

- OpenDocument Text (.odt)
- OpenDocument Presentation (.odp)
- OpenDocument Spreadsheet (.ods)
- OpenDocument Graphic (.odg)

Getting into the habit of using OpenDocument files makes files render better across programs.

For practice, take the Writer file you just created and save it as a .odt file.

Email is standard-based, meaning you won't have any technical issues with one client or another. Choosing your email client can be a purely interface-based decision.

Table 8.1 Which office software should you pick?

Office software	Reason
Choose LibreOffice if …	you want a complete suite of office programs
Choose Calligra if …	you want a complete suite of office programs, and you're using KDE
Choose AbiWord if …	you want a very simple word processor
Choose Gnumeric if …	you want a spreadsheet program
Choose Thunderbird if …	you want a basic email client
Choose Evolution if …	you want to feel like you're using Outlook

8.2 Image editing

Image editing is a simpler process on Linux. For one thing, there are fewer options. But another thing that simplifies it is that the tool you choose depends on what you want to do with images.

The GNU Image Manipulation Program (GIMP), does a lot of things but has a bit of a learning curve. LibreOffice is much more basic, but it's also more straightforward to use.

8.2.1 GIMP

GIMP is a powerful image edit and creation program. It lets you layer images and gives you access to all kinds of things, like filters and color tools. As I said, it's powerful, but it's also very complicated, with a notoriously challenging interface (see figure 8.7). It could be the reason GIMP doesn't ship as default software with all distributions (including Ubuntu), but it's available in all repositories.

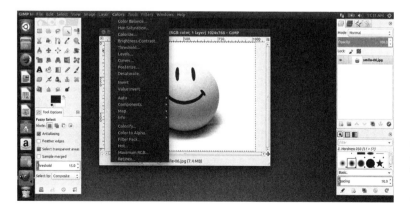

**Figure 8.7
GIMP has a complex interface that makes it both powerful and challenging.**

You'll notice that GIMP has three windows. The window to the left contains the tools you'll use to manipulate your image. This includes things like brushes, color pick-up tools, and erasers. The middle window is where you see your image. The right window controls the layers, which you'll use if you're building a complex image.

There's also a top navigation menu area with a lot of other options. GIMP has a lot of options, which is a blessing and a curse.

The first thing I do with GIMP is go to Windows along the top navigation and put GIMP into Single-Window Mode. This displays one window and makes it much easier to work with (see figure 8.8).

Figure 8.8   GIMP is easier to work with in single-window mode.

The trick to using GIMP is determining which menu has your option. For instance, if you're looking to shrink a photo:

1 Go to the Image menu along the top navigation (see figure 8.9).
2 Click Scale Image…
3 Choose how you want to shrink it. GIMP uses pixels by default but you can also use percentages (see figure 8.10).

The process is simple once you know what to do. But there's a bit of a learning curve.

Figure 8.9   GIMP's top menus control a lot of functionality, including shrinking and enlarging images.

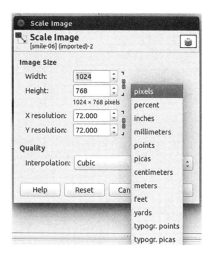

Figure 8.10   The Scale Image menu controls the size and resolution of images.

Download a book cover from Amazon.com and resize it, making it smaller. To save an image, right-click it in your browser and click Save Image As... Make sure you save the image.

I don't have an art or Photoshop background and I use GIMP for all of my image manipulation needs, including the images for this book. I don't use all of the functionality, but I can do what I need to do, and I suspect that's how most people use this. It takes some time to learn GIMP but it's time well-spent if you do any kind of regular work with photos or images.

GIMP is also available for Windows and OS X.

8.2.2   LibreOffice Draw

LibreOffice Draw is much more basic, which makes it easier to use. It's nothing great but if you need to occasionally touch up photos in a minor way, it should be fine.

LibreOffice Draw has a much simpler interface than GIMP (see figure 8.11).

Figure 8.11   LibreOffice Draw has a simple interface, not unlike Microsoft Word's.

If you want to shrink or enlarge a photo with LibreOffice Draw, you click on the image. You'll see some small squares around the image (see figure 8.12).

If you click and drag on the squares, you'll change the size of the image. Take the book cover you just shrunk with GIMP and make it bigger.

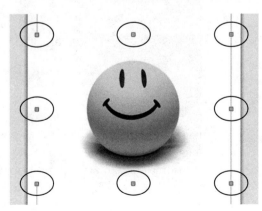

Figure 8.12   Working with the small squares around the image allows you to change its size in LibreOffice Draw.

Table 8.2   Which image editor should you pick?

Editor	Reason
Choose GIMP if …	you're looking for a robust Adobe Photoshop replacement
Choose LibreOffice Draw if …	you want to lightly and occasionally crop photos and images

8.3   Multimedia

Let's be honest for a moment. You're not all about work. Even though you're spending your lunch hour learning Linux, you also enjoy your down time. Maybe you like to watch movies. Or maybe you like to listen to music. This section will help you relax using your Linux desktop.

8.3.1   Movies

Ubuntu doesn't come with a default video player, which I think has to do with how much viewing now happens in the web browser. There was a time when you couldn't stream Netflix from Ubuntu but it's now possible through the Chrome browser on most up-to-date distributions. But if you want to watch your own content, you have options with Linux.

VLC

My favorite video player is VLC Media Player (it can also play music but we'll talk about that later in this section). It handles different formats of videos without much drama or thought. Double-click your video and VLC handles the rest. This isn't the case with all movie players, which sometimes need your help downloading and installing codecs (which you might remember from chapter 4).

VLC's interface is very simple (see figure 8.13). The controls along the bottom are used to work with the video.

Figure 8.13   VLC looks like most other movie players.

There isn't much more to say about VLC because it works so well and so simply. It's also available for Windows and OS X and it's my preferred video player for those operating systems, too, for the same reasons discussed here.

1 Install VLC.
2 Download a video and an audio clip from https://archive.org/ and play both using VLC.

GNOME VIDEOS

There are other movie players for Linux, if for some reason VLC doesn't work for you. GNOME Videos is another one, with a similar look to VLC. However it doesn't have the same kind of codec support VLC does. Luckily, it will offer to go out and download whatever you need to play a given video (see figure 8.14). Try playing the video you downloaded from archive.org in GNOME Videos.

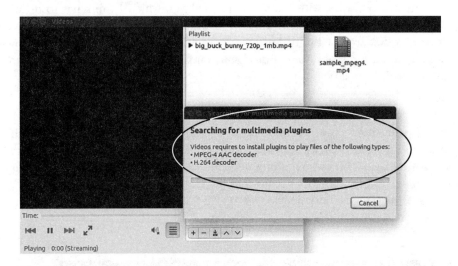

Figure 8.14   GNOME Videos will help you with the codecs needed to play certain videos.

8.3.2   *Music*

Music players, like iTunes, represent a single interface to all of the music on your computer. iTunes isn't available for Linux, but there are quite a few similar programs.

RHYTHMBOX

Ubuntu comes with Rhythmbox by default and it's similar to iTunes, except that content isn't purchased through it (although it does offer a plugin that interfaces with Magnatune, an online music store).

With Rhythmbox, you point it to your music directory (or directories) and it handles the rest. Rhythmbox has a simple interface, with the play/forward/back commands you would expect on a music player (see figure 8.15).

It also has a nice plugin architecture that installs software that adds more functionality, like the aforementioned ability to connect to a third-party music store. Plug-ins can do everything from tweeting what you're playing to automatically importing cover art.

Figure 8.15 Rhythmbox has a standard music player interface.

Rhythmbox is part of the GNOME project, but works across Linux distributions and desktops. Use it to play the audio clip you downloaded from archive.org.

AMAROK

KDE has its own music player called Amarok. It looks similar to Rhythmbox and has most of the same functionality (see figure 8.16). However, it will do things like pull in artist information from Wikipedia. It also keeps statistics on your music habits. Despite being associated with KDE, Amarok is also available for Windows and OS X.

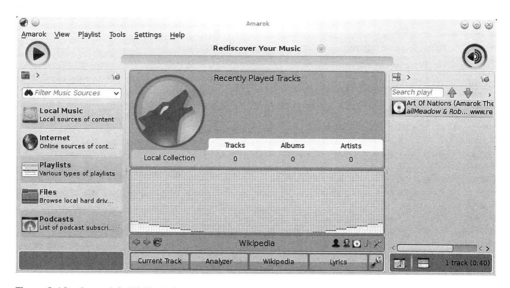

Figure 8.16 Amarok is KDE's default music player, but it works across desktop environments.

There are other music players like Banshee and Clementine. Perhaps more than any other piece of software, different distributions seem to go with different music players.

If you spend a lot of time playing music with your computer, I think it's worth spending time playing with the different players, because the interface is a personal thing and all of them will do the simple job of playing music. Table 8.3 offers suggestions on picking a multimedia player.

Table 8.3   Which multimedia player should you pick?

Player	Reason
Choose VLC if …	you want the simplest way to play videos
Choose GNOME Videos if …	something about VLC doesn't work for you
Choose Rhythmbox if …	you want something relatively simple
Choose Amarok if …	you want a music player with a few more bells and whistles

8.4 *Wrapping up*

The goal of this chapter is to give you an overview of the commonly used software available for Linux. It's based on what people tend to use on Windows and OS X. This list is by no means complete.

The point (and joy) of Linux is the amount of choice you have, so you're by no means limited to what's discussed here. Instead, I selected some of the larger software projects, which are probably good places to start. When I'm resizing a photo or building a spreadsheet, I want a program that simply works. I'm not looking for anything dramatic or exciting. I want my photo to get smaller or my formulas to work. All of the software in this chapter will accomplish that goal. But like desktop environments, you'll want to think about what works for you and the way you like to work.

GLOSSARY OF TERMS

In this chapter I explained:

Office productivity software—Programs typically used for office work, like spreadsheets, word processors, and email clients
Multimedia player—Software for playing audio and video

8.5 *Lab*

Consider these questions before you dive into the lab that follows them. You should also apply these questions to any of the programs discussed in this chapter and in this book:

- What do you like about the interface you're currently using?
- Do you know how to navigate it or are you constantly looking for a feature that you cannot find?
- Do you like the aesthetics of the interface or does it feel ugly to you?

- Does it feel dramatically different from the versions of these programs you use in Windows and OS X?

- What do you like better about these programs?

- Do these interfaces make more sense to you?

- Are there features on these tools that your current tools lack?

- What features and functionality do you feel is missing?

With those questions in mind, let's work with the programs you just learned:

1 Use LibreOffice Writer and create a short document.

2 Use LibreOffice Calc to compute the average of 10, 15, 19, and 18.

3 Download GIMP and try to scale an image from archive.org, this time making it bigger.

4 Use Rhythmbox to install the song lyric plugin. *HINT*: It's under Tools.

Text files and editors

9

A *text editor* is a simple editor that presents text without any formatting like bold, italics, or underline. Text editors only show text and line breaks (some might preserve indenting). Text editors, like Windows Notepad and OS X's TextEdit, are wonderful tools on any operating system but are especially useful on Linux systems because:

- They allow you to edit configuration files in your Linux system.
- They keep you away from proprietary formats that might require certain software.
- They last forever. Long after civilization has ended, text files will still be openable and readable.

This chapter will discuss the power and beauty of text files and will walk you through some common Linux text editors. In the previous chapter, we talked about word processors, which are fantastic tools, but also complex ones. Text editors allow you to work with just text and not formatting, making text files easy to move between operating systems without losing any information. I'm not writing this book in a word processor, but with a text editor. I'll discuss this process later in the chapter.

Text editors also allow you to interact with your Linux system in a way that isn't possible with other operating systems. For instance, I use a ThinkPad with a built-in TrackPoint mouse. Most Linux distributions let me use the TrackPoint wheel to scroll through content without my having to do anything, but some distributions, for whatever reason, don't. In that situation I can enable the TrackPoint scroll by going into a directory, adding a text file to a folder with a few lines I copied and pasted from a guide, and then, after I reboot, the scroll works. Many desktop environments, like Openbox, allow you to make changes to the interface using text

114

files. This power, flexibility, and versatility is what makes text editors so popular within the Linux community.

9.1 Getting to know text editors

This section will introduce you to three text editors, giving you an overview of how they work and the tasks to which they're best suited. The nice thing about text editors is that the product is always the same—a simple file without any formatting. It can be anything from programming to HTML to words in a file. All text editors will do that job fine, so you never need to worry you're using the *wrong* text editor. Any text editor can open the work of any other text editor. With that mental safety net in place, you can simply focus on the one you like to use. Or the ones you like to use, in my case.

One final note: The editors discussed in this chapter are also available for Windows and OS X so if you discover you like using one of these, you can also use them on other operating systems.

9.1.1 gedit

You might remember gedit from chapter 6. It's the default text editor for GNOME and Ubuntu. You also might remember that the interface is simple and straightforward. You type words and they appear on the screen. There are some basic controls along the top navigation panel (see figure 9.1) and some more along the top navigation menu.

The top navigation menu includes the gedit Preferences, found under the Edit menu. Preferences lets you change the look of gedit, including its colors. It also gives you access to some plugins, which give gedit additional functionality like Snippets,

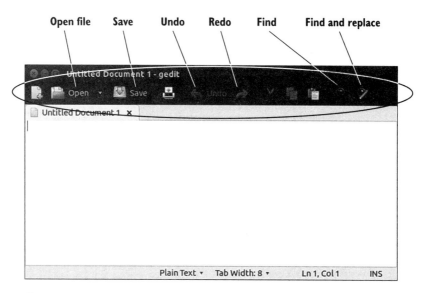

Figure 9.1 gedit has simple editing tools at the top of its interface: undo, redo, find, and find and replace.

which allow you to save frequently used pieces of text and deploy them with either a shortcut key or a tab after a certain word. If you frequently write a complicated word, sentence, or piece of code, you can assign it a letter or word trigger. Then, whenever you type that letter or word and hit Tab, gedit will replace the text with whatever you assigned to that combination.

gedit comes with some plugins, not all of which are activated. You can see them under the Preferences menu also (see figure 9.2).

Because its code is freely available to anyone, you'll find lots of gedit plugins online. The best place to start is the GNOME wiki at https://wiki.gnome.org. There, you'll find links to the various gedit plugin projects.

Figure 9.2   gedit has many plugins that can give it additional functionality.

The permissions-based nature of Linux makes it unlikely these plugins could harm your computer. We'll talk more about permissions in chapter 19.

Let's take a few moments to use gedit again:

1   Launch it via the Dash. You can type `gedit` or `text editor`.
2   Type a sentence into gedit. I recommend `Text editors are fun!`
3   Highlight the sentence. You can use Ctrl-A to select all of the text or use your mouse.
4   Copy the text using Ctrl-C or using the icon along the top bar (it's an icon featuring two pieces of paper).
5   Move to the end of the first sentence and paste this after it using Ctrl-V or the paste icon (it's a clipboard icon).
6   Highlight the second sentence and cut it using Ctrl-X or the cut icon (it's a scissors icon).

All of these steps should feel familiar. It's just like using most word processors, web browsers, or pretty much any other kind of program. I tend to use gedit for most of my writing because it's so simple. I know all of the keyboard shortcuts because they're the same ones most other programs use. The plugins let me do things like add a word count to the screen and preview certain kinds of markup (we'll talk about that in a moment) in a separate window. It's simple yet effective. Now let's move on to Vim, which can do a lot more than gedit, but also has a steeper learning curve.

9.1.2   *Vim*

Vim is another popular text editor with its own syntax that makes it almost like a language. It's not easy to learn, but if you can master it, you can have complete control over your documents and words.

For instance, if you want to remove the third word in the fourth line of a document, there are Vim commands that can do that for you, without you having to move your cursor to that word like you'd need to in something like gedit. Vim is based on vi, a UNIX program that you use within the terminal (Vim stands for vi Improved). If you have access to a terminal anywhere, and you're on a Unix-based system such as Linux or OS X, then you have vi. Vim is a version of vi that's a bit more user-friendly, in that it lets you use the arrow keys to move (vi has you use the H-J-K-L keys because it predates arrow keys!). We're going to work with Vim because it's slightly more user-friendly, but it looks and behaves just like vi, so if you ever find yourself stuck in a terminal, you should be able to survive. You also might recall it from chapter 7 when we installed it.

There are two ways to interact with Vim. The two ways are called *modes* (there are actually more modes but we won't explore them). One mode is for creating text (*insert mode*) and the other is for manipulating it with commands (*normal* or *command* mode).

Insert mode is what you use when you're creating text. It feels like a traditional text editor in this mode in that you're typing words and they're appearing on the screen. However, you can't change the text in insert mode. To do something like copy or move text, you need to switch into command mode. You enter commands at the bottom of your screen; the rest of the screen is for insert mode (figure 9.3).

We're going to learn some Vim commands in a moment. I think of insert mode for creating text and command mode for manipulating text. This is very different from gedit, where everything happens in a single window and in a single mode.

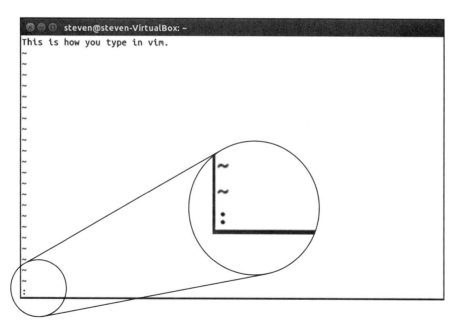

Figure 9.3   Vim's command area is the colon at the bottom of the screen. The rest of the screen is for content.

We're going to spend a few minutes working with Vim. It takes a while to learn and it does a lot of different things well, more than I could even cover here. But if using Vim speaks to you, I encourage you to spend some time learning to use it (I also think it would make a great *Month of Lunches* topic!).

> **CUSTOMIZING VIM**   You'll notice Vim doesn't have a preferences menu (or any menus, really).

If you wish to customize it, in terms of things like colors, fonts, how it wraps lines, or if it starts with the spell check turned on, you create and edit the .vimrc file (with a text editor!) that lives in your home directory (we'll talk more about directories in chapter 14). There are lots of sample .vimrc files online that'll help to get you started.

Let's take Vim for a spin.

1 Launch the terminal via the Dash (you can just type the word `terminal`).
2 Type the word `vim` into the terminal and press Enter. Vim will open.
3 As soon as you start typing, you'll enter insert mode. You'll know this because it says – *INSERT* – at the bottom of the screen. Type `Text editors are fun!` again.
4 Try to highlight and copy and paste the sentence like we did with gedit. Notice that you can't. Instead, enter command mode by pressing Escape and then colon (`:`).
5 Once in command mode, type the letter y, which means yank, or copy, the text.
6 Now type p to paste it. You'll see the sentence on a new line.
7 To remove that extra sentence, type `dd` twice, which will cut the extra sentence.
8 To go back to typing, press Escape and then `i`.
9 When you're done with Vim, click the colon to go into command mode and type `q!` which lets you quit without saving.

Vim comes with its own tutorial. To launch it, type `vimtutor` into the terminal.

9.1.3   *Emacs*

Emacs is, like Vim, a powerful-yet-complex text editor. Like Vim, it has its passionate fans who love its versatility. For instance, Emacs can be used to read and send email. It also has an organization mode that keeps lists and notes. It also has games and a calendar. There are people who live their life through Emacs, and like Vim, learning it could be its own book.

Emacs uses lots of key combinations based upon the Ctrl key, which it abbreviates as C, and the Alt key, which Emacs abbreviates as M. Some people liken using Emacs to playing an instrument, since many of the shortcuts are not unlike making chords on a piano or guitar. You'll notice Emacs has some gedit-like icons along its top (see figure 9.4) as well as some menus.

Open file Emacs tutorial Save   Cut   Copy   Paste

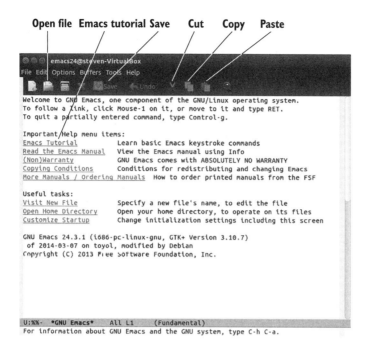

Figure 9.4 Emacs has icons similar to gedit.

Unlike Vim, you can muddle along with Emacs without needing to learn much. Rather helpfully, the menus show the shortcut keys for each command so you learn while you use it (see figure 9.5).

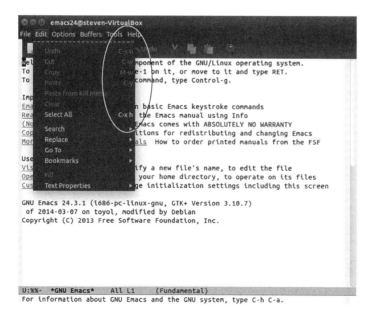

Figure 9.5 Emacs's menus show you shortcuts that you can use instead of menus.

You can customize Emacs via its top Options menu. We're only going to spend a few minutes with Emacs, but like Vim, if you like it, I encourage you to invest time learning to use it. There's a tutorial link in the opening screen of Emacs. You'll see it every time you open Emacs. Let's try Emacs out.

Try it now: Getting started with Emacs

1 Install Emacs (just like we did with Vim in chapter 7), then launch it from the Dash.
2 Open a new file by typing Ctrl-X and then Ctrl-F. You'll be on the bottom of the screen like you were in Vim's command mode. Emacs wants you to name the new file. Just call it test and Press Enter.
3 Now that you're in an empty file, type `Text editors are fun!`
4 Use Ctrl-x and then the letter h to highlight all of the text.
5 Use Alt-w to copy the sentence.
6 Use Ctrl-y to paste it in.
7 To remove the extra sentence, highlight it with your mouse (or shift and the arrow keys) and press Ctrl-w to cut it.

9.2   Working with text editors

Now that you've seen a few text editors, let's talk more specifically about *what* you can do with them.

9.2.1   Writing with text editors

As you saw with those three text editors, writing with them is just a matter of typing. The hard part of that is thinking of things to type. But you can't blame text editors for that. The real challenge of text editors is that they provide you with no formatting, so you can't do anything like add bullets or bold/italicized text to your document. However, there is a solution in certain *markup languages*. Markup languages are ways of formatting documents. Some are complicated like HTML, but others are pretty simple. For instance, Markdown is a popular markup method. You write it in a text file, but if you want to make something bold, you use two asterisks before and after the word or words. So this:

`**bold**`

would look like

bold

To save the file as Markdown, you would put .md at the end of the file name. You would then have a Markdown-formatted text file that you could edit with any text editor on any operating system. But how do you turn a text file into another kind of document? The answer is a utility called *Pandoc*, which transforms text between formats. To use it, you first install it from your repository, and then you use simple syntax to change one kind of file into another. For example, to change a Markdown file called notes.md into an OpenDocument Text file or .odt, which we talked about in the last chapter, you would go into the terminal, navigate into the file's directory (I'll show you how to do that next chapter), and run a command like

```
pandoc notes.md -o notes.odt
```

You would then have a new OpenDocument Text file in the same directory as the original Markdown file. This ability to transform content makes it much more shareable. I might have some great content in an HTML file when I'm suddenly asked to give a presentation on it. I can use Pandoc to change it to a slide format. With Pandoc, file format becomes less of a restriction.

Of course, some people just keep everything in text files without transforming it, which is what allows them to use something like Emacs for everything.

I'm writing this book in Asciidoc, another markup language. What I like about the combination of text files and transformation utilities is that I don't have to worry about rendering or what version of what software someone is using. With text files, you know anyone can open them, on their phone or computer, without any complications.

I like Markdown for similar reasons. I write everything in Markdown and then use Pandoc to change the Markdown into anything and everything from HTML to Word documents, without ever having to shift mental gears in terms of how I work with text.

Markdown and Pandoc are not Linux-only so if you find the workflow helpful here, you can expand it to other operating systems, too.

9.2.2 *Going under the hood with text files*

As I mentioned at the start of this chapter, you can interact with different parts of the Linux operating system using text files. You can change parts of your Linux system by editing certain text files, like the way I fixed my TrackPoint. You can also see what's going on with your system by looking at text files. A quick-and-easy way for us to do that now is checking the log files, which we talked about in chapter 4. The logs are the record of what's going on with your operating system. You'll recall from chapter 4 that Ubuntu has a tool called System Log for viewing log files, but you can use any text editor to view them, too.

If you wanted to look at a log of all of your logs, to see *everything* that's been happening on your system, you could look at the syslog file in a text editor.

To do that in gedit, you would:

1 Use Ctrl-O or click the Open button.
2 Click Computer from the file directory (see figure 9.6).
3 Double-click the var directory (I'll explain that in chapter 14).

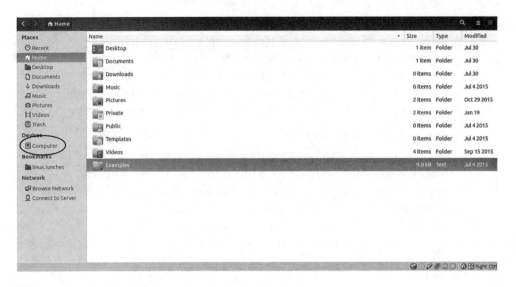

Figure 9.6   Use the Computer link to access your log files.

4   Double-click the log directory.

5   Double-click syslog.

6   The log file will open in gedit.

You can scroll through the file to see all of the things that happen on your computer while you're working. This can help you troubleshoot issues, like unexplained crashes. Simply scroll through the file and see what was happening (or not happening) before the crash.

To open that same file in Vim:

1   Go into command mode (:) and type `edit /var/log/syslog`.

2   The file will open in Vim.

3   Don't forget how to exit Vim: command mode and then q!

To open it in Emacs:

1   Go to the File menu.

2   Click on Open File...?

3   Navigate to the file, as we did with gedit.

9.3   *Wrapping up*

You now have a sense of the power and beauty of text editors. Three specific ones were mentioned here, but like in the previous chapter, there are more that I didn't have time to cover. I briefly touched on a few more in table 9.1. You don't have to spend a lot of time in a text editor on Linux, but it's nice to have one you feel comfortable using, so you're comfortable when you need to use one.

I hope you'll give some serious thought to doing more work in a text editor, because it frees you from the distractions of formatting and is a nice way to force yourself to focus on words or code or whatever it is you're working on.

And which text editor should you pick? By now you know that's up to you! However, table 9.1 might help you decide which one to invest time using.

Table 9.1 Choosing a text editor

Text editor	Pros	Cons
Atom	Simple interface Packages (Atom calls them plugins) add functionality	Linux version is still a little buggy Doesn't render certain markup very well
Brackets	Simple interface Extensions (what Brackets calls "plugins") add functionality	Linux version is still a little buggy
gedit	Simple interface Plugins add functionality Minimal learning curve	Fewest features of the three
Emacs	Powerful Expandable to the point that it's almost an operating system Usable without a mouse	Has a bit of a learning curve Requires a lot of finger stretching to execute commands
nano	*Very* simple interface Terminal-based, like Vim Lists shortcuts on interface	You can't do much more than type, cut/copy, and paste.
Vim	Powerful Can be installed almost anywhere Takes up very little disk space	Has a steep learning curve

GLOSSARY OF TERMS

In this chapter I explained:

Markup—A syntax for formatting documents

Markdown—A form of markup that allows text to easily be changed into other formats, like HTML and word processed documents

Text editor—A simple editor that presents text without any formatting like bold, italics, or underline

9.4 *Lab*

1 Open gedit and write up some notes and thoughts about this chapter.
2 Save the file and open it in Vim, adding one more note.
3 Delete the note you added and save the file.
4 Install Emacs using the terminal.
5 Open the file in Emacs and retype the note you added and deleted in Vim.

6 Delete everything in the file.

7 Undo the deletion.

8 Rank the text editors in order of your personal preference in the file and save it in Emacs.

Advanced lab

1 Open the file in Vim and copy and paste each line so each one appears twice in the file.

2 Use dd to delete the duplicate lines.

Working with files and
folders on the command line

Most of us interact with computers using GUIs, visual ways of working with software. They're what allow us to use a mouse to open programs and change directories. But beneath these visual interfaces are text-based commands. The GUIs translate our clicks into commands, without our having to know the commands. In Linux, you have access to these commands via the terminal. You'll sometimes hear the terminal or command line referred to as Bash or command line interface (CLI).

Most of the time, this graphical way of interacting with our device is convenient. We point at something with our mouse and something happens, whether it's a file opening or a setting changing. But sometimes you need to know the commands yourself. Sometimes, as we saw with Vim in the previous chapter, we need to drop into the command line to issue commands ourselves, without a GUI between us and our operating system. This could be for reasons of convenience, to more efficiently move files around our system, or to repair something on our system that can't be fixed through a GUI.

Linux, which you'll recall is based upon the text-based UNIX operating system, allows you to freely and easily move between the command line and a graphical interface. Also, because OS X is based on UNIX, you'll be able to use these same commands in your OS X command line (Windows has a command prompt, but it's not based on UNIX). Though most commands have graphical equivalents, sometimes it's simply quicker to do something in the terminal.

The purpose of this chapter, and the next few chapters, is to get you comfortable working in the command line and to help you understand how it can make your life easier. The command line often comes in handy when you're trying to fix something with your system. But I also find it helpful when I'm working on an old, slow machine. The command line, in those situations, is much quicker.

My goal isn't to convert you to the command line full-time. The truth is, I spend little time in the command line myself. However, for the few tasks I choose to do via the command line, it's a wonderfully helpful thing to know. In the next chapter, you'll learn how to shut down stubborn programs with the command line. In chapter 12, you'll learn how to move the output of commands into text files. All of these are helpful tools in keeping your Linux system running efficiently. But before we can get to those commands, let's start with the basics.

In chapter 6, we used Nautilus to move, create, and delete files and folders. We're now going to do the same things using the command line.

> **FOR THOSE USING LIVE IMAGES**   If you're using a live image, you'll need to flip back to chapter 6 and put back the linux.lunches folder we put in Documents. Make sure you do that before we begin.

10.1   *Working with files and folders*

Let's start our terminal work by seeing where in our file structure we are. Open your terminal. You should see something like:

```
steven@steven-VirtualBox:~$
```

In this case, my username is steven and the name of my computer is steven-VirtualBox. You'll have something like your logon name @ the name of your computer and :~$. This is called the *command prompt* which references some place in a directory or folder on your computer, but where?

Type ls, for list, hit Enter, and you'll see all of the files and folders in your current directory. This is helpful for orienting yourself.

You should see a list of folders. You know they're folders because they're in a different color than everything else in the terminal. You should see:

- Desktop
- Downloads
- Music
- Public
- Videos
- Documents
- Pictures
- Templates

Now open Nautilus, or another graphical file manager. You should see the same folders. Now you know where you are in your filesystem.

In chapter 6, we double-clicked into the Documents directory. But there's no double-clicking in the terminal. Everything is done via commands. Instead, we'll type `cd Documents` and press Enter (the command prompt is case-sensitive, so make sure the first D is uppercase). `cd` means change directory and Documents is the name of the directory we're changing to. After you type that, you'll notice your command prompt has changed. Now, after the colon, you'll see `~/Documents$`. That means you're now in the Documents directory.

Type `ls` and press Enter again to see what else is in that directory. You should see our linux.lunches folder from chapter 6.

10.1.1 Creating folders

In chapter 6, we used our mouse to create a folder called linux.lunches. Now we're going to use the command line to do the same thing. Let's create another folder called linux.lunches.terminal. To do that, type

```
mkdir linux.lunches.terminal
```

and press Enter. `mkdir` stands for make directory. It might seem like nothing happened, but if you type `ls` again, you'll see two directories in your Documents folder and one of them will be linux.lunches.terminal. This is similar to chapter 6 but with typing instead of right-clicking.

Now, let's go into this new directory so we can add a file. Type

```
cd linux.lunches.terminal
```

and your command prompt will change again. After the colon, you'll now see `~/Documents/linux.lunches.terminal$`. The prompt is showing that you're in the linux.lunches.terminal directory, which is in the Documents directory (see figure 10.1).

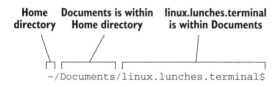

Figure 10.1   The command prompt shows directory hierarchies.

It's important to remember that things done on the command line will appear in our GUI. They're not separate systems. So the directory we created in the command line is visible and accessible via the GUI (and vice versa). Go back to the Nautilus file manager. You'll see this new directory within your Documents directory. Keep Nautilus (or your preferred file manager) open so you can see the changes we make in the command line.

10.1.2 *Creating files*

Now we're going to place a file in this new folder so you can see how to create a file with the command line. The new file will be called mysecondnote. To create it, type

```
touch mysecondnote
```

and press Enter. Now toggle over to your file manager and look in the linux.lunches.terminal folder. You'll see a text file called mysecondnote.touch automatically updates a file, as if you saved it, without having to open the file. It also creates empty files, though, in cases where the file being touched doesn't exist. If you double-click mysecondnote in your file manager, you'll see it's empty. Once again you've created a text file without opening a text editor, which is still kind of impressive! You created a new file in two words of commands without opening or saving anything!

Now that you have the file open, type a brief message like I'm learning the command line. Then, save and close the file, and go back to the terminal. You can open the file in your text editor of choice via the command line.

> **LIVE IMAGE USERS**   Remember: Live image users will need to reinstall Vim and Emacs.

- To open it in Emacs, type emacs mysecondnote
- To open it in gedit, type gedit mysecondnote
- To open it in Vim, type vim mysecondnote

Each time you do this, the file will open in the text editor you indicated.

10.1.3 *Copying folders and files*

The command to copy a file or folder is cp. When you use it, you first indicate a file or folder to copy and then the destination. Let's move mysecondnote into our linux.lunches folder, or directory.

To do that, you'll type:

```
cp mysecondnote ../linux.lunches
```

We're issuing a command to copy the file mysecondnote to the folder linux.lunches (see figure 10.2).

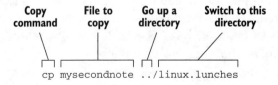

Figure 10.2   The copy command includes the file to be copied and the location to which the file will be copied.

The .. means to go up a directory. And whenever you see a / in a command, you're dealing with a directory or folder. So if we started in Documents/linux.lunches.terminal, we're telling the file to go back up into the Documents folder and then into the linux.lunches one.

Go back into Nautilus and you'll see the file is now in two places.

Now let's copy a folder. Let's copy linux.lunches.terminal into our linux.lunches folder. To do that, you might type

```
cp /linux.lunches.terminal ../linux.lunches
```

But what happened? You should have gotten an error `cp: cannot stat '/linux.lunches.terminal': No such file or directory`. That's because you can't copy a folder or directory from inside of it with `cp`. So you'll need to leave that directory. Remember how we used .. to go up a directory in our copy command? It also works with `cd` command. To move up a folder, type

```
cd ..
```

and you'll find yourself back in your Documents folder. Try your command now (you can remove the .. because you're not going up a directory).

```
cp /linux.lunches.terminal /linux.lunches
```

You should get the same error. The issue is that you need a period before the slash to tell the copy command you're working in the current directory. Add those and try it again. Your command should now look like this:

```
cp ./linux.lunches.terminal ./linux.lunches
```

And now a new error!

```
cp: omitting directory './linux.lunches.terminal'
```

The final piece of the puzzle is that our directory has a file in it, so we need to tell the command to include the files within the directory. When you include the files in a folder or directory, it's called a *recursive copy* so you'll add a modifier, or flag, to the command. Try this (and look at figure 10.3):

```
cp -R ./linux.lunches.terminal ./linux.lunches
```

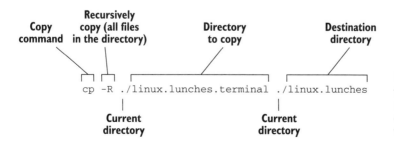

Figure 10.3 The -R flag indicates a recursive copy; you're copying the files within a directory.

You'll now see the linux.lunches.terminal directory, and the accompanying file, in the linux.lunches folder. We'll talk more about flags in chapter 12. For now, I want you to get used to using commands in the terminal.

10.1.4 Moving folders and files

Moving files between directories will be a similar process. The move command is mv. It works the same as cp, in that you specify your source file first and then the destination. You should still be in your Documents folder in the terminal. Move into your linux.lunches.terminal directory with

```
cd linux.lunches.terminal
```

I always like to do an ls to make sure I am where I think I am. I sometimes wish I could do an ls in real life.

Let's move mysecondnote out to our Documents folder. To do that, you'll type:

```
mv mysecondnote ..
```

There's the .. again. That's telling the command to place the file up a directory.

Now let's put it back. To do that, you'll type the following (note the period):

```
mv ../mysecondnote .
```

The .. is pointing to the file, which is in the directory above the current one (see figure 10.4). And the single period indicates the current directory.

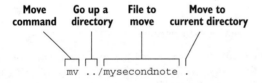

Figure 10.4 The move command is similar to the copy command.

The process is similar for moving a directory. Go back to your Documents directory with a cd ... Then, move the linux.lunches.terminal directory to the Desktop with this command:

```
mv ./linux.lunches.terminal ../Desktop
```

The ./ means we're indicating a folder in our current directory. The folder Desktop is above Documents. And don't forget the commands are case-sensitive. You should now see the linux.lunches.terminal folder on your Desktop. mysecondnote is in it. Unlike cp, mv doesn't need to be explicitly told to be recursive. It included the files within the moved directory automatically.

10.1.5 *Deleting folders and files*

Files are deleted with the `rm` command. Folders are deleted with `rmdir`. A folder can't be deleted until it's empty.

Be very, careful with the `rm` command! When you delete something with the GUI, it winds up in your trash, so files are rarely truly gone. But when you delete something with `rm`, it's gone forever. That means if you accidentally navigate into the wrong directory and delete a file, there's no getting it back. It is for this reason that I rarely use `rm`. I don't trust myself. `rmdir` is safer, since it only works on empty directories. Both commands don't need destination paths since they're removing files and folders.

Let's carefully delete that file and folder from our desktop. We're still in the Documents folder in the terminal. First, we'll have to delete mysecondnote and then we can delete the linux.lunches.terminal directory. To remove the file, we'll use:

```
rm ../Desktop/linux.lunches.terminal/mysecondnote
```

We're sending the command up a directory, via the .., into the Desktop folder and then into the linux.lunches.terminal folder, and removing the mysecondnote file from that folder. Once that file is gone, we can remove the directory with:

```
rmdir ../Desktop/linux.lunches.terminal
```

And just like that, the empty directory is gone. If you get a message the directory isn't empty, that means gedit saved a backup file that will be called mysecondnote~. Go ahead and delete that file and then delete the directory.

> **WILDCARDS** We've been working with one file at a time, but the command line allows you to use wildcards.
>
> Let's say you want to move all of the text files in a directory.
>
> Instead of listing all of the files individually, you could use the wildcard to indicate all files with the same file extension. In this case, it would resemble *.txt, meaning any file that ends with .txt. A *.* would delete any files with a period in their name, including the file extension.
>
> But be careful using `rm` with a wildcard! If your syntax isn't precise enough, you could wind up permanently deleting the wrong file, or files.

10.2 *Wrapping up*

You should now have a sense of how to manipulate files using the command line. I don't expect that you'll stop using a file manager and move to the terminal for all of your file-shifting needs, but I do expect that you understand the process enough to look at commands from other people and understand what's going on.

Once you know how to move and copy files, you'll often find it's quicker and easier than using the file manager. For instance, the wildcard allows you to quickly move all of a certain kind of file into a new directory in the time it takes to open a graphical file manager. This can be a huge time-saver if you have a lot of files to move.

I know we covered a lot of information in this chapter, so I devised table 10.1 to help you remember the commands.

Table 10.1   **A guide to simple Linux commands**

Command	What it does
cd	Changes directory (you need to indicate the directory)
cd ..	Goes up a directory
cp	Copies (use cp -R to get the contents of a directory); includes source first and then destination
ls	Lists files in current directory
mv	Moves; includes source first and then destination
rm	Deletes file; indicates file(s) to delete
rmdir	Deletes empty directory; indicates folder(s) to delete
.	Indicates current directory
..	Indicates directory above current directory
*	Indicates wildcard

GLOSSARY OF TERMS

In this chapter I explained:

Command prompt—The part of the terminal where commands are entered

Recursive—Includes the files and subfolders within a directory in a command

10.3   *Lab*

In this lab, we're going to re-create the tasks from the chapter 6 lab using commands instead of a file manager. Use the terminal to do the following:

1 Create a folder within your Documents folder and call it command_line _homework.
2 In the command_line_homework folder, create a document called homework-file.
3 Move homeworkfile into linux.lunches.
4 Go into linux.lunches and make another file called homework2.
5 Copy homeworkfile into Documents.
6 Delete homework2 from linux.lunches.
7 Delete command_line_homework.

Advanced lab

1 Create three .txt files in a single directory called recursive.
2 Copy recursive to your Desktop.
3 Use a single wildcard command to delete all three recursive .txt files at once.

Working with common command-line applications, part 1

Doug McIlroy, a programmer who worked on UNIX, is credited with coining what is considered the UNIX philosophy: "Do one thing and do it well." For UNIX, that meant programs that did only one thing, like moving or copying files but not both. This approach is very different from most software programs, where one tool might serve multiple functions. Programs that only do one thing: that is where Linux shines.

Think back to our file manager: It displays files, it moves files, it copies files, and it deletes files. And that model works for us because it does all of those things perfectly fine. In the previous chapter, you learned some basic-but-essential commands that do very simple things. You also might have noticed that each command we used did one thing. For example, when we moved files, we used the mv command, but when we copied files, we used cp.

We often want to do more complex tasks than moving and copying files. The previous chapter was about getting you comfortable with the command line. This chapter is about learning to use five specialized command line programs for very specific tasks: top, which tracks system usage; xkill and killall, which shut down programs and processes; wget, which downloads files; and grep, which searches files. These are five applications I use a lot, because they're much faster than their graphical equivalents. Once you have these commands under your fingers, you'll wonder how you ever lived without them.

11.1 top

We've all had the experience of our computers slowing down due to some unknown issue. Most operating systems have a task manager that lets you see what programs and processes are running and the percentage of the CPU they are taking up, as well as how much memory. Ubuntu's task manager is called System Monitor (most desktop environments and distributions have something equivalent, if not the same—otherwise you can download one out of the repositories). To launch it, type `System Monitor` into the Dash. You'll see it has three tabs. We're interested in the Processes tab (see figure 11.1).

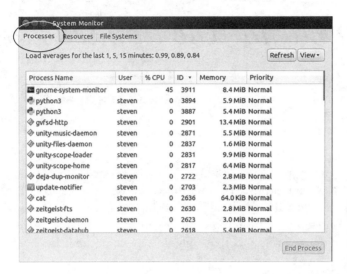

Figure 11.1   System Monitor shows you what processes are running on your computer and how much memory and CPU percentage they are using.

If your system slows down, you can use System Monitor to learn/discern the cause. You'll know the problem because it'll be taking up more memory or CPU than anything else on your system. You can see what's taking up the most of either resource by clicking the column for either % CPU or Memory. System Monitor will sort by accordingly.

Let's say I see that Firefox is taking up most of the memory or CPU percentage on my computer. I can close Firefox myself and free up some memory. But sometimes programs are taking up so much memory or CPU that they won't close. In this situation, the program is using so much memory or CPU, the computer has nothing left to use to close the program. Your computer is choking on a program. In that situation, you can close the program through the System Monitor. Right-click on the process and you get a list of options (see figure 11.2).

You'll see options to End Process and Kill Process (the Stop Process pauses the program). You usually want to start with End Process, which has the computer try to properly close the program for you. If that doesn't work, Kill Process forces the offending program or process to close. Killing is like pulling the plug out of a socket to turn off an appliance. It's tough but effective.

The `top` command does the same thing as System Monitor. So why use it? Because it's fast.

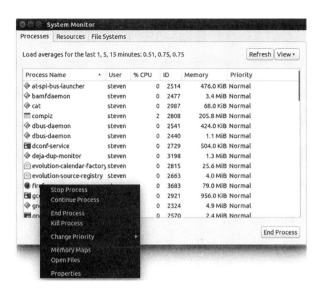

Figure 11.2 System Monitor lets you end processes that are slowing down your computer.

When you open System Monitor, you're using system resources, and if your computer is stuck due to an unresponsive program, opening *another* program, especially a graphical one, which is more system-intensive than a command, is making things worse. Just how bad it can make things depends on the specs of your computer hardware. However, with `top`, you open a terminal and type the command. You're using fewer resources and getting the same functionality. Let's look at `top` in action. Open a terminal and type `top`. You should see something like figure 11.3.

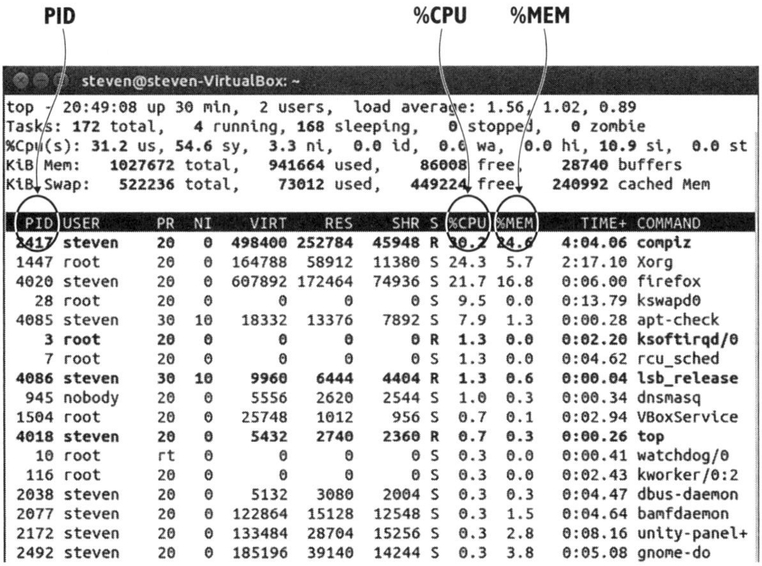

Figure 11.3 The `top` command lets you see system resources without using up too many system resources.

The layout is similar to what we saw in System Monitor. You'll notice columns for %CPU and %MEM, which represent memory. You'll see the name of the program or process in the far right column. You'll also notice the far left column, which is called PID. That stands for *process ID*. Every process running on your computer has a unique PID. We're going to talk about that in a moment.

Back in System Monitor, to sort by CPU or memory usage, you clicked the column. But that doesn't work in the terminal. If you want to sort by CPU percentage usage, type P (make sure it's capitalized). The sort will change instantly. To sort by memory usage, type M (make sure it's capitalized).

All of the columns are sortable, and we'll talk about how to find out about the sorts and configurations available in these kinds of commands in chapter 12.

Now what about killing the process or program that's holding up your computer? To do that, you're going to look at the PID for the offending process. It'll have very high %CPU or %MEM usage—probably the most on your computer. If you go back to figure 11.3, you'll notice Firefox has a PID of 4020. So to kill it, we're going to type k. You'll see a message like this above the columns (see figure 11.4):

```
PID to signal/kill [default pid = 2808]
```

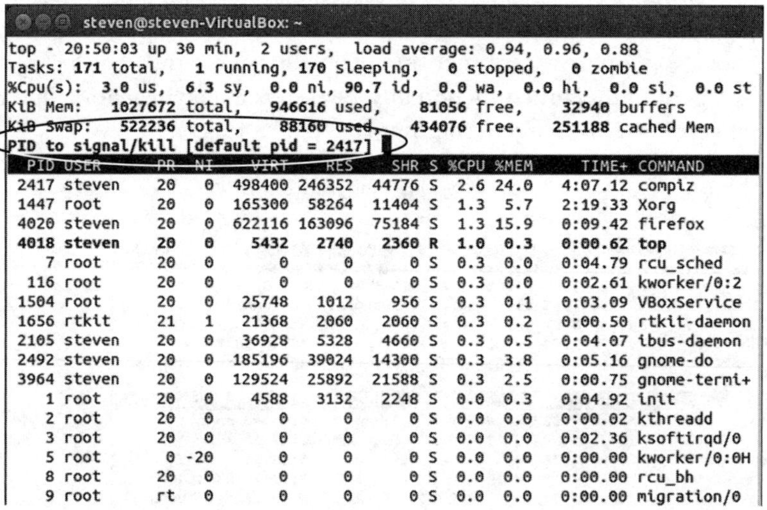

```
steven@steven-VirtualBox: ~
top - 20:50:03 up 30 min,  2 users,  load average: 0.94, 0.96, 0.88
Tasks: 171 total,   1 running, 170 sleeping,   0 stopped,   0 zombie
%Cpu(s):  3.0 us,   6.3 sy,  0.0 ni, 90.7 id,  0.0 wa,  0.0 hi,  0.0 si,  0.0 st
KiB Mem:   1027672 total,   946616 used,    81056 free,    32940 buffers
KiB Swap:   522236 total,    88160 used,   434076 free.   251188 cached Mem
PID to signal/kill [default pid = 2417]
  PID USER      PR  NI    VIRT    RES    SHR S %CPU %MEM     TIME+ COMMAND
 2417 steven    20   0  498400 246352  44776 S  2.6 24.0   4:07.12 compiz
 1447 root      20   0  165300  58264  11404 S  1.3  5.7   2:19.33 Xorg
 4020 steven    20   0  622116 163096  75184 S  1.3 15.9   0:09.42 firefox
 4018 steven    20   0    5432   2740   2360 R  1.0  0.3   0:00.62 top
    7 root      20   0       0      0      0 S  0.3  0.0   0:04.79 rcu_sched
  116 root      20   0       0      0      0 S  0.3  0.0   0:02.61 kworker/0:2
 1504 root      20   0   25748   1012    956 S  0.3  0.1   0:03.09 VBoxService
 1656 rtkit     21   1   21368   2060   2060 S  0.3  0.2   0:00.50 rtkit-daemon
 2105 steven    20   0   36928   5328   4660 S  0.3  0.5   0:04.07 ibus-daemon
 2492 steven    20   0  185196  39024  14300 S  0.3  3.8   0:05.16 gnome-do
 3964 steven    20   0  129524  25892  21588 S  0.3  2.5   0:00.75 gnome-termi+
    1 root      20   0    4588   3132   2248 S  0.0  0.3   0:04.92 init
    2 root      20   0       0      0      0 S  0.0  0.0   0:00.02 kthreadd
    3 root      20   0       0      0      0 S  0.0  0.0   0:02.36 ksoftirqd/0
    5 root       0 -20       0      0      0 S  0.0  0.0   0:00.00 kworker/0:0H
    8 root      20   0       0      0      0 S  0.0  0.0   0:00.00 rcu_bh
    9 root      rt   0       0      0      0 S  0.0  0.0   0:00.00 migration/0
```

Figure 11.4   To kill a signal with top, you need to know its PID.

Then you'll type in the PID of whatever you want to shut down. In my example, it's PID 4020, which is assigned to Firefox. Type in 4020 and click Enter. You'll be asked if you want to send the signal. It will look something like this:

```
Send pid 4020 signal [15/sigterm]
```

Press Enter. Whatever was assigned to that PID (in my example, Firefox) will close.

When you're done with `top`, type `q` to close it. Make sure it's lowercase. `top` is useful for seeing what's going on with your system without slowing anything down. The ability to kill programs and processes is especially convenient, although in the next section, we'll explore other ways to kill programs and processes from the command line.

11.2 Kill commands

Sometimes a program gets stuck. For whatever reason it won't respond and it won't close. In those instances, you want to execute a kill command. In this section, you're going to learn two commands to kill programs that are in your way.

11.2.1 xkill

`top` is useful when you're not sure what's slowing down your computer. But often you know right away when a program is hung up. You can still use `top` to get the PID and kill it, but it's a multi-step process. For times when I know what I want to shut down, I use the `xkill` command. `xkill` is brilliant in its simplicity. You type it into the terminal and your cursor turns from an arrow into an X (see figure 11.5).

Once it's an X, click on any program and it will close. This is very useful for unresponsive programs that won't close by normal means. As I mentioned, it's a terminal command, but you use it on your desktop, making it slightly different from the other commands in this chapter.

Figure 11.5 `xkill` turns your cursor into an X. You can then use it to close programs.

You launch `xkill` in the terminal, but you don't use it there. Because of that difference, you can launch it in a slightly different way. Rather than going into the terminal, you can use Alt-F2, which is a shortcut for entering a command into the terminal, without launching the terminal first. This shortcut is fairly standard across Linux distributions and desktop environments. In Ubuntu, it looks like you've summoned the Dash, but if you look in the search bar, you'll notice it says Run a command (see figure 11.6). In our example, this saves us time because we don't need to see anything in the terminal. We're running our command and then leaving the terminal so this saves us the step of having to close the terminal later.

Figure 11.6 Alt-F2 allows you to enter a command into the terminal without opening the terminal first.

In another desktop environment, the input area might look a little different. For instance, in Xfce you get a small box from which to run the command (see figure 11.7).

Figure 11.7   **Alt-F2 in Xfce gives you a small box and the option to run the command in the terminal.**

Try it Now: xkill

1 Launch Firefox.
2 Press Alt-F2 to launch the terminal box.
3 Enter xkill into the box. You'll notice your cursor is now an X.
4 Click Firefox to force it closed.

Using xkill is faster than going into your System Monitor, and also quicker than using top.

11.2.2 *killall*

Sometimes you know which program or process is slowing down your computer, but you can't see it. For instance, I'll sometimes shut down my Chrome or Firefox browser, but it will continue running in the background, slowing down my system. Or sometimes I'll have trouble with my sound and I know I need to shut down PulseAudio, the program that controls the sound. In these cases, I know what the problem is but xkill won't work, because there's nothing to click. The issue is the program is running in the background. In those cases, I use killall, a command-line utility that lets me shut down a program by name.

For instance, from time to time I'll close Firefox and try to open it later. When I go to open it, I'll get a message like Firefox is already running, but isn't responding. I could go into top and get the PID of the Firefox process that is still running, or I can save some myself the trouble of running top and finding the PID by going into the terminal and typing:

```
killall firefox
```

This command will shut down all instances of Firefox. What's nice about killall is that if multiple processes with the same name are running, let's say multiple instances of the Chrome browser, it will shut down all of them. This is convenient for when

Chrome is frozen, because each open tab is a separate process with its own PID. `kill-all` knocks them all out for you.

Something to keep in mind is that when you kill programs like with `killall` and `xkill`, you're not properly shutting down the programs. When you shut down a program with `killall` or `xkill`, you run the risk of losing data and will often reopen the program to find an error message. These kill utilities are for when you can't properly shut down a program or process.

11.3 *wget*

`wget` is a command-line application that downloads files from the internet. The files could be HTML pages, sound files, or PDFs. You point the command to the file or site, and `wget` handles the rest. I know what you're thinking—doesn't the web browser do this same thing? You're right! The web browser downloads files. But what I like about `wget` is that I don't have to leave my browser open when I download big files, which keeps my computer running faster. I also don't have to worry about the download getting corrupted, which sometimes happens when you download very large files via the browser, which isn't designed for that kind of downloading. And `wget` is much faster than the browser download.

I don't use `wget` often. I mostly use it to download very large files (smaller files download so quickly, it's rarely worth using `wget` instead of the browser).

For instance, when I'm downloading a Linux image file, like we did in chapter 3, I use `wget` to pull down the file. First, I locate the web address of the image file, which is a .iso. Then I go into the terminal and navigate to the folder where I want to download the file. For instance, if I wanted to download an image from example.com into my Documents folder, the syntax would look like this:

```
1  cd Documents
2  wget http://www.example.com/sample.iso
```

I could then close my web browser and leave the file to download. Or I could work on something else. The file will download in the background while I work.

Another thing I like about `wget` is that if there are any issues with the download, it keeps trying to finish the job. If the download is interrupted, it'll resume on its own.

Some people use `wget` to download websites, meaning not specific, single files, but entire sites. I've never had a need for that, but if for some reason you did, you would use a flag, which we mentioned in chapter 10. To download all of the website www.example.com, you'd use:

```
wget -r http://www.example.com
```

The `-r` means recursive. It's what we did with the `cp` command in the last chapter, but with a lowercase r instead of a capital.

`wget` has lots of options, from saying how it should appear to a server (you can make it look like a web browser to a server because a server might object to a command, and not a human, downloading content) to how long to wait between downloads. I rarely have a need for these in my day-to-day work. Instead, `wget` is tremendously helpful for getting big internet files, especially big Linux image files, onto my computer without having to keep my browser open.

11.4 *grep*

grep is a command-line tool for searching through text files. It's like a Ctrl-F that can search through hundreds of text files in the blink of an eye. It's very powerful because it allows the users to search with *regular expressions* (also known as *regex*), which is a complex syntax that lets you search patterns, like certain words, certain amounts of spaces between words, and even words containing certain letters in certain places.

I rarely use grep unless I'm troubleshooting an issue with my computer. For me, it's a utility I understand, but it's not something I have a regular need for. It's incredibly helpful for pulling text out of logs and files, and when you're trying to find that needle of text in a haystack of text files, you'll be glad you understand it, too.

Remember the lspci command from chapter 4? It shows you hardware on your computer. It's a great overview, but often you want one specific thing. Maybe you want to know your graphics card. So rather than scrolling through the whole list, you can execute lspci and then use grep to search for specific terms. That command would look like this:

```
lspci -v | grep Graphics
```

You're running the lspci command like we did in chapter 4 and then using grep to search for the word Graphics. grep is case-sensitive, which is why the G in Graphics is capitalized. The | is a pipe. We'll talk about pipes more in chapter 12. The result of that command is you're not sifting through unhelpful text. grep is bringing you only the text you want to see at that moment.

You can also use grep on log files. In chapter 4, we talked about using System Log or a text editor to view a log file. But that's a lot of content. You can use Ctrl-F in a text editor to find certain words, but with grep, you can search those words before you even open the log. Let's say you're computer is crashing and you want to find out why. You can search the system log for the word fail. That search will look like this:

```
grep fail /var/log/syslog
```

The first part, grep fail is your search term. The second part, /var/log/syslog is the file you're searching. Together, you're saying to search the syslog file in the /var/log/ directory for the word fail (see figure 11.8).

Figure 11.8   grep requires a search term and a place to search.

Maybe you want to search that syslog file for the word fail or crash. That search would look like this:

```
grep 'fail\|crash' /var/log/syslog
```

In grep, OR is represented by \|. You put the search terms in single quotations (') (see figure 11.9).

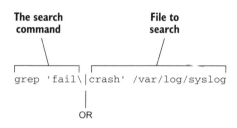

The search command   **File to search**

```
grep 'fail\|crash' /var/log/syslog
```

OR

Figure 11.9 grep can use Boolean operators, like OR.

If you discovered a text editor you love in chapter 9 and are now working with lots of text files, you could also use grep to search through text files in a directory. To do that, you would have a search like this:

```
grep -r searchterm .
```

The -r makes the search recursive, looking through subdirectories. The . is searching the current directory, which you might remember from the previous chapter.

> **FLAGS AND COMMANDS** Flags are text added to commands to give them further instructions. I like to think of them as an options menu that uses dashes and letters rather than clicks. For instance, we used -r earlier to make grep and wget recursive.
>
> Flags are important because commands don't have graphical menus. If you want a command to be modular, like searching recursively as opposed to just searching the current directory, you need a way to modify the command. Flags are that method. In the next chapter, you're going to learn about the man command, which is a way to learn more about how commands work. Part of the information provided will be the flags for a command. The flags are how you know to use -r with grep but -R with cp. If the default behavior of a command isn't working for you, see what flags are available either by searching online or using the man command, which you'll learn all about tomorrow.

11.5 *Wrapping up*

These are a few of my most frequently used commands. As I've mentioned, I don't use them daily, but I do use them often enough that I consider all five to be indispensable. Some, like top, have graphical equivalents, but the command line is much quicker and less system-intensive. After spending some time with these commands, you might discover your own uses. In the next chapter, we'll talk about how to find out more about commands. Table 11.1 outlines everything we just discussed:

Table 11.1 Useful Linux commands

Command	When to use it
grep	Finds text in text files. Useful for parsing files and for extracting key information from long screens of output.
killall	Kills processes and programs by name. Useful when you know the program you need to shut down.
top	Shows you what's taking up CPU and memory; also lets you kill it by PID. Useful when you're not sure what's slowing down your computer.
wget	Good for downloading large files that might become corrupted in your browser.
xkill	Lets you close unresponsive programs using your cursor. Useful when the program you need to force closed is open in front of you.

GLOSSARY OF TERMS

In this chapter I explained:

Flag—Text added to commands, preceded by a dash, to give them further instructions. They're a way to change the default behavior of a command.

Process ID (PID)—Unique number assigned to every process and program on your computer

11.6 Lab

1 What command would you use to shut down all instances of Firefox? Open Firefox and use that command to force it closed.

2 What command would you use to find audio information in your hardware configuration? Run that command to locate yours.

3 What command would you use to download a PDF of the U.S. Constitution from http://mng.bz/o25h? Use wget to download it.

4 Which command requires the PID of the process to shut it down? Open Firefox and use that command to shut it down.

5 Open a program and use xkill to kill it. HINT: If you're not sure of the name of a program, you can use another command to see the names of everything running.

Advanced Lab

1 Use wget to download the plain-text version of *Debian GNU/Linux : Guide to Installation and Usage* from Project Gutenberg (http://www.gutenberg.org/ebooks/6527.txt.utf-8).

2 Use grep to search the file for the word linux, but make the search case-insenstive.

Working with common command-line applications, part 2

The previous chapter discussed a few command-line programs that are useful for keeping your system running smoothly. This chapter picks up right where chapter 11 left off, getting us into a few more programs that have systemwide implications.

The commands we'll discuss in this chapter are powerful ones. We're going to work with the su and sudo commands, which let you do a lot of administrative tasks on your system. We're also going to talk about installing and removing software using commands, rather than a graphical package manager. And then we're going to finish off the chapter by learning about pipes and how to use different commands together.

The previous two chapters have been about getting you comfortable with the command line and showing you what the command line can do. This chapter is going to prepare you to work with your system. These are commands that you need to know and understand to be an effective Linux user. For instance, you need su or sudo to do most administrative tasks on your system. But don't let that scare you! The work of the previous two chapters has gotten you ready for this moment. Let's get started.

12.1 su and sudo for administrative tasks

Linux systems are permissions-based. That means only certain kinds of users can make changes to the system. This includes adding and removing software, but also editing and changing certain files. It's a safety and security precaution that we'll discuss more in chapter 19.

So even though you installed Linux yourself and even though you might be the only user on your system, your Linux installation still doesn't trust you! But that's a good thing. That means it's all that much harder for you to accidentally break your system or for someone else to do it deliberately.

You might recall from chapter 7 that to install software, either with Synaptic or the Ubuntu Software Center, we had to enter a password. That's because Ubuntu grants the account creating the system full administrative privileges, which in Linux is called *root*. The root account has full access and permission to do anything and everything on a system. Not all distributions give the main user account root access, though. Some have the users create their own account, but also a separate root password (the root login is always root). This is an extra level of security.

For instance, let's say my regular account password is changeme and my root password is bosco. If my regular account is hacked, or if I forget to logout of my system before someone playful or malicious jumps on, they can't make any major changes to my system without my root password.

The su and sudo commands are methods of bringing the administrative password in without logging out of your session and then logging in as root. The commands are very similar. Let's take a look at what they do and how you use them.

12.1.1   su

The su command stands for superuser. Or switch user. (These things are sometimes hard to determine.) Technically, it allows you to switch to another user's account. But if you don't specify an account, it allows you to switch to the root (or superuser) account, assuming you know the password. From there, you can do things like install software and change systemwide configurations.

Ubuntu locks the root account, so su won't work for root access with that distribution. The philosophy behind locking it is that it protects the root password from being compromised by anyone, but users can still work with their system using sudo, which we're going to discuss next.

12.1.2   sudo

The sudo command is similar to su, in terms of what it does, but it works in a slightly different way. You use sudo to get administrative privileges on your computer, but you're not using root. Instead, there is a file, called sudoers, that controls which accounts have access to the root privileges. But instead of using the root password, you'll authenticate with your own.

The difference between the two commands is that su has you logging in as root and sudo has you on a list of users that can act as root, but are not root itself.

The difference doesn't matter, though. Just know that for Ubuntu, if you want to install software via the command line, which we'll do in the next section, you're going to use the sudo command.

If you're on a system without sudo, you can install it and add users to the file. To do that, you would use su first, to become root, and then add the user using the adduser command, which adds users to different groups, with the different groups having different permissions (we'll talk about this more in chapter 19). The steps would look like this:

```
su
```

Your command prompt would then turn to something like root@yourcomputer. By now you've probably noticed that the prompt has your *username@the name of your computer*. With su, you're switching to the root account, which changes the command prompt.

From there, you would use

```
adduser user sudo
```

to add the user named in the command to the sudo list. The user named will then be able to use the sudo command to do things like install software.

To see this process on your system:

1 Go into the terminal.
2 Type sudo adduser *your login name* sudo.

You'll get a message that you're already a member of sudo, because you are, but the steps would be the same for adding other users on your system.

And now the million dollar question—which command is better? As you saw, not all distributions will allow you to use su, which means you have to use sudo. The sudo command requires you to add users to the group and while it only takes a minute, some people don't appreciate the extra step. I'm a sudo user myself, since I learned Linux on Ubuntu-based systems. Which tool you use isn't as important as making sure you're mindful of what you're doing when you're using your root-level access.

We're going to work more with sudo in the next session because you can't use a text-based package manager without it. But before we move on, I'll leave you with an xkcd comic (see figure 12.1) that might help you to understand sudo a bit better.

Figure 12.1 The sudo command isn't exactly magic, but it sometimes feels that way. Image via https://xkcd.com/149/.

12.2 Installing and removing software with the command line

If you recall, in chapter 7 we talked about package managers. Different distributions use different package managers. You'll recall that Debian-based distributions use Apt, and others like Fedora and OpenSUSE use RPM. There are also text-based commands associated with these package managers. In Debian-based distributions, like Ubuntu, that command is `apt-get`. In Fedora, the command is `dnf`. Since we're using Ubuntu here, I'll use `apt-get` for most of the examples. But things don't vary too much between commands. For instance, if you're on a Debian-based system, and you want to install the Clementine music player, you would just type

```
sudo apt-get install clementine
```

You'd enter your password and the software would install. If you try `apt-get` without `sudo`, you won't have the permissions required to install software.

So `sudo` is setting your permission and `apt-get` is the name of the package manager program. We're telling `apt-get` to install with the word `install`. And `clementine` is the name of the package we want to install (packages are always lowercase).

If our system didn't have `sudo`, we'd use `su` to become root and then install the software with `apt-get install clementine`.

With `dnf`, it's almost the same:

```
sudo dnf install clementine
```

As before, `sudo` is setting the permission, `install` is saying to install the program, and `clementine` is the name of the program to install. The only difference is the name of the package manager being used.

You might remember in chapter 7 that Synaptic and Ubuntu Software Center took care of additional software needed by the software we were installing. It's the same thing with `apt-get`, `dnf`, and any other command-line package managers. They all install any programs needed by the program. In fact, when you go to install via the command line, package managers will show you what other packages will be installed, how much space they'll take up, and will ask you to confirm you want to install the software.

Removing software with the command line is a similar process. Let's say after installing Clementine, you realize it's not for you. On a Debian-based system, you'd type

```
sudo apt-get remove clementine
```

We're using `sudo` the same way we did before—to let the system know we have the authority to remove software. We're using `apt-get` as our command and `remove` is telling `apt-get` that this time software is coming off the computer. And `clementine`, as before, is the name of our program.

On Arch Linux, another distribution, that command would be

```
sudo pacman -R clementine
```

Even though it's a different package manager, and even though the commands and terms are different, conceptually you can see it's the same command. We're still using `sudo`, as we did with `apt-get`. Arch's package manager is named `pacman`. Instead of the word `remove`, as we did with `apt-get`, we're using `-R`. And we're ending with the name of the program to be removed.

We'll talk more about package managers in chapter 17. For now, be aware that the command line is another option for installing software. It's a great option if there's an issue with your system and you can't get graphics to render. Knowing how to use package management commands allows you to fix programs without a GUI. Also, remember that package managers work together. That means you can install something with Synaptic and remove it with `apt-get`. You can move freely between them all.

Let's move on to learning how to learn more about commands.

12.3 Read the manual with the man command

You've noticed in our discussion of commands that there are lots of flags and options and modifiers. How do you know them all? The reality is most people will use an internet search to learn more about commands. You're reading this book and by the end you should have a firm grasp of lots of commands and flags. Any commands you want to know more about, you'll probably explore with sites like the ones I mentioned in chapter 4. But UNIX systems have a built-in help mechanism that's pretty amazing.

It's a command called `man`, which stands for manual. To use it, type `man` and the name of the command you wish to learn more about. Go into your terminal and type

```
man apt-get
```

You'll get a lot of information (see figure 12.2).

```
●●●  steven@steven-VirtualBox: ~
APT-GET(8)                        APT                        APT-GET(8)

NAME
       apt-get - APT package handling utility -- command-line interface

SYNOPSIS
       apt-get [-asqdyfmubV] [-o=config_string] [-c=config_file]
               [-t=target_release] [-a=architecture] {update | upgrade |
               dselect-upgrade | dist-upgrade |
               install pkg [{=pkg_version_number | /target_release}]... |
               remove pkg... | purge pkg... |
               source pkg [{=pkg_version_number | /target_release}]... |
               build-dep pkg [{=pkg_version_number | /target_release}]... |
               download pkg [{=pkg_version_number | /target_release}]... |
               check | clean | autoclean | autoremove | {-v | --version} |
               {-h | --help}}

DESCRIPTION
       apt-get is the command-line tool for handling packages, and may be
       considered the user's "back-end" to other tools using the APT library.
       Several "front-end" interfaces exist, such as aptitude(8), synaptic(8)
       and wajig(1).

 Manual page apt-get(8) line 1 (press h for help or q to quit)
```

Figure 12.2   The `man` command tells you about a command line program. It's the manual.

You'll get a description of the command, a list of the options available, like using it to install or remove software, and examples. You'll notice some flags at the top, too. You'll recall from yesterday that flags are a way to change the default behavior of a command. You know they're flags because they begin with a -. The `man` page is showing us ways to change the apt-get command. For instance, if we wanted apt-get to only install software from a certain repository, we could use the -t flag to tell it which repository to use.

Use your arrow keys to scroll through to the install section of the manual. Now use the k key to scroll back to the top. You can use your up and down arrows to scroll through, as well as the j and k keys, which you might remember from Vim in chapter 9. A lot of the information from man is available online, but if you're in the terminal already, it's often easier to use man than to open a browser and search for the information. When you're done with man, you type q to quit.

In the previous chapter, we talked about the top command and how you could sort by CPU usage with the letter P and by memory with M.

Try it now: Using man

1 Type man top into the terminal.
2 Scroll through and find the section on *SORTING of task window* and the other sort options, such as by PID (N) and time (T).

You might have noticed it took a lot of scrolling to find the sort information. Let's try a different way.

1 Quit the man page with q and then reopen it.
2 Use Ctrl-f to find the word sort. But you can't! Ctrl-f only moves the page forward. To find terms in man, you need to use the / key.

Now type

```
/sort
```

and you'll see all of the instances of the word sort, or words starting with sort, highlighted. Type the letter n to move, or navigate, between them all.

One of my favorite things about man is it doesn't discriminate. If you want to learn more, type man man and you'll get the manual for man! You can also learn more about moving through man by clicking h from the opening screen.

Now that we know how to research commands, let's work on putting commands together.

12.4 Grow commands with pipes and redirects

A pipe is a way to join two command-line programs. It's a way to save time and typing. Rather than typing one command, pressing Return, manipulating the output, and then typing another command to work with the output, you can use pipes to make one-line programs made up of commands. You're feeding the output of one command into another, all in the one line. For instance, in the last chapter we used a pipe to combine lspci and grep. Rather than running lspci, putting the output into a file, and then searching for the word `graphic`, we were able to do the same thing in one simple line:

```
lspci -v | grep Graphics
```

The | is the pipe.

Commands can also have their output redirected into files. What that means is rather than information appearing on the screen, you can move the content into a file, which often makes it easier to read.

Going back to our `lspci` command, the results wound up on our screen. If we wanted it in a file, we would use a > to redirect it into a file. That command would look like this:

```
lspci -v | grep Graphics > output.txt
```

Now, instead of the information from `lspci` showing up on the screen, it's in a file called output.txt.

Remember the `ls` command from chapter 10? It's the command that lists what's in your directory. You can use `grep` with `ls` to list all of the files with a certain word in their titles. This is helpful when you're looking for a bunch of files. For instance, because of this book, I have a lot of files with "Learn" in the filename. When I want to see them all, I sometimes use this command:

```
ls | grep Learn
```

I'm left with a list of the files with "Learn" (note the case) in their filenames. If I wanted a file with those file names, I would just redirect the output into a file. That command would look like this:

```
ls | grep Learn > filelist.txt
```

That would leave me with a text file featuring all of the files in my directory that have "Learn" in the filename.

Pipes and redirects are helpful for manipulating files and for getting complex command output off of your screen and into a file, where it's usually easier to work with. I don't use pipes and redirects often, but it's worth understanding for trouble-shooting your system, and for saving yourself work. Many times you'll have to do something dull and repetitive, like change a bunch of file names or combine a bunch of files into one larger one (as a librarian often working with barcodes in text files, I do this fairly regularly). A few minutes of internet research (perhaps in some of the places I mentioned in chapter 4) might reveal a way to do it using commands and pipes, so if nothing else, understanding how they work gives you lots of options.

12.5 *Wrapping up*

This chapter touched on a few advanced concepts with commands. Some, like `su` and `sudo`, are immediately essential for using Linux. Others, like `man` and pipes, will reveal their utility as you use Linux more and more. In the next chapter, we'll talk about ways to use the command line productively. Table 12.1 summarizes what we covered today.

Table 12.1   Useful Linux commands

Command	When to use it
man	Manual for a command
su	Switch to the root user; used for installing software
sudo	Perform something administrative with the same access as a root user; used for installing software
|	Joins two commands
>	Puts output of a command into a file

GLOSSARY OF TERMS

In this chapter I explained:

Pipe—A way to join two command line programs

12.6   Lab

You learned a few different commands and processes today. This lab will make sure you understand how to use the commands and know how to use pipes and redirects to work with commands.

1 Install the Midori web browser on your computer using the command line. HINT: The package name is `midori`.
2 Remove it using the command line.
3 Find all of the mentions of root in the manual for `sudo`.
4 Use a single-line command to copy the `sudo` manual text file called sudo.txt.

Advanced lab

1 Return to your downloaded copy of *Debian GNU/Linux : Guide to Installation and Usage* from Project Gutenberg (available via www.gutenberg.org/ebooks/ 6527.txt.utf-8).
2 Pipe the output of your `grep` search from the previous lab (a search for Linux or linux) into a text file called linux.txt.

Using the command line productively

We've spent the past three lunches talking about the command line, focusing on the commands themselves. In this chapter, we're going to talk about ways to be effective and productive when you're using the terminal. This chapter will cover two alternative terminal interfaces: customizing your terminal and techniques to help you recall and reuse commands without having to retype them each time.

This chapter is about creating a command-line environment that makes you comfortable and gives you the information you need. As you saw in the previous chapters, the command line, at its core, is a way to save time. Rather than working through a GUI, you're in essence talking directly to your system. It makes sense that in an environment where you're trying to work efficiently, you'd want tools to help you be even more efficient. This chapter is about those tools. Let's start with the most basic of tools—the terminal interface.

13.1 Alternative terminal interfaces

When you're using the terminal on Linux, you're actually using an emulator, or program. That means it's an interface between you and your system. You're not talking directly to your operating system when you're in the terminal, even though it sometimes feels that way. Because the terminal is a program, that means there are different versions of terminals you can use that will all do the same thing. Conceptually, terminal interfaces are like desktop environments. They can have different looks and feels. The big difference between desktop environments and terminals is that the terminal is much simpler, so terminal interfaces aren't going to vary all that much. But they do vary enough that you might want to play with a few to see if you like one better than the default Ubuntu one, which is called GNOME Terminal.

151

But don't forget—which terminal interface you use doesn't matter in terms of commands. Everything you do in one terminal interface, you can do in another.

13.1.1 *Guake*

Guake borrows from the classic first-person shooter video game Quake. In that game, there's a menu that rolls down from the screen. When you're done with it, you roll it back up. Guake is exactly the same. You use F12 to summon it and F12 when you're done.

I like Guake because it embeds itself in my desktop. Since it's practically transparent, it almost feels like my whole computer is a terminal (see figure 13.1). But then, when I'm done, it's out of my way. Let's install it, so you can see what it looks like.

Figure 13.1   Guake is almost transparent, so it stays out of your way when you're working.

As you might recall from the last chapter, you can install it with

```
sudo apt-get install guake
```

Using Guake is slightly different from using the standard terminal we've been using. The first time you use Guake, you need to type Guake into the launcher. After that first time, you call Guake with the F12 key.

Now that you have Guake installed, you'll see it works just like the GNOME Terminal we practiced with. If you type ls, you'll see it lists everything in your directory. The only difference between the default terminal and Guake is you can call Guake up a bit quicker. And when you're done with Guake, you can press F12 to roll it up and out of the way.

You'll notice Guake has a bar at the bottom. The icon on the far right is used to generate new tabs. The box on the left represents different terminal windows, or sessions (see figure 13.2). You can have multiple terminals open, all doing different things, with one terminal downloading a file from one site and another terminal

Figure 13.2   Guake has a bottom bar that lets you track different terminal sessions.

downloading a file from a different site. (This is also possible in GNOME Terminal, which allows you to open new terminal windows or tabs—Guake puts all of the tabs and windows in one place for you.) To move between sessions, click the box representing the session you want. If you've got a lot of sessions open, you can right-click a session and give it a name.

Guake can also be customized. The customization options are in a separate program called Guake Preferences. To launch it, type `Guake preferences` into the Dash.

The options (figure 13.3) can do things like change the height of your Guake window, change the key you use to launch it (if you don't like using F12, the default), and even change the level of transparency, if you'd like the terminal to appear lighter or darker.

I like Guake for its speed. When I need a terminal, it's right there. In some ways it's very well suited for people who don't spend a lot of time in the terminal, because it's

Figure 13.3   Guake has a number of customization options, from color schemes to the launch keys.

almost designed to disappear. As someone who doesn't spend a lot of time in the terminal, I find it very useful. And as someone who spent far too much of college playing Quake, I also appreciate the feeling of nostalgia using it gives me.

Now let's look at an interface for people looking to spend *more* time in the terminal.

13.1.2 *Terminator*

Terminator is more like GNOME Terminal. The main difference is its ability to handle multiple windows, allowing you to tile them. That means the windows are all open and arranged in front of you, like tile on a floor, except windows might be different sizes. Figure 13.4 shows Terminator tiling windows.

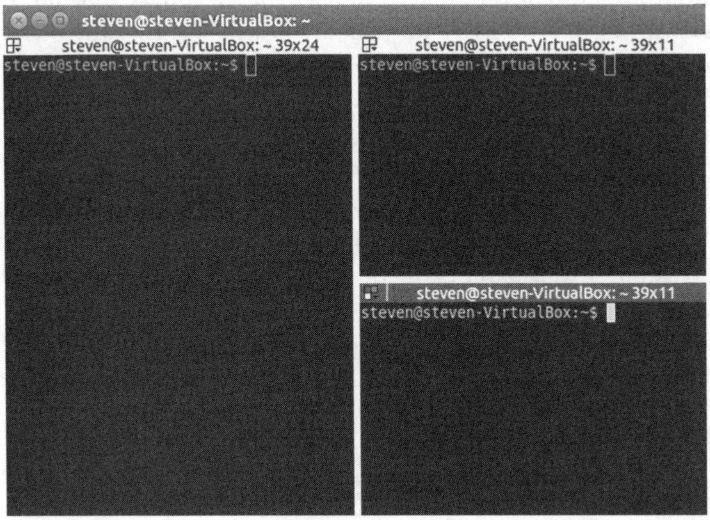

Figure 13.4   Terminator tiles terminal windows so you can see everything.

Terminator works more like the terminal we're used to. It just has some additional features. Let's work with it a little.

First, install it with `sudo apt-get install terminator`. Once it's installed, you can open it in the Dash.

It looks just like GNOME Terminal. If you type `ls`, you'll get the same output you would expect to get in any terminal. Let's look at what makes Terminator different from the other tools we've used.

> **Try it now: Tiling with Terminator**
>
> 1 Type Ctrl-Shift-e. You'll notice the terminal splits in half vertically. If you need help remembering this, think of the second letter of vertical.
> 2 Now type Ctrl-Shift-o. Now the terminal has split horizontally. If you need help remembering this, think of the second letter of horizontal.

If you're doing work in multiple terminals, like perhaps writing something in Vim in one terminal while you install software in another, and you want to see everything at once, Terminator is a great option.

You can move between windows with Ctrl-Shift-n (next) and Ctrl-Shift-p (previous). You can also use your mouse to select and drag windows around.

Another neat thing about Terminator is its broadcast option. This lets you type the same thing into every terminal window at the same time, rather than typing the same thing one window at a time. This functionality is useful if you want to use the same commands on different directories. Let's look at how to do that:

1 Click the four squares in the top left corner (see figure 13.5).
2 Click Broadcast All.
3 Type your command. In our case, type `exit`. Notice that as you type, the letters are appearing in each window. When you hit Enter, everything closes because `exit` is the command to close a terminal window. We entered the same command once, but it was executed three times in three different terminal sessions.

Terminator is probably best-suited for people spending a lot of time in the command line or people who use multiple terminal windows. But even if you don't work that way, there's something neat about having a bunch of open terminals. It will definitely impress people in coffee shops.

We just looked at two additional terminal interfaces. If you want to know more about other terminals, Wikipedia has a nice list you can work your way through: https://en.wikipedia.org/wiki/List_of_terminal_emulators#Linux. Now let's talk about ways to customize the terminal.

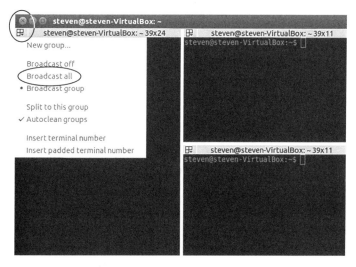

Figure 13.5 Terminator allows you to send the same command to all terminal windows simultaneously.

13.2   *Customizing the terminal*

Earlier we just saw how to customize the look of Guake. You have that same ability with the GNOME Terminal. To look at your options, go to the Profile Preferences option under the top navigation's Edit menu (see figure 13.6).

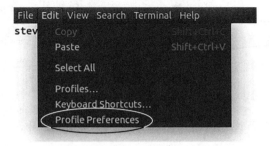

Figure 13.6   The default terminal allows you to customize its look via the Profile Preferences menu.

As you might have gathered, GNOME Terminal allows you to have profiles, meaning you can have your terminal configured for different people, or for different activities. We'll get to the profile element in a moment. For now, you should see something like figure 13.7 in front of you.

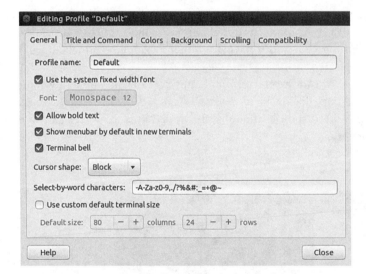

Figure 13.7   The different tabs of the Profile Preferences menu of GNOME Terminal.

Using these menus, you can change quite a few things about your terminal. Customizing your terminal is important in terms of making it easier for you to use. If you have trouble seeing the default white text on purple background, you can change that to something you find easier to read. You can also change your fonts. To do that:

1   Uncheck the Use the System Fixed Width Font option so you can choose your own font and font size for the terminal.
2   Once you've unchecked the box, click the word Monospace (Monospace 12 is the default terminal font and font size) and change the font, the font size, or both (see figure 13.8).

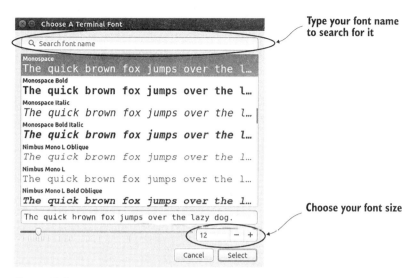

Figure 13.8 Your terminal font and font size can be changed.

3 Change the font size to 20, click Select, and return to the terminal. Your terminal should look different now, with a much bigger font.

4 Go into Profile Preferences again and change your font back to 12.

You can also change the colors being used by your terminal. Let's do that together

1 Click the Colors tab (see figure 13.9).

2 Uncheck the Use Colors from System Theme box.

3 Select Black on White from the Built-in Schemes.

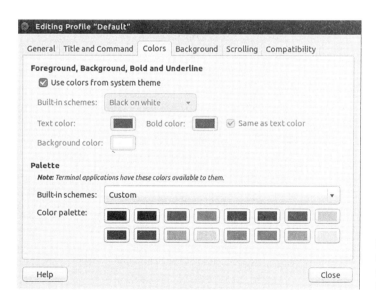

Figure 13.9 Your terminal has some built-in color schemes, or you can choose your own colors.

Your terminal should now be white instead of purple, with black text instead of white. You could also choose custom background and text colors by using the Custom scheme option and then choosing your own colors.

Finally, if you click the Background tab you can choose an image for your background instead of a color (see figure 13.10). I don't recommend this option since it's hard to read text against images. However, if that's your preference, it's available.

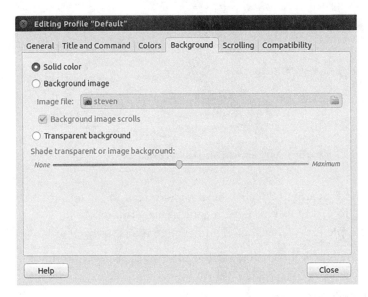

Figure 13.10   You can make your terminal semi-transparent, just like Guake.

You can also give yourself a transparent background, just like Guake uses. I like this option because it lets me see through the terminal to my screen, which is very helpful when I'm looking up commands online. To change the transparency of your terminal, check the Transparent background option. Use the slider to change the amount of transparency. Your terminal will get less transparent as you move from none on the left to maximum on the right. This is another personal setting depending upon your vision and workflow preferences. To learn more about GNOME Terminal's preferences, click F1 to open the Help menu and then click Preferences.

With all of the options you have, you might have different terminal color schemes and configurations for different kinds of activities. For instance, you might want a larger font when you're writing in Vim. Or you might want a different color scheme when you're installing software, so you remember to be careful. You can use profiles to keep them separate. To create a profile, click the File button on the top navigation and then click New Profile…. You'll see a little pop-up window asking you to name the new profile and asking you which existing profile to base the new profile on. Since you only have one profile, you'll base your first new profile on Default.

If reading white-on-purple text makes your eyes tired, you might prefer a reading profile that's white-on-black, in a larger font, that you use for reading man pages. You might make a transparent profile that you use when you're researching commands online. As you use the terminal more, you might find it helpful to create profiles that allow you to customize the terminal without having to reconfigure it every time you change activities. To change your start-up terminal profile, go to Edit and then Profiles and then change the Profile Used When Launching a New Terminal setting (figure 13.11).

Figure 13.11   You can also change which profile is used when you start the terminal.

The next section is going to show you a few shortcuts that will help you save time when you're working in the command line.

13.3   Saving time in the terminal

As you read about Linux and work with it, you'll pick up lots of tips. This section is going to walk you through a few of the most useful tips I know. They represent all of the things I wish I had known sooner about the command line. The common thread in these tips is that they all help you to recall commands you've already used or help you to type a bit less.

13.3.1   Last command(s)

You've probably already run into the situation where you type a command and manage to insert a typo. It's not a big deal for relatively short commands, but as they get longer and more complex, the thought of retyping from scratch can seem demoralizing. Luckily, you don't need to retype! Instead, use the up arrow to call up your last command in the terminal. And what if you need a command from earlier? Just keep pressing the up arrow. And if you accidentally go past the command you needed, use the down arrow to move forward. This process is great if you mistype a small part of a complex command. You can use the arrow to find the command and edit it rather than retyping it.

13.3.2   history command

The up arrow is good if your command was used fairly recently, but if you're trying to find something you used days ago, you might need a way to see more commands. The history command gives you a printout of your previously used commands. Every terminal has a different default number of commands saved. Mine is set up to save the last 950. You can change this variable in the .bashrc file, which we're going to talk about in the next chapter. Type history into your terminal to see all of the commands you've run so far.

You probably noticed that the command gives you a giant list of commands on your screen. You can certainly scroll through them, but it's not easy to read or work with. Luckily, in the last chapter, we learned how to send text from the terminal into a file. If you go back to your terminal and type

```
history > ../Desktop/commands.txt
```

you should now have a text file full of commands on your desktop, with each command on its own line.

13.3.3 Searching commands

The final use case we'll discuss is when you remember *something* about a command you used. In that situation, you can search through your commands by typing Ctrl-R. You'll get something that looks like this in your terminal:

```
(reverse-i-search)`':
```

Type whatever part of the command you remember and you'll see a command matching your search appear. Use Ctrl-R to cycle through all of the matches and press Enter when you see the command you wish to execute. If you want to tweak the command, use the right arrow to put it in your terminal without launching it. You can then edit the command before pressing Enter.

13.3.4 Autocompleting commands

The terminal can also save you some typing by autocompleting your command. To autocomplete, you start to type a command and use the Tab key to either finish it or see what your options are. I typically use it to avoid typing entire directory names. For instance, go into your terminal and type

```
cd Dow
```

Now press Tab. The command should now read:

```
cd Downloads
```

The Tab finished the command. If you had typed cd D and pressed Tab, nothing would have happened until you pressed Tab again. At that point, you would've seen the directories that start with a capital D (Documents and Downloads). Using Tab to complete your commands can save you lots of typing.

13.3.5 Copying and pasting

It is possible to copy and paste text into and out of the terminal. In most interfaces, you use Ctrl-X to cut, Ctrl-C to copy, and Ctrl-V to paste. In the terminal, it's Ctrl-Shift-X to cut, Ctrl-Shift-C to copy, and Ctrl-Shift-V to paste (see table 13.1). This means that if you found the command you needed in that text file we created using history, rather than retyping it into the terminal, you could copy it out of your text editor and paste it in with Ctrl-Shift-V. You can also paste out of websites and into the terminal but *be very careful running commands you don't understand!* You can accidentally damage your system. Make sure you go through a command and understand what each section is doing before you run it. We'll talk more about running commands safely in chapter 20.

Table 13.1 Shortcuts for copying and pasting type

Terminal shortcut	Action
Ctrl-Shift-C	Copy out of terminal
Ctrl-Shift-X	Cut out of terminal
Ctrl-Shift-V	Paste into terminal

13.4 Wrapping up

This is not the end of our work in the terminal, but it is the end of our extended focus on it. Now, as you move through the rest of the book, we'll move between GUIs and the terminal, using whichever tools do the best job, but also giving you options, when it's appropriate. You now have enough knowledge to understand commands and to create them. You also know enough to create a terminal environment that feels comfortable. Finally, you now know a number of ways to review and reuse commands. Put together, you now have the tools to feel comfortable using the terminal for different tasks.

GLOSSARY OF TERMS

In this chapter I explained:

Tile—Desktop windows are all open and arranged in front of you, like tile on a floor, except windows might be different sizes

13.5 Lab

This lab is going to walk you through the customizations and time-saving tricks you just learned:

1 Install Guake and Terminator using the command line, if you haven't already done so.
2 Use autocomplete to move into your Documents directory.
3 Go back into your home directory.
4 Now, pipe the output of `history` into a text file. What are your last three commands?
5 Go into Guake and look at your history. How does it compare to the output from the default terminal?
6 Configure Guake to launch with the F11 key.
7 Split Terminator into four windows in a grid of 2 x 2.
8 Type `apt` and then Tab twice. What happens? What does that output mean?

Explaining the Linux filesystem hierarchy

14

We've spent some time exploring different Linux commands, working within your home directory (I'll explain home in just one moment). But there are other directories on your system containing information related to everything from your program files to your system's configuration files. In this chapter, we're going to explore those directories, learning what's in them and what you can do with them. While this process is helpful in troubleshooting issues with your systems, I want to emphasize that it's just as important for personalizing your system. So knowing and understanding these directories isn't only about fixing what's broken. It's also about improving what already works.

Before we begin, I want to note that Linux directories are different from Windows directories, in that they don't use letters to identify hard drives or partitions. So while your Windows installation lives on a C: drive, Linux (and OS X) simply use directory names, like /home.

You might think you know your home directory pretty well, based upon the amount of time we've spent in it, but there are some interesting secrets hidden within Linux directories. Let's take a deeper look at home.

14.1   /home

The /home directory on Linux systems is the user's personal directory. As you've seen over the past few chapters, your /home directory has your personal folders:

- Desktop
- Downloads
- Music
- Public
- Videos
- Documents

- Pictures
- Templates

These are folders for your content. You can use them however you wish. There's nothing stopping you from putting your music in your Documents folder. You can even delete any of these folders. But /home itself is a system folder, meaning it was put there by your operating system and serves a specific purpose. It can't be deleted without destroying your system. You could *probably* save personal files in system folders using root permissions, but there's a chance the files could be deleted or could interfere with a process, so it's best practice to keep your personal files within home. Let's take a look at home:

- Go into your terminal and type `cd ..` You should see something like this:

  `steven@steven-VirtualBox:/home$`

  You are now in your system's /home directory, which contains the /home directories of all of the users on your system.

- Type `ls` to see what directories are in /home. You should see your username as a directory (you can tell it's a directory because it's bold and in a different color than the file names).

That's your personal home directory with your personal settings and configurations, and that's the purpose of /home. Just like your physical home is where you live, the /home directory is where your personal files and configurations live. It's the folder we've been working in and the default place when we launch our terminal or graphical file manager.

Let's go back into it:

- Type `cd` and the name of your personal /home directory.
- Once you're in it, type `ls`. You'll see the usual directories we've seen before.
- Now type `ls -A`. This stands for *list all*. What happened when you typed it?

You should see a lot more folders and files, all of them starting with a `.` (see figure 14.1).

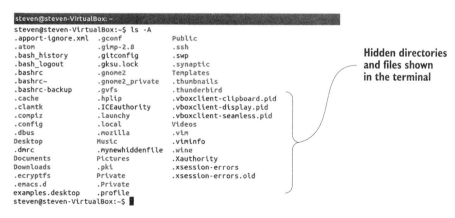

Figure 14.1 The `ls -A` command shows hidden folders and files in the terminal.

These are system files that are used by you personally. For instance, you'll notice a .mozilla folder. If you don't see it in your Live session, open and close Firefox and it will appear.

That folder contains your Firefox profile information. These hidden files and folders within your /home directory are used by Linux to personalize your experience. Before we work with hidden folders and files, I want to show you one other way to see them, if you're more of a graphical user.

To see these hidden folders and files in Nautilus:

1 Open Nautilus. You'll see your usual directories.
2 Type Ctrl-H. Ctrl-H is a global shortcut across Linux file managers for showing hidden files.

You should now see a list of previously hidden folders and files in your file manager. It should look something like figure 14.2.

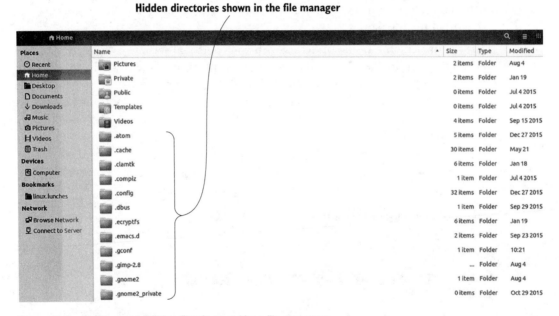

Hidden directories shown in the file manager

Figure 14.2   Ctrl-H reveals hidden files in most Linux file managers.

In Linux, a file or directory can be hidden by beginning the file or directory name with a period. For instance, to hide a file in the terminal, you would type

```
touch .mynewhiddenfile
```

The file won't appear unless you use `ls -A` or view hidden files in the file manager.

There are lots of interesting hidden files to play with. For instance, you'll recall in the last chapter that we customized our terminal using the Profile Preferences menu.

But you can also customize it by editing a hidden file called .bashrc. Let's add information to our terminal prompt. Before we do that, let's make a backup of our .bashrc file, just in case something goes wrong. Go back to your terminal and type:

```
cp .bashrc .bashrc-backup
```

This is an important habit to cultivate. If we somehow wreck our .bashrc file, we can delete it and rename the backup .bashrc. Now that we've made a backup, we can start changing things with a text editor. You could use any text editor, as you might recall from chapter 9. I'm using the gedit text editor because I only need to make a quick edit. The takeaway here is not about customizing terminal prompts, but that your /home directory has these configuration files and folders that allow things like your terminal prompt to be changed. To open the file with gedit, use this command:

```
gedit .bashrc
```

1 Scroll to the bottom of the .bashrc file and type export PS1="\u@\h:\w \d\\$ \[$(tput sgr0)\]". This command is changing the variables that display in our command prompt (figure 14.3).

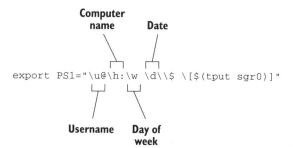

Figure 14.3 The command prompt is made up of variables you can select.

2 Save the file.

3 Exit the terminal with the exit command and then relaunch the terminal. Your prompt should now feature the date:

```
steven@steven-VirtualBox:~ Thu Nov 12$
```

If you were to create another user account on your system, that user would have the stock terminal prompt until they decided to change it. So things you change in /home only apply to that user—nothing else changes for other users on the system. Coming up in chapter 16, we're going to create keyboard shortcuts to launch certain applications. Those shortcuts are going to use the .gconf directory which lives with /home. We'll be changing the way part of our system works, mapping certain key combinations to certain programs, but we'll only be impacting a single user—not the entire system.

These configuration files are also portable. Some users carry their .bashrc file with them, so when they're on a new system, they can copy over their own .bashrc file and have a customized terminal in an instant.

Now let's take a look at your systemwide files.

14.2   / (root)

Your entire filesystem resides in an area called root. It's represented by a / and not the word root. These are the highest-level directories on your system. There is nothing beyond root. To see these files, go into your terminal and type cd /. That command is saying to change the directory to root.

You can also see root from your file manager by clicking the Computer link on the left navigation panel (see figure 14.4).

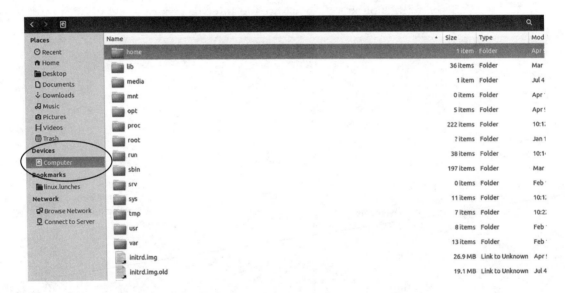

Figure 14.4   Your root directory can be seen from your file manager.

There isn't anything to do, per se, in root, but it's important to know about because it's the path to all of your system folders. Also, as you browse the list of folders within root, you'll notice a directory called root. This is the home directory of the root user. We talked about root in chapter 12. You'll recall root is the master account for all Linux systems. Because it's such an important account, there's not much you can do with it, which protects the integrity of your system. But it is confusing that root is used in two different ways like this. It's safe to assume that if someone is talking or writing about a root directory, they're talking about / and not about the root user's home directory.

14.3 /usr, /bin, and /sbin

One of the more confusing things about Linux is that you don't have a sense of where your programs are. The package managers handle the installation, and you, as the user, are less involved in where programs go, which is different from Windows, which tends to keep programs in one place and often even asks you where you want a program to be installed.

The /bin directory, which is short for binaries, contains commands. A binary is a program and can't be edited directly the way a configuration file can. So while we were able to tweak .bashrc ourselves with a text editor, the files in bin, /sbin, and /usr can't be edited by us as end-users.

Let's look at /bin, which will make things clearer. If you're in root, move into /bin and view the files. Scroll through the list and you should see some familiar names—cp and grep. These are the commands we've worked with. When we use them in the terminal, the commands call into the /bin directory to execute and do what we're asking. So when we use cp to copy a file, the cp program is launching from our /bin directory.

The /sbin directory is similar, but the commands, used by your system are administrative. They usually require root access to run.

These are two directories you'll rarely, if ever, work with, but they're good to know about in terms of understanding what happens when you use a command like mv. You're launching a program through the terminal and the program lives in a directory like /bin.

The /usr directory holds the so-called user applications, which I find confusing since I'm a user and I often use the programs within /bin. Navigate into /usr and you'll see it has its own /bin and /sbin folders, which also contain binaries.

These three directories control much of our computer. And we can see how they're structured and what they contain. It's pretty amazing. It reminds me of those anatomical models with clear skin, where you can see how all the parts of the body look within the body. It's sort of like x-ray vision for your computer in that you can get a sense of how it works.

But now let's look at a directory we can actually edit!

14.4 /etc

The /etc directory stands for et cetera! It contains your systemwide configuration files. These aren't binaries. These are files you can edit, although because they're systemwide and important you always want to tread carefully.

A great example of an editable file can be seen with GRUB, the program used to boot your computer. If you're dual-booting your computer, you might have to edit GRUB files. But even if you're not dual-booting, there are reasons you might want to edit the file.

For instance, when you shut down or turn on your computer, you might see text telling you what's going on with your system. By default, Ubuntu turns this feature off, so you don't see any messages, but other distributions leave it on. If you're trying to troubleshoot an issue with your system, these messages can be helpful so in general, you probably want it off when things are working, but on when something isn't working. Let's edit the file using the terminal to see the difference between editing a file from home, which only impacts a single user, and editing a file from /etc, which impacts the whole system. We're using the terminal for this because we're going to need administrative access to the file which requires the sudo command.

Try it now: Editing GRUB

1 Open your terminal.
2 Type `cd /etc`. This will put you in the /etc directory.
3 Type `cd /default`.
   This will move you into the default subdirectory of /etc (you could also type `cd /etc/default` to move directly into that folder in step 2).
4 Type `ls` to see the files in the directory. We're going to edit the GRUB file, which is conveniently named grub.
5 Type `sudo vi grub` to edit the file.
6 Once the file is open, you'll see a line that reads `GRUB_CMDLINE_LINUX_DEFAULT ="quiet splash"`. Quiet splash means no messages are shown when the computer turns on or off.
7 Delete quiet splash so it reads `GRUB_CMDLINE_LINUX_DEFAULT=""`. By deleting it, we're turning off the quiet splash option, which means we'll see system messaging.
8 Notice that the top of the file says `If you change this file, run 'update-grub' afterwards to update.`
9 Save and quit Vim (`:wq`).
10 Once you're back in the terminal, run the command recommended, which requires root permission. It will look like `sudo update-grub`.
11 Once GRUB updates, restart your computer.

Use root privilege / **Use vi text editor** / **Edit this file with vi** — `sudo vi grub`

You need the sudo command to edit the grub file.

As you shut down, you'll notice lots of code running down your screen, telling you everything that's happening as your computer shuts off. You'll also see this as you boot up, unless you're using a LiveCD, in which case the setting won't be saved.

The purpose of this section is not to teach you about GRUB, although GRUB is *very* useful, but to show you the type of systemwide configuring you can accomplish in the /etc directory. In this section, we changed a small behavior in terms of how our computer shuts off and turns on. The /etc directory also holds configurations for everything from which repositories we use (which we'll talk about in chapter 17) to how fonts render. Don't forget—our .bashrc editing in our home directory only impacted a single user but the GRUB tweak we made in /etc will impact all users.

14.5 /tmp

The /tmp directory represents temporary files. These aren't system files or configuration files. Files placed here by your system often disappear between reboots.

I mention it because sometimes programs will place files here. For instance, when I take a screenshot, the default file saving location is the /tmp directory. There were times, before I knew this, when I would accidentally save a screenshot too quickly and then I couldn't find it.

So consider this final section a public service announcement. Sometimes things are saved in /tmp. If you're not sure where something is, it doesn't hurt to check there.

14.6 Wrapping up

This chapter walked you through what I consider to be the most important directories. The /home directory is probably the most important one, since that's where your files and settings are, but as you saw with the GRUB example, the /etc directory can also be useful for changing things on our system. The reality is that most of the time, we interact with /etc through different third-party system tools.

If we want to change our keyboard layout, we do it through the GUI, but if we're so inclined, we can also manually edit a file in /etc/default. Understanding how these directories work helps us to understand our system—especially if something isn't working as expected. Most Linux users won't immediately know which directory to visit when they're trying to fix or configure something, but now, when you see a file location, you'll understand immediately what kind of setting you're dealing with. And in situations where you're not quite sure what you're looking for, you'll have a better sense of which directory might contain the answer.

Table 14.1 recaps what you learned today. I also mention a few other directories we'll discuss in greater detail in chapter 17.

Table 14.1 An explanation of useful directories

Directory	Purpose
/	The directory holding all of your directories. Called root.
/bin, /sbin, and /usr	Your binary applications, or programs, which you can't edit.
/etc	Your systemwide configuration files.
/home	Your personal files and personal configurations.
/lib	Your systemwide libraries (we'll talk about this more in chapter 17).
/opt	Applications installed from outside of your software repository (we'll talk about this more in chapter 17).
/root	The home directory of the root user.
/tmp	Your temporary files. Files saved here usually disappear between reboots.

GLOSSARY OF TERMS

In this chapter I explained:

> *Binary*—A program that can't be edited directly by the user
>
> *Hidden files*—Files that can't be seen by default

14.7 *Lab*

In this chapter we went into a few directories to change personal settings and system-wide ones. Now, you're going to put everything back!

1 Return your terminal prompt to its original state.

2 Return your GRUB to its original state, so it boots and closes without any messages.

3 Use the terminal to delete your hidden file (mynewhiddenfile).

4 Pipe a list of all of the files and directories in your /home directory, including the hidden ones, into a hidden file.

5 Save a file called important.txt in your /tmp directory and restart your computer. What happens to the file? Why does it happen?

Windows programs in Linux

The challenge of using any operating system is when you need a specific program that's only available on a different operating system. For instance, the U.S. government has a nice savings bond calculator, Savings Bond Wizard, that tells you how much interest bonds are earning and when they come due. Linux has its own version, called GBonds, but the files aren't compatible between the two programs, and I originally created the file in Savings Bond Wizard. So I need Windows to use my file.

There are times when there's no Linux alternative for a program and your only option is the Windows version. This has been common with games, although that's changing as more games are available on the Steam platform. Luckily, moving between Windows and Linux isn't that complicated. In this chapter I'm going to discuss two options for moving between the Linux and Windows worlds.

One interesting thing to note is that as I've spent more time in Linux, I find myself needing to go into Windows less. Just about every Windows program I need has a good Linux equivalent. But knowing how to easily get into Windows on a Linux machine is convenient for those rare occasions you might need Windows. We're going to explore two ways of running Windows programs within Linux. One is virtualization, where we run a full Windows installation within Linux, just like we ran Linux in a virtual machine back in chapter 3. The other is Wine, where aspects of Windows are emulated within our system.

15.1 *Virtualization*

We talked briefly about virtualization in chapter 3, where we used VirtualBox to install Ubuntu within Windows, but we didn't have much time to discuss what we were actually doing. Virtualization is the process of simulating hardware. You're basically tricking software into running on hardware that doesn't exist. In chapter 3, we "built" a computer in VirtualBox and then installed Ubuntu on that computer. Ubuntu thinks it's running on a physical machine with whatever RAM and memory we designated, but it's really running in VirtualBox. Put simply, a virtual machine is a computer within a computer, and knowing how to install different operating systems without needing different pieces of hardware is a useful skill.

Just as you installed Ubuntu within your Windows or OS X installation, you can also install Windows in a similar way. The process is the same as we used in chapter 3. First, you would install VirtualBox on your Linux machine. Then, you'd build a virtual computer in VirtualBox. Then, you'd install Windows in that virtual computer.

The process is simple. The challenge is that to install Windows virtually, you need a Windows image. You'll recall from chapter 3 that we downloaded our Ubuntu image from the Ubuntu site. Ubuntu is free and open source, meaning the code is publicly accessible to everyone, but also that it's cost-free. Windows is a paid product, though. You can download a limited trial version of it but you can't permanently install it for free (at least not legally).

And because installations are tied to product keys, if you have a copy of Windows, you can't use it if you're already using that product key.

One option for getting Windows is to purchase it. But explore other options. For instance, I work for a university that provides Windows images and product keys to faculty and staff. I've also heard of some students having access to Windows images and product keys through their universities. It could be worth asking around your school and/or workplace to see if there's a legal copy of Windows that could be given to you.

Of the two options I'll discuss in this chapter, this is probably the easiest way to deal with Windows: When I need Windows, I just boot into it through VirtualBox and do what I need to. Then, I close it and return to Linux. It's simple and non-disruptive. There are rarely, if ever, any complications with software, because I'm running a full version of Windows. While it does require having the Windows image to implement, which isn't trivial, once you have the image, it's pretty much like having a Windows machine that doesn't take up any physical space.

I realize not everyone will have access to a Windows image, but I want to quickly review the steps to install it. If you do have an extra Windows image, follow along:

1 Make sure your Windows image is a .iso file. Mine came as a .img file so I just changed the last three letters to .iso and I was all set.
2 Open VirtualBox and create a machine (see figure 15.1).
3 Give the image a name and indicate the version of Windows you're using in the pulldown menu. I recommend at least 1024 MB base memory because newer versions of Windows can be memory intensive.

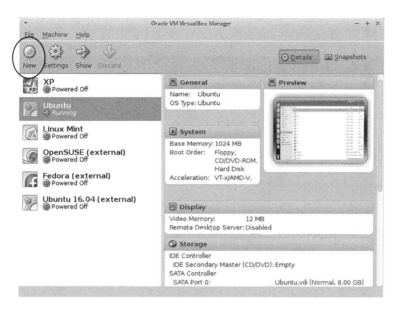

Figure 15.1   VirtualBox allows you to create machines within your existing operating system.

4   Create a new hard disk and start-up disk (see figure 15.2).

5   Use the VirtualBox Disk Image (VDI) for your file type.

6   Use a dynamically allocated disk file.

Figure 15.2   You're creating a new machine for Windows, but not a new physical machine.

7   Allocate at least 25 GB for the size of the disk. A dynamically allocated disk file
    won't use the full 25 GB at once.

8   Click Create twice and your virtual machine is configured.

9   Double-click your virtual machine which will trigger the First Run Wizard.
    Choose the location of the Windows image as your Media Source (see figure 15.3).

Figure 15.3   Point VirtualBox to the location of your disk image.

10   Click Next and then Start and you should boot into Windows.

11   From there, follow the on-screen instructions to install Windows.

When you're done, it'll be like you have a Windows-only machine that you can boot
into through VirtualBox. It's completely separate from your Linux system. If that virtual Windows machine gets infected with a virus, you can delete it. While it's possible
it could impact your Linux system, it's unlikely.

   You can install Windows software into the virtual machine. Returning to my Savings Bond Wizard, I could install it in the virtual Windows machine. When I want to
use it, I'd go into VirtualBox, boot into Windows, and then launch Savings Bond Wizard from there.

   Before we move on to another method to use Windows within Linux, I want to
point out that virtual machines don't care what operating system you're using. In the
preceding example, I showed how you could install Windows into Linux. If you
wanted to play with other Linux distributions, you could create virtual machines for
those in your existing Linux system.

15.2   *Wine: Using Windows without full-blown virtual machines*

Wine is a tool used to run Windows software directly within Linux. You don't have to boot into Windows. Instead, you use Wine to install the programs and then they become regular programs in your Linux system. So why would anyone virtualize when you can use Wine? Because unfortunately, not every Windows program runs in Wine and not all of them run well.

Luckily, Wine has a neat system for tracking how well things work. The project maintains a database of programs that work (and don't work) with Wine, identifying issues and assigning a score. The database, available at https://appdb.winehq.org/, uses a five-point scale to rate how well programs run in Wine. Platinum means absolutely no issues and garbage is, well, garbage. Visit it now to get a sense of what programs work well with Wine. A list of the top 10 platinum programs is right on the home page.

Let's install a Windows program in our Linux machine. Because you've heard so many great things from me about Savings Bond Wizard, download it. You can find it on the U.S. Treasury site at treasurydirect.gov. The file you need can be found at https://www.treasurydirect.gov/indiv/tools/sbwsetup.exe.

Also, because you know exactly where the file is, this is a great use case for `wget`. Why open your browser if you don't need to? Use `wget` to download the file. You'll also need to install Wine. When you install Wine, you'll have to agree to an end-user license agreement, which is something we haven't encountered yet. It will come up during the installation. Once you accept it, the installation will continue.

After that, you can install Savings Bond Wizard:

1   Double-click the .exe file you downloaded. Wine will open and guide you through an installation process that looks just like the Windows installation process (see figure 15.4). If it doesn't, right-click on the file and open it with Wine.

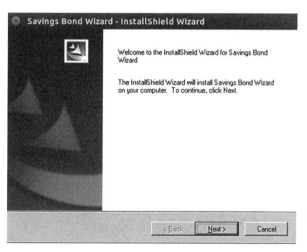

Figure 15.4   Wine allows you to install Windows programs within Linux. The installation is just like using Windows.

2   Go through the options to accept the license and install Savings Bond Wizard. It's fine to use all of the default settings.

3   Once you're done, you'll see a shortcut on the desktop to launch it. You can delete that if you're trying to keep your desktop nice and clean.

4   To launch Savings Bond Wizard, just type its name into the Dash.

5   The program will launch. It'll look just like a native Linux program (see figure 15.5). When you launch it, Wine is automatically working in the background to run the Windows program.

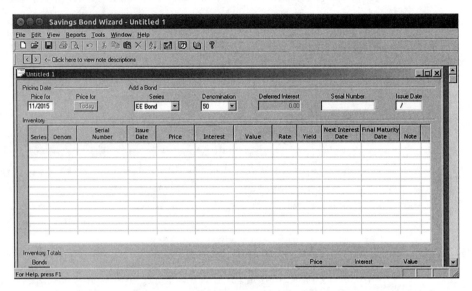

Figure 15.5   Once a program is installed with Wine, you launch it like any other program.

If you want to uninstall a program you installed with Wine, type `Uninstall Wine` into the terminal to launch the uninstaller (see figure 15.6). Click the program you wish to uninstall and click the Remove button.

Wine allows you to customize it however you see fit. The customizations are accessed by typing `Configure Wine` into the Dash.

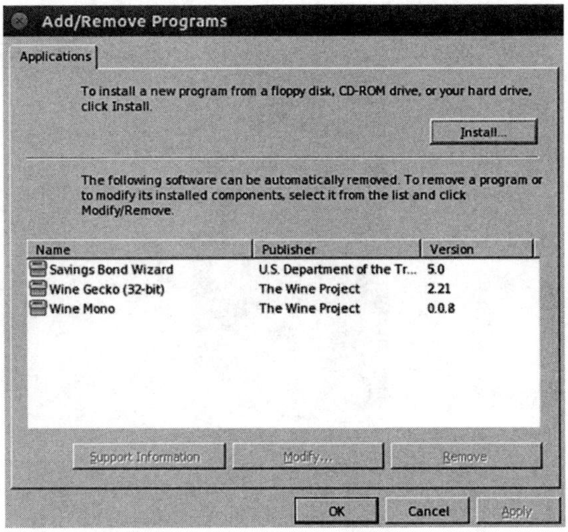

Figure 15.6   Wine also uninstalls programs for you.

The Applications tab allows you to choose which version of Windows is being emulated by Wine, either at the application level or for all of Wine (see figure 15.7). I've never had to override Wine's default choices, but it could be necessary if you're using a piece of software that needs a specific version of Windows to run.

The Drives tab lets you add additional drives to Wine. This means you can change the install location of programs and create different Windows drives for Wine to work with. This could be helpful if you wanted to keep Wine files on an external hard drive for space purposes. By default, Wine creates a fake C: drive on your computer. It's a folder called drive_c that's in a hidden folder called .wine in your home directory. Recall from the last

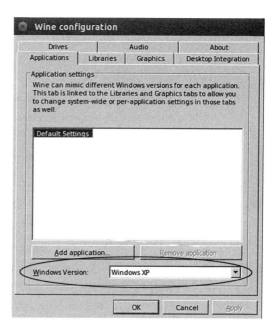

Figure 15.7   Wine lets you choose which version of Windows it's emulating, either at the application level or globally.

chapter that because it's in your home directory, that means that while other users on your system will have access to Wine, they won't have access to any programs you install. Let's take a look at that directory so you know where to look if you have trouble finding something you saved with Wine:

1   Go into the terminal and type `ls  -A` so you can see your hidden files. You should see a .wine directory.
2   Go into it with `cd  .wine`.
3   Type `ls` to look around. You should see `drive_c`. That's where Wine is keeping your Windows programs.
4   Go into `drive_c` and you'll see the Windows Program Files directory which is where your Wine programs are.
5   Go into Program Files. Press tab after you type `cd  P` so the terminal will complete the Program Files folder name for you.
6   Use `ls` to look around again and you can now see Savings Bond Wizard.

15.2.1   *Winetricks*

Some Windows software is problematic to install with Wine. Because of that, Wine comes with a program called Winetricks, which is a collection of scripts designed to help you with difficult-to-install software. If you have trouble getting something to work in Wine, try Winetricks. Winetricks works like a repository, in that it will download many of the required files for you and then install the program. Not every program is represented in Winetricks, but it's a good place to look if you're having trouble installing something. Let's take a quick look at it:

1 Open Winetricks via the Dash.
2 Click Install an App and click OK.
3 You'll see a list of all of the programs available, much like Synaptic. A Media status of download means Winetricks will download the program for you. A Media status of manual_download means you'll have to download the program yourself (see figure 15.8). Winetricks usually tells you where to go and where to install files if it doesn't download them for you.

Winetricks will download file.

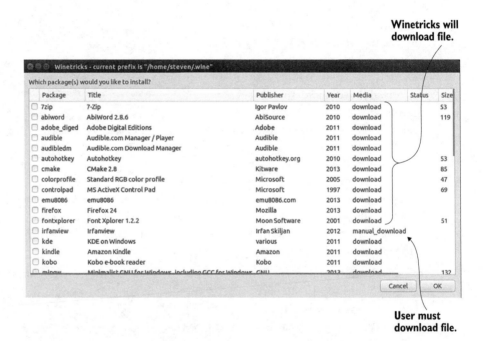

User must download file.

Figure 15.8   Winetricks will handle most downloads for you and indicates the programs it can't download.

As you review the list, you'll probably notice there isn't much worth installing. But if you're desperate to get older Windows software running in Linux, which is a pretty specific situation, Winetricks could be represent your answer.

I've used Wine without any issues for years but there is a paid version of the software called CrossOver that provides more support. If you can't get a certain Windows program to run in Wine, it might be worth seeing if it runs better with CrossOver. The CrossOver site is www.codeweavers.com.

15.3   *Wrapping up*

Between virtual machines and Wine, you shouldn't have any problems getting Windows programs running in Linux. But before you spend too much time exploring these options, I hope you'll think about the software we explored in chapter 8. The Linux software ecosystem is impressive, and you should find that most Windows programs have a strong Linux version.

At this point, you might be wondering which of the two options we discussed here you should choose for those times when you need Windows to run a program on your Linux system? My suggestion would be to use both, which is what I do! I use Wine for my bond program because it runs well and it opens like any other program. But I also keep a virtual Windows machine for times when Wine doesn't work. Both options work great side-by-side and one doesn't take away from the other.

GLOSSARY OF TERMS

In this chapter I explained:

> *Virtualization*—The process of simulating hardware

15.4   *Lab*

1   Use Wine to uninstall the Savings Bond Wizard.
2   Use Wine to create a D: drive on a USB, as you might do if you want to keep your Wine programs off your main hard drive.
3   Visit the online Wine database and find a platinum Windows program to install.
4   Download and install Amber Pyramid Solitaire using Wine (it's a free game). It can be found at www.gametop.com/download-free-games/pyramid-solitaire/.
5   Play one game of Solitaire. If anyone asks what you're doing, tell them it's homework for this book.

Establishing a workflow
16

By this time, you should be starting to put the pieces of your Linux system together. You can now:

- Find and install software.
- Use Unity's GUI to interact with your system.
- Use the terminal to create, move, copy, and delete files.
- Understand how your computer's filesystem is organized and how the various files control different aspects of your system.
- Run Windows programs within your system.

In other words, you have a sense of how you like to work in Linux. You probably even have a preferred text editor! This next part is going to show you how to really make your system your own. We're going to discuss two concepts today:

- *File/application launchers*—Tools to help you quickly open files and launch programs. We talked about them a bit in chapter 5, but we're going to go more in-depth in this chapter.
- *Keybinding*—A way to assign certain programs and tasks to certain keystroke combinations, which can help you use your computer more efficiently. Rather than clicking through menus you're using a key combination to open the program you need.

Application launchers and keyboard shortcuts are great ways to make the programs you use frequently readily available to you in only a few keystrokes. In terms of how I work, I prefer application launchers because they cover *everything*, where keyboard shortcuts have to be configured in advance. Unity's Dash launcher is great for lots of people, but if you're looking for something with a little more functionality than Dash, you might consider Kupfer or GNOME Do (we'll discuss them in the next section), which not only open files and folders, but also allow you to use them to move files and folders.

This chapter is the chance to think about the programs you use most and the fastest, easiest way to get them open. And what if you're happy with the default workflow? Then great! But work through this chapter and bookmark it, because eventually you probably will want to tweak your Linux workflow.

16.1 File/application launchers

Why am I discussing application launchers when Ubuntu comes with one? There are a few reasons you might wish to go beyond Unity's Dash. One would be if you decide to move to a desktop environment without a built-in launcher. You'll recall that in chapter 5, we ran through a few desktop environments. Some, like KDE, GNOME, and Unity, have built-in file/application launching functionality. But others, like Xfce, do not. So if you decide to leave a desktop environment with a built-in launcher, it's useful to know how to replicate that functionality in a different desktop.

Application launchers are also useful if you don't like the one that ships with your desktop environment. We've been using Unity's Dash for quite a while, but it might not be to your taste. Personally, I find it a little slow and I don't like how it takes over my whole screen when I use it to open something.

Your tastes might be different. You might love Dash. And that's fine! You don't have to switch. But we're going to look at two other launchers, to give you a sense of other tools available to you.

Before we begin, you're going to need to install the launchers. You can use the command line, Synaptic, or the Ubuntu Software Center. The two programs you need to install (with the package name in parenthesis) are:

- GNOME Do (gnome-do)
- Kupfer (kupfer)

16.1.1 GNOME Do

GNOME Do launches applications and opens files and folders. What makes it different from Dash is that it allows you to combine these two activities within its interface, so that you can do things like open a specific file with a specific program and move/copy files and folders. Before we can try it out, we need to configure it. This will let us choose how GNOME Do looks and will allow us to select the key (or keys) used to launch it. Go into the Dash and launch GNOME Do. You'll see it open in the middle of

Figure 16.1 The GNOME Do launcher needs to be configured before it's usable in Unity.

your screen. To customize it, click the triangle in the top right corner and go into Preferences (see figure 16.1). Let's create a keyboard shortcut to launch GNOME Do.

The Preference area is where you'll modify GNOME Do's behavior. You'll see four tabs (see figure 16.2):

- General, which controls startup behavior
- Keyboard, which is how you change which keys control which parts of GNOME Do's behavior
- Plugins, which gives GNOME Do additional functionality (we'll discuss that later in this section)
- Appearance, which controls the look of GNOME Do

Figure 16.2 GNOME Do's preferences area lets you configure the launcher's behavior.

Click Keyboard so we can assign a launch key (see figure 16.3). I'm going to use Ctrl-space but it can be any combination not being used by something else on your system:

1 Double-click the shortcut next to the Summon Do action. It might take a couple of tries to get the click speed just right so that Disabled changes to New Accelerator….

2 Once you see New Accelerator…, you can assign a launch key combination by typing it. Use Ctrl and space together for the key combination. It should look like figure 16.4.

3 Close GNOME Do and type Ctrl-space. GNOME Do will now launch.

To launch an application with GNOME Do, type the name into the GNOME Do box and press Enter. For instance, type Firefox into the GNOME Do box and you'll see the Firefox icon appear (see figure 16.5). Press Enter and Firefox

Figure 16.3 Summon Do allows you to assign a keyboard shortcut to launch GNOME Do.

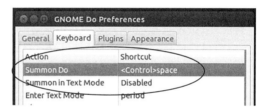

Figure 16.4 Ctrl-space will now launch GNOME Do.

will launch. You can still use Dash to launch programs. The two applications don't conflict.

Figure 16.5 GNOME Do lets you launch programs, much like Unity's Dash.

I mentioned that you could use GNOME Do to launch folders and files. That isn't a default behavior, though. Let's activate it so GNOME Do will always launch folders and files:

1 Go back into GNOME Do's preferences. You should be in the Plugins tab.

2 Put a check in the box next to Files and Folders (see figure 16.6). This will activate the plugin that allows GNOME Do to open individual files as well as folders.

3 Click Close and close GNOME Do.

Now launch GNOME Do and type docu-ments. You'll see the Documents folder come up in the left pane. In the right pane, you'll see it says Open. Press Tab and you'll move from the left pane into GNOME Do's right one. Then, use the down arrow to reveal all of the things you can do to that folder with GNOME Do, from opening it, to copying it, to moving it, to creating an empty folder inside it (see figure 16.7).

Let's create a new file with GNOME Do. This will be the third way we've created an empty file without opening an editor. The first way was with the file manager, which you learned in chapter 6, and the second was with the touch command, which you learned in chapter 10.

1 Launch GNOME Do.

2 Type documents again (capitalization won't matter here, unlike in the terminal).

3 Once your Documents folder comes up, tab over to the right pane.

4 Use the down arrow to scroll until you reach the Create New File option.

5 Press Enter.

6 GNOME Do will immediately give you the option to open the file, which it named Untitled.

Figure 16.6   GNOME Do lets you launch files and folders once you activate a plugin.

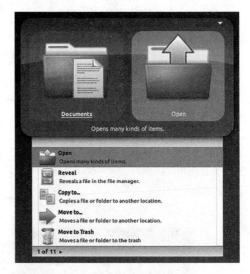

Figure 16.7   GNOME Do doesn't just open folders and files. It also lets you manipulate them.

7 Press Enter to open the file.

8 The file will open in gedit.

9 Save the file as gnomedotest and close out.

This kind of workflow is helpful if you're starting a new project. You would begin your project by using GNOME Do to create a file in your working directory. You could then use Save As to give the file a more meaningful name than Untitled. However, if you happen to want a file called Untitled, this is amazingly convenient.

While the application launching functionality of GNOME Do is comparable to Dash, the ability to use it to also work with files and folders is convenient. To move files with Dash, you need to launch a file manager, whereas with GNOME Do, you can move the files directly, without a file manager. By now, you've probably noticed a lot of this book is about saving time and keystrokes. GNOME Do is a nice tool in that time-saving arsenal, because rather than finding a file in the file manager and then copying it somewhere else, you can do it all within the GNOME Do interface, similarly to how we did it in the terminal.

Of course, GNOME Do is just one launcher. Let's take a look at Kupfer, which is similar but designed for KDE systems.

16.1.2 *Kupfer*

Kupfer, a KDE application launcher, will work on any desktop environment. The KDE part is only significant in that it requires some programs that aren't in other desktop environments by default. When you install it, those files are automatically downloaded (we'll talk more about this in chapter 17), but Kupfer takes up a little more space because of it. It's not a major issue, though.

You can launch Kupfer via GNOME Do, by typing Kupfer.

You'll notice Kupfer looks a lot like GNOME Do. The two tools are very similar, which you'll see shortly. For now, let's assign a key combination to launch Kupfer.

To do that, click the gear icon in the top right corner (see figure 16.8) and then click Preferences.

Figure 16.8 Like GNOME Do, Kupfer has a configuration option.

Figure 16.9 Kupfer's preferences area is similar to GNOME Do's.

As with GNOME Do, you'll see a configuration area with four tabs (see figure 16.9):

- General, which controls startup behavior
- Keyboard, which controls the keyboard shortcuts
- Plugins, which controls which Kupfer plugins are used
- Catalog, which lets you select which settings and files Kupfer searches

It's very similar to GNOME Do. To assign a key combination to Kupfer:

1 Click the Keyboard tab (see figure 16.10).
2 In the Show Main Interface area the shortcut is Ctrl-space. Since we're using that combination for GNOME Do right now, double-click Ctrl-space and assign Alt-Ctrl-space to Show Main Interface.
3 Click Close.

Figure 16.10 Kupfer lets you choose which key combination you use to launch it.

You can now launch Kupfer with Alt-Ctrl-space. As with GNOME Do, you can use any key combination not being used by something else on your system.

In addition, you can launch applications, like Firefox, simply by typing the name of the program.

Unlike GNOME Do, Kupfer can open files and folders by default. However, it doesn't index your Documents directory by default. Let's configure Kupfer so we can use it to open files and folders in our Documents directory:

1 Go to Kupfer's Preferences.

2 Click the Catalog tab.

3 Click Add (see figure 16.11).

4 Double-click Documents.

5 Click OK.

You should now see your Documents folder as one of Kupfer's indexed folders. That means you can launch any file or folder within Documents.

Figure 16.11 Kupfer lets you launch files and folders by default, but you have to indicate which directories you wish it to index.

The indexing can take a few minutes. If you want to speed up the indexing, you can quit Kupfer and relaunch it.

Once your Documents folder is indexed, you can type gnomedotest and you'll be presented with the option to open the file (see figure 16.12).

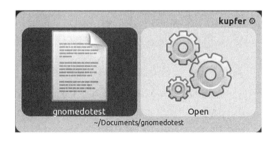

Figure 16.12 Kupfer lets you open files once you've told it where to look for them.

As with GNOME Do, you can tab over to the right pane, use the down arrow, and manipulate the file from the Kupfer interface. Let's use Kupfer to move our gnomedotest file to the Desktop:

1 Launch Kupfer.

2 Type gnomedotest.

3 Tab to the right pane.

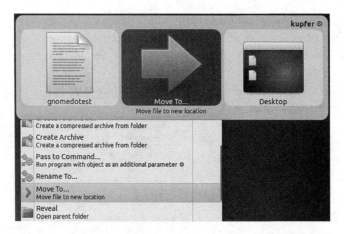

Figure 16.13   Kupfer, like GNOME Do, lets you move files and folders through its interface.

4 Use the down arrow to scroll through your option until you get Move to….

5 Tab over to the third pane that will appear and select Desktop (see figure 16.13).

6 Press Enter.

You'll now see your gnomedotest file on the desktop.

In terms of which one to choose, Kupfer tends to be used by people using KDE, whereas Xfce and GNOME users tend to use GNOME Do. You can customize the appearance of both, so one appearance option might appeal to you more. That would dictate the launcher you would use. But both are *very* similar. The differences between the two launchers are subtle.

Now that you've spent time with application launchers, let's finish up by learning how to create global keyboard shortcuts that will allow you to launch specific applications.

16.2 *Keyboard shortcuts*

If you just want to quickly open certain programs, keyboard shortcuts could be a good option for you. We use keyboard shortcuts within applications all of the time. For instance, Ctrl-X is a universal way to cut text out of most applications. Linux also allows you to launch programs with shortcuts.

Some shortcuts are already configured for you. The Windows/meta key opens the Dash area for you. Press Alt-Ctrl-T right now and a terminal window will open. But you can also create your own shortcuts. In this section, I'm going to walk you through the process in three different desktop environments. We're going to map the key combination Ctrl-Alt-F to Firefox. This way, when you want to open that browser, you use a shortcut, rather than a launcher or clicking. While the process is similar in each desktop environment, they're different enough that it's helpful to have a guide.

16.2.1 *Unity/GNOME*

The process in Unity and GNOME is the same.

Try it now: Creating a keyboard shortcut

1 Launch Settings (GNOME) or System Settings (Unity). If you don't have a System Settings option in Ubuntu, install the unity-control-center package.
2 Click Keyboard.
3 Once in the Keyboard area, click the Shortcuts tab. If you want to change an existing keyboard shortcut, like the terminal one, you can do it from here. To create a new shortcut, click Custom Shortcuts.

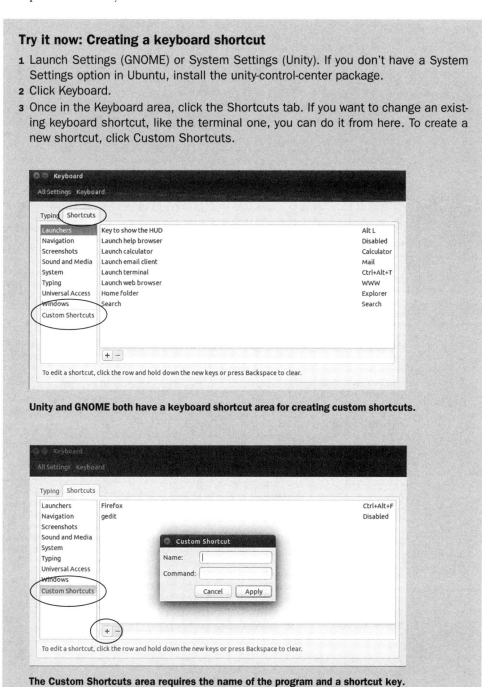

Unity and GNOME both have a keyboard shortcut area for creating custom shortcuts.

The Custom Shortcuts area requires the name of the program and a shortcut key.

(continued)

4 Click the + sign to create a shortcut. To create a shortcut, you need to know the name of the package. In the case of Firefox, the package is `firefox`. If you're not sure of the name of a package, you can look it up in Synaptic.

5 Use Firefox for the name (which is a descriptor so you know what the shortcut does) and `firefox` (the name of the package) for the command.

6 Press Enter.

7 Click once on the word Disabled.

8 When the text changes to New Accelerator, press the Ctrl-Alt-F keys together.

9 Close out of the Settings tool.

Press Ctrl-Alt-F together to make sure the shortcut works.

16.2.2   *KDE*

To create a keyboard shortcut for an application in KDE, the process is slightly different. Here you're going to use the KDE Menu Editor. Here is how you would make that same Firefox shortcut in KDE:

1 Right-click the KDE menu icon.

2 Select Edit Applications... (see figure 16.14).

3 You'll now see a list of programs arranged by what they do. Since we need Firefox, click Internet, then Web Browser, then Firefox (see figure 16.15).

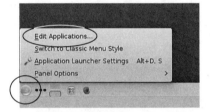

Figure 16.14   KDE users create shortcuts using the KDE Menu Editor.

4 Go over to the right pane and click the Advanced tab.

5 Click where it says Current Shortcut Key and set the shortcut to Ctrl-Alt-F.

6 Click Save and exit the menu editor.

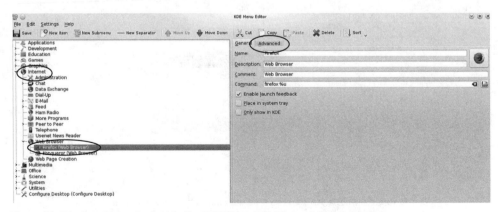

Figure 16.15   Creating a shortcut in the KDE Menu Editor is an Advanced option.

You can now launch Firefox with Ctrl-Alt-F.

16.2.3 Xfce

The process for setting keyboard shortcuts in Xfce is similar to the GNOME/Unity process:

1 Click Settings.
2 Click Keyboard (see figure 16.16).

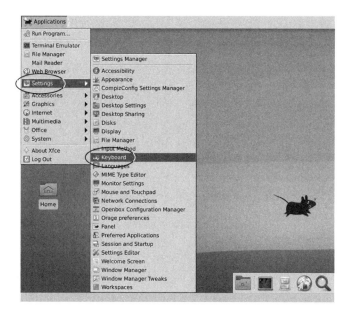

Figure 16.16   Xfce, like Unity and GNOME, has a dedicated area for keyboard shortcuts.

3 Click the Application Shortcuts tab.
4 Click Add (see figure 16.17).
5 Use `firefox` for the command. It'll be all lowercase because it's the name of the package.
6 Xfce will then ask you to set a shortcut. Press Ctrl-Alt-F and it'll assign that combination to Firefox.
7 Close out of the keyboard settings box.

You can now launch Firefox with Ctrl-Alt-F.

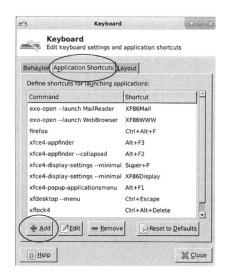

Figure 16.17   Add a new shortcut using the name of the package, which might be different from the name of the program.

16.3 *Wrapping up*

Launchers and keyboard shortcuts take some time to learn, but pay off in terms of saving time while you work. There are other application launchers, like Launchy and Synapse. We'll talk about Synapse in the next chapter, but to find out about other launchers, you can check out Wikipedia: http://mng.bz/XfJH. And don't forget that you can use all of these tools and techniques together. For instance, you might open files with an application launcher but launch programs with a keyboard shortcut. Linux is all about creating a workflow that works for you. And now, you have a few options to consider in terms of setting up your workflow.

GLOSSARY OF TERMS

In this chapter I explained:

> *File/application launchers*—Tools used to quickly open files and launch programs
>
> *Keybinding*—Assigning certain programs and tasks to keystroke combinations

16.4 *Lab*

1 Use GNOME Do to create a folder on your Desktop called testfolder.
2 Use Kupfer to move that folder into Documents.
3 Use GNOME Do to create a file on your Desktop called linuxlunches.doc.
4 Use Kupfer to open the linuxlunches.doc file with `gedit`.
5 Map `gedit` to Ctrl-Shift-G.
6 Of the launchers and shortcut techniques we explored in this chapter, which can you see yourself using regularly?

Advanced lab

Assign a key combination to the `xkill` command we used in chapter 11. Use that shortcut to kill an open program.

Part 3

Home system admin on Linux

This third and final part of *Learn Linux in a Month of Lunches* shows you how to be a system administrator for your home Linux setup. This section is all about taking care of your system, just like SysAdmins do, but on a much smaller and more manageable level. You'll learn how to keep your system up-to-date, how to set up printing, and basic networking concepts. This section is your advanced Linux class. In this final section, you'll learn about:

- Package management
- Updating your operating system
- Linux security
- Connecting to other computers
- Printing (a surprisingly interesting chapter!)
- Collaboration using version control

An in-depth look at package management and maintenance

Welcome to part 3 of our journey! You just finished part 2, which was about learning to work with Linux as a day-to-day user. That's why we learned about commands and text editors and software. Those are things you need to do your personal work.

In part 3, we're going to explore the administrative aspects of running Linux. This section will help you with your own work, but will also help your system to run smoothly. And just to be clear, when I say administrative, I mean systems administration and not the people at work who boss you around. Although, in a sense, you will be learning to boss around your system. So maybe the term works on a few levels.

We talked about installing and removing software in chapter 7 with a focus on using the repositories of software that come with your Linux system. In this chapter, we're going to further explore installing and removing software, with a focus on three areas:

- *Installing software from outside of the repository.* The ability to install software from outside of the repository is useful for situations where the software you want isn't included with your distribution. You'll recall from the previous chapter that I mentioned a launcher called Synapse that isn't in the Ubuntu repositories. In this chapter, you're going to learn how to install it.
- *Package dependencies.* This section will help you to understand your Linux system and how it runs programs. You understand the mechanics of installing software, but now it's time to learn what goes on underneath that. Many software issues are caused by dependency problems, meaning the programs needed by other programs. This section will help you to understand those challenges.

- *Advanced commands to install and remove software.* Advanced commands will help you keep your system free of unnecessary dependencies that, at best, take up memory on your computer and, at worst, can interfere with other programs.

This chapter will also help prepare you for chapter 18, where you're going to update and upgrade your system, which also involves the package manager.

Let's get started installing Synapse, which is not in the Ubuntu 14.04 repositories.

17.1   Installing software from outside of the repositories

In chapter 7, you learned about the convenience of the software repository. All of the software you need is in one place, and is either a click or a command away. But what about when the software you want *isn't* in a repository?

This happens for many reasons. Sometimes a piece of software doesn't make it into a particular distribution release. Sometimes a piece of software isn't in the repositories for licensing reasons. For instance, Dropbox, the popular file syncing/sharing program, is commercial software that's not available in any repositories. What if you wanted Dropbox installed on your system?

There are usually three options for installing software that's outside of the main repository:

- Installing software via a package file.
- Adding another repository to your system and then installing the software via your package manager.
- Installing software from source code. There are lots of different ways to do this. The software often has instructions on how to install it, usually in the form of a README file that contains installation directions. Because this process is so idiosyncratic, I'm not going to explore it in this chapter.

The method you choose depends upon how the software is available. Most of the time, you don't have a choice, so you use whichever option is available. Let's start with package files.

17.1.1   Installing software with package files

Software package files are like the .exe files you use to install Windows software. Debian-based systems, like Ubuntu, use .deb files, whereas other systems use other formats. Fedora and OpenSUSE both use .rpm files. Installing software via this method is as simple as downloading a file and then opening it. As an example, the Brackets and Atom text editors, which we talked about in chapter 9, are both available via software package files, as is Dropbox. Let's install Dropbox (don't worry if you don't have a Dropbox account; you won't need one for this exercise):

1. Go to www.dropbox.com/install?os=lnx.
2. Click download for Ubuntu (.deb) 32-bit.
3. Save the file to your Downloads folder.

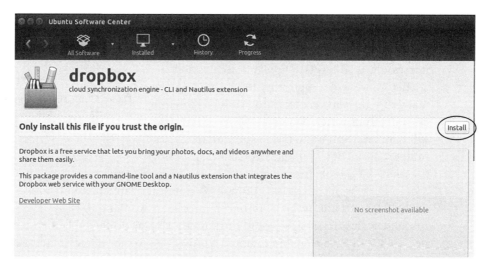

Figure 17.1   Ubuntu will install .deb files with Ubuntu Software Center.

4   Double-click the .deb file and Ubuntu will install Dropbox using the Ubuntu Software Center (see figure 17.1) after you enter in your password.

5   You'll see a green check once Dropbox is installed. You can now delete the .deb file from your Downloads folder.

INSTALLING .DEB FILES   If you don't like using the Ubuntu Software Center to install .debs, you can install GDebi, which is a tool for installing .deb files. I prefer GDebi to Ubuntu Software Center, which always feels kind of slow to me. Once you have GDebi, right-click on the .deb, click Open With… and choose GDebi to use it as the default for opening .deb files.

This is a fairly painless way to install software on your system. However, always take care when installing software packages. You could potentially be installing something harmful on your system. Research the origins of the software package file. If it's coming from a business you've heard of, like Google or Dropbox, then it should be fine. But if it's a standalone file on a site or message board you're not familiar with, then you should probably avoid using it—at least until you have confirmation, based on researching what others have said about the package, that the file won't harm your system.

Now that you know how to use software package files, let's explore how to install a repository.

17.1.2   *Viewing and adding repositories*

When you download software out of a repository, it feels like you're pulling software from one big collection. But the reality is that you're working with multiple repositories and interacting with them through a single interface, like Synaptic. When you add a repository to your system, it's like you're connecting a hose to your package manager and the hose is bringing in new packages from that repository you just added (see figure 17.2).

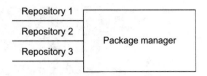

Figure 17.2   **The package manager connects to multiple repositories.**

Before we add a repository to our system, let's make sure the software we want to add isn't in our current repositories. Don't worry! Nothing bad will happen if you try to install software that's not in the repositories. You'll just get an error message.

First, let's look for Synapse. Go into Synaptic and look for a package called synapse. It won't come up, though. It's another launcher but unlike Kupfer and GNOME Do, it's not in the Ubuntu repositories. If Kupfer and GNOME Do didn't quite resonate with you, Synapse could turn out to be your preferred launcher. Software is a personal choice, and before I choose a tool, I like to take a few for a test spin.

To see repositories on your system

Before we add the Synapse repository, let's look at our current repositories and see which ones are included.

1   Go into Dash and launch Software & Updates. This is a tool to manage your repositories. We used it in chapter 4 to look at our drivers. If you change a repository here, it's changed across your system—even if you use a different package manager. The opening screen shows you the four repositories that make up our system's software list: main, universe, restricted, and multiverse (see figure 17.3). We talked about this in chapter 7, but to review:

  - *Main* is free and open source software maintained by the Ubuntu developers.

Figure 17.3   **Ubuntu's software list is made up of four repositories.**

- *Universe* refers to software contributed by the community but not officially supported by Ubuntu.
- *Multiverse* refers to non-free, proprietary software (there is no way to purchase software through Synaptic so it doesn't refer to cost).
- *Restricted* refers to proprietary drivers.

Now we're ready to add the Synapse repository.

TO ADD A REPOSITORY USING GRAPHICALLY

Adding a repository is a two-step process:

1   Click the Other Software tab. Anything with a check in the box is software in your repository, but that isn't an official part of the Ubuntu project. For instance, you'll see the Dropbox repositories in there now that we installed it (see figure 17.4). Anything without a check in the box is not in your repository, but can be added with a check.

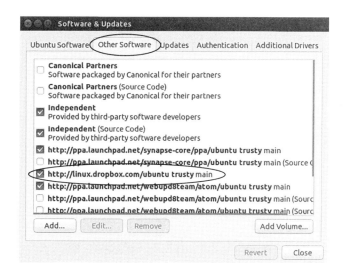

Figure 17.4   Other software shows you repositories from beyond the main Ubuntu project.

2   Click the Add button. A pop-up will open asking you to Enter the Complete APT Line of the Repository That You Want to Add as Source. You're going to type in `ppa:synapse-core/ppa`. The PPA information comes from the project page on Launchpad.net, which is where Canonical hosts different software projects.

Ubuntu will use that information to pull in the web address of the repository for you:

1   Click Close. Ubuntu will now prompt you to reload its software because it's out-of-date.
2   Click the Reload button. Ubuntu will now re-index the repositories. Software & Updates will close when it's done.

3 Return to Synaptic.
4 Click Reload to refresh Synaptic's holdings.
- Search for synapse again.
- The package is now available for you.
- Install it just like we installed Vim in chapter 7.
- Once Synaptic finishes, close out of it.
- Go into Dash and launch Synapse. It's another great launcher to play with if you didn't get enough of launchers in the last chapter!

When you typed in the repository information, you used the initials PPA. It's an abbreviation for *Personal Package Archive*, which is a repository maintained by a project or individual, rather than the distribution. PPAs are specific to Debian-based systems but other distributions have similar concepts. Returning to the hose analogy at the start of this section, a PPA is the hose that brings packages into your system. Most distributions have methods of adding repositories that are conceptually similar to PPAs. For instance, Arch Linux has *AUR*, which stands for *Arch User Repository*. This is where Arch users can place software not in the main Arch repository and share it with the Arch community. OpenSUSE has a comparable concept it calls the *Open Build Service*.

TO ADD A REPOSITORY USING COMMANDS
As you might expect, there are also commands to add a new repository (see figure 17.5):
- `sudo add-apt-repository ppa:synapse-core/ppa`
- `sudo apt-get update`
- `sudo apt-get install synapse`

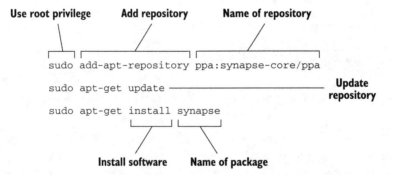

Figure 17.5   As you might expect, there are also commands to add a repository and install new software.

Now that you know the different ways to install software, we're ready to move into dependencies, which are the programs needed by other programs to run. In the next section, we're going to look at what dependencies are, how they work, and how you can remove unneeded dependencies to save space on your system.

17.2   *Dependencies*

I've talked about package dependencies at different times in this book. Dependencies are files and libraries (modular software shared and used by multiple programs) needed by a program to run it. Part of the job of the package manager is to take care of the dependencies for you. It looks at what files a package needs to run, making sure you have them on your system and installing them if you don't. The package manager even makes sure you have the correct version of a program or library, since sometimes a piece of software needs a specific version of a file or library.

When you just installed Synapse, you didn't only install Synapse. You also installed the programs and libraries it needs to run. What are they? Let's take a look:

1   Open Synaptic and search for Synapse.

2   Right-click on it and click Properties. This area will tell you all about a package.

3   Click the Dependencies tab (see figure 17.6) to see other programs Synapse needs to run. The number in parenthesis means the version of the package or library needed by Synapse. For instance, the program libgee2 needs to be version greater than or equal to 0.5.0. This is useful if you're having trouble with a program. Sometimes the package manager is using the incorrect version of a dependency. Looking at the dependencies yourself gives you the ability to see what the issue might be—whether it's a missing dependency or the incorrect version of one.

4   Close out of properties and close Synapse.

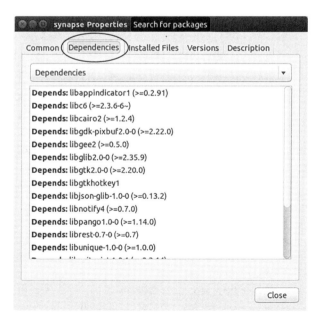

Figure 17.6   The Synaptic package manager allows you to see dependencies.

Of course, if you were to remove Synapse from your system, you would no longer need some of these dependencies but they would remain on your system, taking up space. In the next section, you'll see how to remove them.

17.2.1 *Using advanced commands to remove dependencies*

Before you can remove dependencies, you have to remove the program. If you try to remove a dependency, the package manager will also remove software using the dependency. This won't break your system, but it's annoying if a program you use gets removed because then you have to reinstall it.

First, let's remove Synapse using the command line. In chapter 12, we used the command `sudo apt-get remove` to uninstall software on our system. That command removes software but leaves behind configuration files. A more complete way to remove almost everything about a program is to use `sudo apt-get --purge remove` and the name of the package. This is the command I usually use to remove software in order to keep my system as clean as possible. Go into the terminal and remove Synapse with `sudo apt-get --purge remove synapse`.

If you look at your terminal text, you'll see a message at the top that you might not have noticed previously when removing software:

```
The following packages were automatically installed and are no longer
    required:
  consolekit libck-connector0 libgtkhotkey1 libpam-ck-connector pastebinit
  python-gnome2 python-pyorbit
Use 'apt-get autoremove' to remove them.
```

Those packages were used by Synapse and aren't used by anything else on your system, so you don't need them. All they're doing is taking up space. If you install another piece of software that needs one of those programs, the package manager will reinstall what it needs. Go back to the terminal and type `sudo apt-get autoremove` to get rid of those unneeded dependencies.

> **AUTOREMOVE** `autoremove` can be a controversial command in that it occasionally removes packages needed by other packages, thus breaking your system. I have never run into this issue personally, but I have read about other users running into it. The only time I would skip autoremove is when working with:
>
> - *A metapackage*—A metapackage is a preconfigured collection of programs that allows you to easily install something complex, like a desktop environment, without having to install lots of packages one-by-one.
>   The packages bundled in a metapackage aren't necessarily dependencies. Instead, they make software more usable to the user by pre-selecting everything needed to make it work well. If I removed a metapackage, like `xfce` or `kde`, which are both desktop environments, I wouldn't follow-up with `autoremove`. Instead, I would leave whatever packages were left behind on my system.

- *GNOME applications*—The GNOME desktop environment has a lot of software tightly integrated with it, like the Evolution email client and GNOME Videos, the video player. These programs are tightly integrated into GNOME and it seems that when you remove those programs and then their dependencies, you often wind up breaking GNOME. When dealing with GNOME applications and the GNOME desktop, I leave the dependencies alone. You can see a list of GNOME applications on the GNOME wiki: https://wiki.gnome.org/

Other than those two situations, I use `autoremove` constantly and have never run into an issue with it personally.

You'll remember we looked at Synapse's dependencies and saw a program called `libgee2`. It wasn't on the `autoremove` list, so that means at least one other program on our system uses it. Let's see what happens when we try to remove `libgee2`. Go into the terminal and type `sudo apt-get --purge remove libgee2`.

You'll see a *long* message beginning with:

```
The following packages were automatically installed and are no longer
    required:
```

These are all the programs that also use `libgee2`. If we remove `libgee2`, the package manager will remove *all* of the programs that use it. Handling dependencies this way is useful behavior since it prevents us from removing programs needed by other programs. Rather than leave us with broken software, the package manager offers to remove everything that would be broken were the dependency removed.

It's also why you need to be careful removing programs, because if you blindly said yes to removing both programs, you might wonder what happened to that huge list of software shown in the terminal message. That's why it's important to always carefully read system messages. Type `N` and press Enter to cancel removing `libgee2`.

17.3 Wrapping up

You now know different ways to install software when the software you want isn't in a repository. This will open up your Linux world even more. You also should have a sense of how dependencies work and how to remove them from your system when they're no longer needed, which helps to save space. All of this work will come in handy in the next chapter when we talk about updating and upgrading your system, which also relies on your package manager.

GLOSSARY OF TERMS

In this chapter I explained:

Arch User Repository (AUR)—A repository containing packages submitted by projects or individuals, rather than the Arch distribution.

Dependency—Files and libraries (modular software shared and used by multiple programs) needed by a program to run it.

Personal Package Archive (PPA)—A repository maintained by a project or individual, rather than the distribution. PPAs are specific to Debian-based systems.

Software package files—The Linux version of the .exe files you use to install Windows software. Debian-based systems, like Ubuntu, use .deb files while other systems use other formats. For instance, Fedora and OpenSUSE use .rpm files.

17.4 Lab

This chapter was a lesson about installing and deleting software from your computer:

1 Use only commands to install the Atom text editor. Its PPA is ppa:webupd8team/atom and details can be found on the project page at https://launchpad.net/~webupd8team/+archive/ubuntu/atom.
2 What dependencies does Atom have?
3 Remove Kupfer and its dependencies. If you're using a live session, you'll have to install it again, which we did in the previous chapter.

18

Updating the operating system

Keeping your Linux system up-to-date is important for security reasons but also for functionality reasons. When you update your system, you're updating the operating system, but also the software, which means you're getting new features and improvements as they come into your repository.

You're also fixing any security vulnerabilities that have been discovered and corrected. Programmers are human. They make mistakes in their code and sometimes these mistakes can compromise the security of our computers. Updates often occur because someone found a mistake and then fixed it. Keeping your system up-to-date is important to keep your system running well.

UPDATING AND UPGRADING YOUR SYSTEM It's considered best-practice to update and upgrade your system regularly, starting from when you first install a new distribution. I update mine around once a week.

We didn't do that in our case because I wanted to build up to that activity.

But when you next install another distribution, make sure you upgrade it right away!

In the previous chapter, we used the package manager to add new repositories, and now we're going to use it to update our system. In this chapter, we're going to talk about two concepts:

- *Updating* the system, where we make sure all of the latest packages are in our repository.
- *Upgrading* the system, where we install all of those new packages.

We're also going to learn to do both tasks graphically and with commands. Let's start with updating our system, which needs to happen before we can upgrade.

18.1 Updating Linux

You'll recall from chapter 17 that after we added the Synapse repository to Synaptic, we reloaded Synaptic so the Synapse package would show up in it. That was an *update*. An update is when you tell the package manager to go out and get all of the latest versions of packages. The package manager looks at which packages are new to your system and targets those as ready for an update. Package managers usually handle this on their own, although you can go out and force a repository to update, as we did with Synapse. You might have noticed Ubuntu telling you about updated packages. You'll see a pop-up message like figure 18.1.

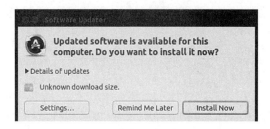

Figure 18.1   Unity shows you when packages have been updated.

This is the Ubuntu Software Updater. It also appears on your left navigation dock (see figure 18.2)

Different desktop environments show packages have been updated in different ways. For instance, in Cinnamon, you get a notification in your bottom taskbar (see figure 18.3).

Figure 18.2   The Ubuntu Software Updater icon also appears on the navigation dock when it has detected updated packages.

Figure 18.3   The Cinnamon desktop shows updated packages in its bottom taskbar.

KDE also gives you a notification at the bottom of the screen (see figure 18.4).

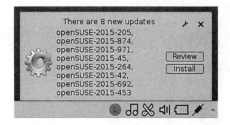

Figure 18.4   The KDE desktop also shows updated packages in its bottom taskbar.

The desktop environment doesn't impact *how* your system is updated and upgraded. It controls the way you are informed that it has happened.

You can control how frequently your system checks for updates and even which software is automatically upgraded by clicking the Settings button on the Software Updater (see figure 18.5).

This Updates screen (figure 18.6) is confusing because although it uses the

Figure 18.5   You can control how frequently Ubuntu checks for upgrades and which upgrades it allows by clicking the Settings button.

term "updates," it's updating the repository and not the software on your system. This screen is checking for new packages and then bringing them into your package manager without your direction. The final installation of the software, which is technically an upgrade, is up to you, the administrator.

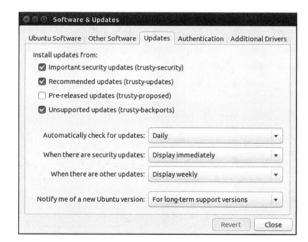

Figure 18.6   The Updates screen refers to updating the repository, not the software on your system.

The top part of the Updates screen are the packages that are automatically updated. I would leave these as is. The Important security updates are important for keeping your system secure.

The Recommended updates are important for keeping your system stable. The confusingly named Unsupported updates allow you to install newer major releases of software. When a version of Ubuntu is completed, it's seen as a finished product, with newer versions of software being saved for future releases. Unsupported updates allows you to get newer versions of software without moving to a new release. We'll talk more about releases in a bit.

The bottom part of the screen lets you choose how often Software Updater checks for updates and how often it shows you that updates are available. Personally, I leave these as is, so I can keep my system up-to-date without having to remember to update the package manager myself. But I know lots of people who turn this off and manually update and upgrade once a week when they have set aside time to maintain their system. The important thing is that your system is regularly updated and upgraded. You know the best way to accomplish that.

Finally, click on When there are security updates pulldown menu (see figure 18.7). Here you can configure the Updater to automatically install software for you. Personally, I like to see what upgrades are being installed, but automatic updates are a good option for a non-technical user who you want to exclude from the upgrade/update process. In that situation, non-technical users will have a system that upgrades itself.

If you were to install Ubuntu on your brother's computer and he's not very good at keeping up with things like software maintenance, you might configure it to handle the updating and upgrading for him.

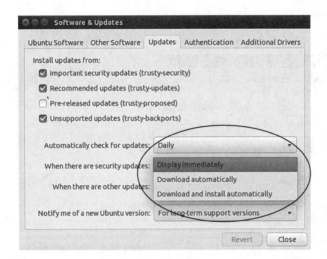

Figure 18.7   You can set security updates to automatically install, which is a good option for non-technical users.

As you might expect, there's also a way to update your system using a command. Let's take a look at that next.

18.1.1   The update command

There are two reasons to update using a command:

- Updating via the command line is fast.
- Updating via the command line works across all desktop environments, even when you don't have a desktop environment.

If you're upgrading with a command, which we'll learn how to do in the next section, you should run the update command first, so you have all of the latest software in your repositories. When you're updating graphically, the Software Updater checks for updates automatically.

The `update` command is also helpful if you've disabled all of the automated updating and notifications that we looked at in the previous section. If you're the type of person who wants to do your updating and upgrading once a week, then the `update` command is a fast way to get all of the latest packages. It frees you from having to wait for your computer to tell you updates are ready.

Finally, as I mentioned before, the display of upgraded packages depends upon the desktop environment. But some desktop environments don't show you when packages have been upgraded. So the `update` command is a good way to make sure you have all of the latest packages *before* you do an upgrade if you're using one of those kinds of desktop environments. The beauty of the command is that it *always* works on any system. You never have to worry about what kind of GUI the updater uses.

Your software repository is probably up-to-date from when we installed Synapse (unless you're using a live session), but just to be sure, go into the terminal and type

```
sudo apt-get update
```

You'll see all of your repositories updating. Now, you're ready to upgrade your system.

18.2 Upgrading Linux

Once your repositories have been updated, you're ready to upgrade your system, which means installing the updated packages onto your system.

UPGRADING IN THE LIVE ENVIRONMENT If you're running Linux from a live CD or USB, you'll be able to upgrade your system, but those upgrades will be gone when you reboot, unless you set up a persistent environment that allows you to save changes.

There's no harm in upgrading in a live environment and it's good practice, but don't be surprised when all of those upgrades are gone when you reboot:

1 Open the Software Updater.
2 Click the triangle next to Details of Updates (see figure 18.8). Any package with a check will be upgraded. This is the area where you could exclude a package from being upgraded. This is also where you can see the type of upgrade. There are Other updates, which are software updates that are not security-related.

Everything under the Security heading is a security upgrade and should be

Figure 18.8 You can manually choose which packages to upgrade.

allowed to upgrade. But if for some reason you didn't want to upgrade something that was a security upgrade, it's within your power to prevent it:

1 Click Install Now to upgrade your system. This might take a few minutes because we haven't upgraded in a while. VirtualBox users might see a message about replacing a file. Click Replace.

2 When the upgrade finishes, you'll need to restart your computer. You don't always have to restart after upgrades. Usually a restart is required after a kernel upgrade, because that's a major change. Otherwise, upgrading isn't disruptive at all.

3 Restart your computer. (If you're using a live image, your computer will revert to the pre-updated state after the reboot, but that's fine for the next exercise.)

When your computer restarts, you should get a message that more upgrades are available. That's because we waited quite a while to update our system, so not everything could be upgraded at once.

Some packages couldn't be upgraded until after your reboot, but the reboot wasn't required by your system. Instead, it was patiently waiting for the next best opportunity to upgrade your computer without disrupting your work.

And don't worry if you didn't get a message that there are more upgrades available. Your system might not have checked yet. Because we only have an hour, we're going to pretend it notified you. Let's go ahead and finish the job with the upgrade command.

18.2.1 *The upgrade command*

The reasons for using the upgrade command are the same for using the update command. It's a way to upgrade your system using three words. To finish the upgrade:

1 Go into the terminal and type sudo apt-get upgrade.

2 After entering your password, you'll see all of the packages left to upgrade. Press y and Enter to finish upgrading.

Your system is now totally up-to-date. Moving forward, you'll be notified when there are more updates in the repository. You can go ahead and install those updates on your own to keep your system secure and so that you're always using the latest versions of software.

All the way back in chapter 2, we talked about how our version of Ubuntu is supported for five years. That means updates will keep coming for five years (2019 in our case, since Ubuntu 14.04 was released in 2014) and then Ubuntu will no longer submit updates for our version of Ubuntu. In the next section, we're going to compare standard, version-based releases, like Ubuntu, to rolling releases, which are continuously updated. As we head toward the end of this book, it's an important distinction for you to understand, as it will help you to choose your own distribution.

18.3   Rolling releases vs. standard releases

Standard Linux releases are supported for a fixed amount of time, meaning they get updates until the support period is over. Then, you can either live with an operating system that isn't getting anymore updates, which isn't a great idea from a security perspective, or you can move to a new standard release.

Rolling releases are continuously updated systems. That means they're constantly getting updates and new versions of software for the life of the system. Compare that to our version of Ubuntu, which is only getting updates until 2019. Some distributions are supported for even less time. For instance, Fedora releases only get updates for around 13 months.

I think of the difference between rolling and standard as comparable to the difference between a manual and automatic transmission. A rolling release is like a manual transmission. You have more control but that control requires more attention. Something like updating and upgrading your system will require some work.

A standard release is like an automatic transmission. Your system is handling work for you, in this case making sure upgrades won't hurt your system, but at a cost of control and performance. For instance, sometimes a rolling release will require certain packages to be upgraded in a certain order. Standard releases handle that sort of thing for you. Let's take a closer look at both models.

18.3.1   Standard releases

Some distributions allow you to move between standard releases. For instance, when a new long-term stable release of Ubuntu is ready, your Software Updater will give you the option to upgrade your entire system from 14.04 to 16.04. However, I've always found this kind of Ubuntu upgrade between versions to be more trouble than it's worth, because a lot of stuff winds up needing to be fixed and reconfigured. They can be small things, like shortcuts I've set up to launch programs, or bigger things, like programs that no longer work.

I find it easier to start with the clean slate of a completely new installation. When I'm ready to move to a new Ubuntu standard release, once support has run out, I install Ubuntu from scratch and copy my files over. I find starting fresh results in much better performance and it's something I only need to do every five years.

> **INFORMATION ABOUT NEW RELEASES**   Curious about what's new and different in the latest standard release? Linux news sites usually cover the differences well, letting you know what's changed. For this kind of news, I usually visit:
>
> - LXer: http://lxer.com/
> - The Linux Subreddit: www.reddit.com/r/linux/
> - OMG!Ubuntu (for Ubuntu news): www.omgubuntu.co.uk/

Fedora has a tool called DNF system upgrade that helps users to upgrade between different Fedora releases, which occur about every six months.

Linux Mint has an interesting update philosophy. It strongly recommends not upgrading to a new standard release unless you're dissatisfied with the current one!

Standard releases tend to be stable, because the people who work on a release know all of the software in a repository and can see if a particular upgrade breaks anything. The downside to standard releases, however, is that you're often not working with the most recent version of software, because newer software is more likely to break older systems. The goal of standard releases is to keep your system running, but the cost of that stability is often older software.

18.3.2 *Rolling releases*

Examples of rolling releases include Arch, openSUSE Tumbleweed, and Gentoo. There are no fixed versions of these distributions. Some fixed release distributions have a rolling option that can be enabled. openSUSE, Fedora, and Debian can all be configured to be rolling releases.

Instead, new software is constantly flowing into these repositories. The benefit of this, as we discussed in chapter 2, is the latest versions of software and never having to install a new version of your distribution. The downside is the potential for instability. Rolling releases aren't inherently unstable, but they do require more attention to keep stable. You saw how we kept an eye on our upgrades and updates with Ubuntu, but with a rolling release, more active research is often required to make sure a given upgrade won't break your system.

When a release-based distribution like Debian or Ubuntu rolls out upgrades, they've been tested to make sure they don't break anything on your system. But the testing is easier because there's a smaller number of software versions to deal with. Everyone's system is relatively similar with standard releases. However, with rolling releases, there's a lot more variety in the versions of software people are using, because that depends upon when they last updated. That makes it harder to test new software and to see what it might break. There are simply more variables with rolling systems, making it harder to predict how upgrades might impact a system.

To get a sense of how different the software versions can be, let's compare our version of LibreOffice to what's in the Arch repositories, which are viewable in your web browser:

- To see which version of LibreOffice you have, go into the terminal and type `libreoffice --version`. As of this writing, the version is LibreOffice 4.2.8.2. Yours might be slightly different based upon how much updating and upgrading has occurred with that package.
- Compare this to the version found in the Arch repositories, which are at www.archlinux.org/packages/. Search that repository for libreoffice. You'll see two versions: `libreoffice-still`, the stable version of LibreOffice, which as of this writing is at 4.4, and `libreoffice-fresh`, the development version of LibreOffice, with newer features but possibly some bugs.

This is at version 5, a huge jump for software, since the first number in a release is used to indicate significant changes between versions.

18.3.3 Which is better?

The decision to use a rolling release or a standard release boils down to two questions:

- How much time do you want to spend managing your system?
- How important is new software to you?

If you don't want to spend a lot of time researching updates, a standard release is a better choice, since the updates tend to be tested more than is possible with a rolling release. However, if you want the most up-to-date software, and are willing to risk the possibility of breaking your entire system, a rolling release is probably a better option. To be fair, a rolling release is also a great way to learn Linux, since it gives you a lot of opportunities to fix things!

18.4 Wrapping up

You now know how to update and upgrade your system, which is an important part of Linux. Table 18.1 shows the difference between updating and upgrading.

Table 18.1 Updating versus upgrading

Term	Explanation
updating	Moves all of the latest packages into your repository
upgrading	Installs the packages

Performing both tasks makes sure you're working with the latest versions of software, and eliminating bugs in previous versions and keeping your computer more secure, because installing updates allows security vulnerabilities to be fixed. We're going to talk more about security in the next chapter.

We also spent some time discussing the difference between rolling releases and standard releases. As we head toward the end of this book, now is a good time to start thinking about what your future distributions might look like. One of the variables to consider, and which we touched on in chapter 2, is the amount of time you have to spend keeping your system updated and the importance of the newest software.

GLOSSARY OF TERMS

In this chapter I explained:

Rolling release—A continuously updated systems that's constantly getting updates and new versions of software for the life of the system.

Standard release—A Linux release supported for a fixed amount of time, meaning it is updated until the support period is over.

Update—Moves all of the latest packages into your repository.

Upgrade—Installs the packages onto your system.

18.5 *Lab*

Today's lesson is all about keeping your operating system as up to date as possible.

1 What version of Firefox is on your system? What version is in the Arch repositories? What does this tell you about how frequently Firefox is updated for Ubuntu?

2 What is the difference between the `update` command and the `upgrade` command?

3 Configure the Ubuntu Software Updater to automatically download security updates.

4 Configure the Ubuntu Software Updater to immediately show non-security related updates.

5 Go to the Gentoo repository at https://packages.gentoo.org/. How do its Firefox and LibreOffice holdings compare to Arch and Ubuntu? Are they older or newer? By how much?

Linux security 19

Security is an important but complex topic. The challenge is that it's an ever-changing idea. Software we think of as secure can become insecure as hackers figure out how to break though whatever safeguards were once coded in. For users, it means being vigilant—staying on top of your system and considering security a recurring task rather than something you do once and can then be considered finished.

In this chapter, I'm going to run through the best practices for keeping your system secure. I'm not a hacker or a security expert so I'm not going to get very detailed. Instead, I'm going to explain some basic, fundamental, and essential security concepts and give you a few manageable things to do to keep your computer secure.

In this chapter, we're going to discuss:

- The user and superuser concept and how and why it keeps your computer secure
- Linux viruses (and anti-viruses)
- Linux firewalls
- Privacy on Linux, including encrypting your hard drive, to protect your personal data
- Best practices in running commands safely

But don't forget the important security lesson you learned in the last chapter: Make sure your system is always up-to-date. Regular security updates help to protect your system by constantly repairing any security issues. Security issues can send personal information, like logins and passwords, to malicious third parties. These issues can also give these same bad people access to all of your personal files.

Think of security bugs as a hole in your home. With the hole there, things, like burglars, can get into your home. And think of security updates as patches for the holes. With the holes covered, it's much tougher for someone to get in.

Now let's talk about other ways to keep your system secure. Let's start with the Linux user and superuser concepts. This idea is the key to keeping Linux systems safe.

19.1 *Users and superusers in Linux*

If you think about it, security is about preventing someone from doing something without your permission. In real life, it could be someone stealing something from you, which by definition happens without your permission. With your computer, it could be someone stealing data from you, again, without your permission.

In chapter 12, we talked about the idea of superusers in Linux. Superusers are users with certain privileges on a system. These privileges are permissions. Superusers have permission to do certain things on a system, like install software, configure internet access, and even print.

That's why you need to enter your password before you add or remove software. Because you don't want just anyone installing software on your system. Otherwise, they could install something mean and nasty.

Linux has a list of users who can perform certain tasks and if you're not on the list, you can't do those tasks—like installing or removing software. Malicious programs work by installing something without your consent. These malicious programs can then do anything from destroying your data to sending out all of your private data, including valuable pieces, like passwords. The Linux permissions concept makes it hard for someone to install something without your consent.

Linux has a bunch of user groups with certain permissions, or access rights, based upon the user group to which they're assigned.

This is helpful on systems with more than one user, like if you share your laptop with someone (or a group of people). Every person can have their own set of permissions, which prevents an unauthorized or unknowledgeable person from doing something that might harm the computer.

Let's pretend you're going to share your computer with someone who doesn't know much about Linux. You're going to want to make a new user with restricted permissions. Let's do that so you can see what that process looks like, and so you can get a sense of how these permissions keep your computer safe.

Try it now: Creating new users

1 Go into Dash and launch User Accounts.
Click Unlock and enter your password (see the next figure). Also, note that your account is an Administrator one, which means you control your system (unless you're using a Live session, in which case you won't see any accounts, although you can still create them).

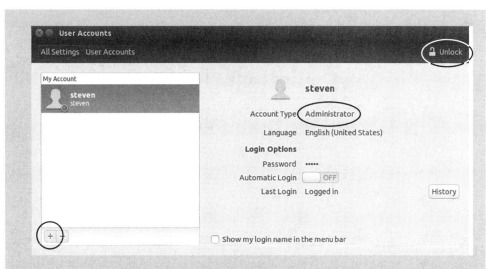

Once you unlock the Ubuntu User Accounts tool, you can add new users to the system.

2 Click the + sign in the bottom left corner to add a new user.
3 Name the new user george (if your username is already george, you may use jerry) and select Standard for the Account Type.
4 Click Add to create the account. Once you've created the account, click where it says Account Disabled next to Password.

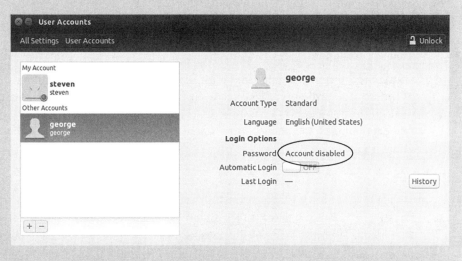

When you create an account, you can give it a new password, which is a best security practice we're skipping for now.

(continued)

5 Set the Action to Log in Without a Password and click the Change button (see the next figure). Suffice it to say this is not a good security practice, but we're not going to keep the account. It's purely for demonstration purposes.

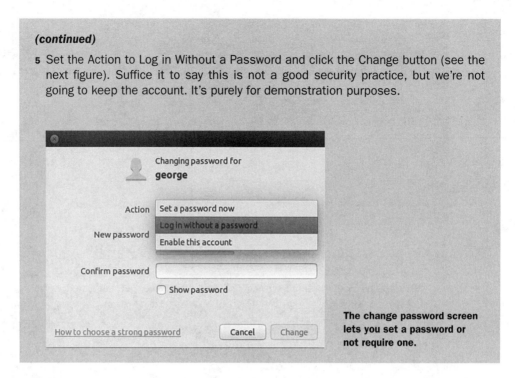

The change password screen lets you set a password or not require one.

But what does it mean to have a standard account? Now let's see to which groups george belongs. This will show us what parts of the system a user can access.

Groups control access to certain parts of the system. In chapter 12 we saw how to add a user to the sudo group. A group is just a list of users who can perform certain tasks. In the case of sudo, it's access to the sudo command. To see which groups george belongs to, go into the terminal and type:

```
groups george
```

Our george account belongs to two groups: george and nopasswordlogin. Being a part of the nopasswordlogin is what makes us able to log in to the account without a password. If the george account were to leave that group, we'd need a password to get into that account. Let's see how george's access compares to our own. Go back to the terminal and type:

```
groups your user name
```

(or just groups for Live Session users).

You should see more groups including the sudo group, which we discussed in chapter 12. Now let's see what the george account can and can't do with your system:

1 Now that you've created a new account, you can log in to it directly by clicking the logout cog in the top right corner and clicking on the george account (see figure 19.1).

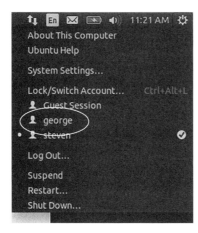

Figure 19.1   You can log in to an account using the Ubuntu cog in the top-right corner.

2   Once in the george account, go into the terminal and type:

```
sudo apt-get install leafpad
```

Leafpad is a small text editor. But what happens when you enter your own password? Nothing! Because, as we saw, george isn't on the sudo list. That means the account can't use the sudo command. In the case of Ubuntu, the george account could still install software via Synaptic, if George had your password, but otherwise the account is limited in what it can do to your system. (Of course, if your system password is compromised, your computer and security are also compromised.)

Let's get rid of that fake george account. Log out of the george account and then log back into yours. Don't use the cog shortcut we used to get into the account before—otherwise the george account will still be active and we won't be able to delete it. Use the logout option instead.

Log back into your personal account. Let's delete the george account with a command. To remove an account from the system use:

```
sudo userdel -r george
```

(Unless you named that account something else.) The userdel command deletes the account and the -r deletes the home directory that was created (so be careful using this command on your day-to-day system). You'll get a mail spool message you can ignore. The george account is now gone.

The concept of groups and users is what keeps Linux systems secure. Only certain accounts can do certain things. It's as limiting the people who have the keys to your home.

As you can see, it's tough for anything to be installed on your system without your approval. A computer virus is a great example of something you wouldn't want installed on your system. Let's take a closer look at Linux and viruses.

19.2   *Viruses and Linux*

Computer viruses are pieces of software that replicate themselves on a computer. The replication means a virus is distributing itself all over your computer, making it tough to get rid of. Viruses seem to understand that there's safety in numbers.

Viruses can destroy data or send it out to a malicious third party, meaning someone creepy could be viewing your passwords, your financial documents, and even your photos.

Computers become infected in any number of ways, but the commonality is that the user is tricked into installing it, either by visiting a dangerous site, installing a piece of software, or downloading an email attachment.

19.2.1   *Is Linux immune to viruses?*

Antivirus is an important part of Windows security but because Linux is constructed differently from Windows, it's less important. But don't interpret that as "Linux is immune to viruses." It's not. Users can be tricked, which is why I emphasized caution in chapter 17 when we talked about installing software from outside of repositories. (Software from repositories could, in theory, become infected with a virus, but it's highly unlikely.)

But in general, Linux tends to be safer from viruses than Windows. Why? Part of it is the nature of Linux, which as we just learned, assigns permissions to users. If you're a Linux user with administrative rights, you probably know enough to avoid viruses. Contrast that with other operating systems, where it might be easy to trick anyone using the computer into installing a virus.

Another part of what makes desktop Linux safer than Windows is that the market share is relatively small, not a lot of creepy people are designing viruses for it. This is not to say that getting a virus on Linux is impossible. It's not. But there's enough security between you, the knowledgeable user, and your system, which has its own protections, for you to feel reasonably safe.

19.2.2   *Linux antiviruses*

But what if reasonably safe isn't enough? What if you want to be *exceptionally* safe, like wearing suspenders and a belt? I respect your caution!

Linux actually has some antivirus tools. The most popular program is called ClamAV. It's cost-free for Linux (and for Windows; the OS X version is a paid product).

ClamAV detects viruses on your system that you can then remove. It's a terminal-based program but there is a graphical front-end called ClamTk you can install. It lets you use ClamAV as a graphical program, which is why it has a slightly different name. Some users might find the graphical program easier for configuring preferences. Let's install the graphical version and work with that.

Try it now: ClamTk

1 Install ClamTk with `sudo apt-get install clamtk`.
2 Update its virus definitions with the command `sudo freshclam`. You might get a message about your version of ClamAV being outdated. That's because Ubuntu doesn't always have the most recent version in the repositories. It's not ideal but don't worry about it for now.

If you want the most recent version, you can install it from the CalmAV site: www.clamav.net/. The virus definitions, which are used to find and identify viruses, will be up-to-date either way.

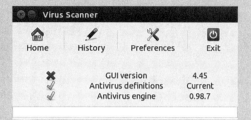

ClamTk is a graphical interface to the ClamAV program. Make sure your antivirus definitions are current with the `sudo freshclam` command.

Once it finishes the update (it might take a while, so this might be a good time to eat some of your lunch), launch it via the Dash. The antivirus definitions should read as Current.

To run the antivirus, click the Home button, which will scan your home directory. You can configure a more specific scan by using the Scan menu (shown in the figure at right).

3 When it's done, you'll get a report of files scanned and threats found.

Any viruses can be quarantined by ClamTk and manually removed by you. Just be careful that you're not deleting something important.

How do you know if it's important? If it's from one of the system folders we looked at in chapter 14, it might be

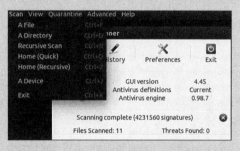

ClamTk lets you choose which folders or files are scanned.

worth researching the infected file and making sure you're not getting a false positive, meaning ClamAV thinks something is a virus but it really isn't. To research a ClamTk report, do an internet search for the infected file and see what other users have reported about the nature of the file. There's a list of research tips in chapter 23, too.

If the file is something forwarded to you by that friend who forwards you everything, it's probably safe to assume it actually is a virus.

I don't use an antivirus application on my Linux machines because I don't see viruses as a risk. We learned how to update our systems in the last chapter and that's really what protects our operating system, as does being careful what we install on our computers (these same practices keep our Windows installations safe, too). But if running

ClamTk or ClamAV brings you comfort and peace of mind, then by all means use it. It won't hurt anything. Wikipedia has a list of other Linux antivirus tools: https:// en.wikipedia.org/wiki/Linux_malware#Anti-virus_applications.

Now, let's talk about firewalls, which are another tool used to protect your computer from outside intruders.

19.3 *Firewalls*

Unless your computer isn't connected to the internet, it has traffic coming in and out of it. Traffic is just another word for network activity.

When you go to a website, traffic is leaving your computer. If you connect to your computer from another computer, then traffic is coming into your computer. The traffic travels through ports, which are basically numbered exits and entrances on your computer. There are thousands of ports used for specific purposes, like sending email, chatting, and even printing.

A firewall is what's used to control this kind of traffic, for users who want granular control over their system. For instance, browser traffic uses port 80 or 443.

If you didn't want internet traffic on your computer (I'm shivering in terror as I type that sentence), you could block ports 80 and 443 so traffic can't pass through them. This would mean your web browser couldn't receive anything from the outside world. You would block the outgoing port, so you can't access web pages.

However, if you wanted to deny incoming traffic to your computer, meaning you can go out for content but no one can connect to your computer from the outside, a firewall is a useful thing. Configuring a Linux firewall requires a certain degree of knowledge. You have to know which ports and IP addresses you want to block or allow.

It gets more complicated if you remotely connect to your computer from another computer. If you have a simple setup like me, where you only use your computer for accessing the internet, you can turn on the firewall and not tweak it. If you have a more complex setup, I'll show you how to learn more at the end of this section.

Linux comes with its own configurable firewall called iptables. However, because it's so configurable, it's also complicated. To help with that, Ubuntu ships with a command-line program called ufw, which stands for uncomplicated firewall.

The ufw program controls iptables, but simplifies the process. By default, ufw is not enabled. To turn it on, type `sudo ufw enable`.

Now that it's on, you might want to see what it's blocking and allowing. To do that, type `sudo ufw status verbose`. You should see something like this:

```
Default: deny (incoming), allow (outgoing)
```

This means your firewall is denying all incoming traffic and allowing all outgoing traffic. This is secure, unless you want to connect to your computer.

This next bit might get slightly technical for people who don't connect to their computer from another computer. If you do need access to your computer, you need to open an incoming port in your firewall. For instance, if you use Secure Shell (SSH) to connect to your computer, you're going to need port 22 open since that's the port used by SSH. We're going to talk about this more in the next chapter. SSH is useful if you want to connect to another computer, to exchange files, or if you're working with a remote web server. To allow SSH, type:

```
sudo ufw allow ssh/tcp
```

To see the new firewall configuration, type `sudo ufw status verbose` again. You'll see port 22 is now allowing in traffic. This means you could connect to your computer from another computer. As I said earlier, we'll talk about this more in the next chapter. If you change your mind about the rule, and want to deny SSH traffic, you can change the command to:

```
sudo ufw deny ssh/tcp
```

But how does one learn all of these options and commands? A good place to begin is with our old chapter 12 friend, the `man` command. Entering `man ufw` will give you a sense of the options and parameters to tweak your firewall, if that's something that interests you. For instance, if you don't want someone on your system to use chat, you could figure out which ports their chat service uses (an internet search will reveal that) and block the outgoing traffic for that particular port.

And if you misconfigure your firewall? The command `sudo ufw reset` will get rid of all of the rules you created and disable ufw, so you can turn it on and start over with a clean slate.

There's a graphical interface to ufw called Gufw that has preconfigured rules. We're going to explore that in the lab. Let's move on to encryption, another security measure.

19.4 *Encryption*

Encryption is a way of keeping data safe by making it unreadable to the naked eye. If we double-click an unencrypted file, it opens and we can read it. However, if we open an encrypted file, we can't read what's in it. Encrypted files need to be transformed in some way, usually using a key, which is sort of like a code that changes the encrypted file into something you can read.

It is another level of protection beyond your password.

Your Linux system has a user and password that prevents unverified users from running administrative commands. It also has a password that prevents people without the password from accessing your system. However, there are other ways of getting access to your data. For instance, someone else can run a live session and gain access to your files. That requires physical access to your computer and technical knowledge, but it is still a risk. However, if your home directory is encrypted, someone needs to know a passphrase to gain access to your files. Even with physical access to your computer.

You might remember in chapter 3 that when you were installing Ubuntu for the first time, there was a question about encryption (see figure 19.2). That is one way to encrypt your home directory—to do it at the time of installation. However, if you

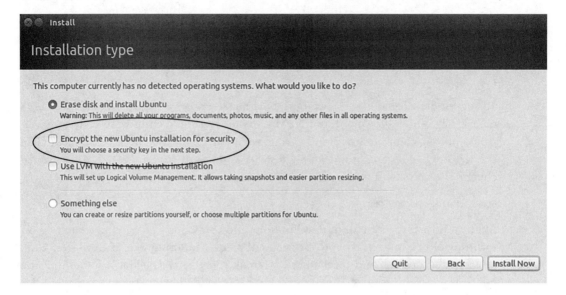

Figure 19.2   You can encrypt your home directory when you install your operating system, or you can do it after the fact with eCryptfs.

didn't think of it at the time, or if you change your mind, you can still encrypt your home drive using a program called eCryptfs.

We're not going to encrypt your home directory because it requires a lot of disk space. Some people encrypt their home directories to keep all of their files safe, rather than having to decide which ones they want to protect.

Instead, we're going to encrypt part of our home directory. This would be a safe place to hold important files you wouldn't want compromised without encrypting the entire directory.

For me, disk space is usually the deciding factor in terms of whether to encrypt the entire home directory or just part of it.

However, if you have the space and the inclination, eCryptfs has a convenient step-by-step process for encrypting your home directory after you've installed your operating system. It's called the `ecryptfs-migrate-home` command. The ArchWiki (https://wiki.archlinux.org) has some great information on how to use it. But for now, let's create an encrypted folder in our home directory:

1   Install eCryptfs. The package name is `ecryptfs-utils`.
2   Run the command `ecryptfs-setup-private --nopwcheck --noautomount`. This command will create an encrypted directory that requires a password (nopwcheck) other than the login password (see figure 19.3). The directory will also be inaccessible by default (noautomount).

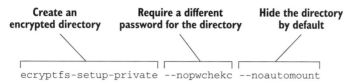

Figure 19.3 `encryptfs-setup-private` **allows you to specify a password and mount behavior with flags.**

3 You'll be asked to enter your login passphrase. This is the password you'll use to open the encrypted directory. Keep the password someplace safe! If you lose it, you'll lose access to your files. Sadly, this isn't a password you can reset like your Netflix one.

4 You'll be asked to enter your mount passphrase. Click Enter so one is generated for you. This will generate a file that will be used to give you access to the directory. If the file is lost or corrupted, you'll lose access to the directory, like losing the key to a box. We'll talk about how to backup this file in a moment.

5 Once the directory is created, log out and log in again.

6 You'll see a directory named Private in your home directory. It'll have a lock on it. To use it, go into the terminal and type `ecryptfs-mount-private`. You can now click into the Private directory since you mounted it, or made it available.

7 Save a blank file in the Private directory.

8 Unmount the directory with `ecryptfs-unmount-private`.

9 Now go into the directory. You can no longer see the file since the directory isn't accessible. If you reboot, you'll have to mount the encrypted directory again.

You can see how encryption keeps your data safe. There's a private directory that only you can unlock. Anyone with your computer can't get into that encrypted directory without a password. We just encrypted a part of your home directory, but as I mentioned, you can also encrypt your entire home directory.

Before we move on, there's one last thing. I mentioned keeping a backup of the passphrase used to mount your encrypted directory, in case something happens to the key file. To reveal the passphrase, type `ecryptfs-unwrap-passphrase`. You'll be asked to enter your passphrase, which is the password you created in step 3. Enter it and you'll get a string of letters and numbers. Print it and keep it someplace safe, just in case there's an issue with the key file (or if you forget the password you created).

Now that you know how to keep your data private, let's get into the final part of Linux security, which is running commands safely.

19.5 Running commands safely

We talked about running commands safely in chapter 13, but it's an important enough topic to recap here. As you've seen, the real security dangers with Linux are social ones. If someone tricks you into revealing your password or running the wrong command, they can assume control of your system.

Security vulnerabilities often come about because of something the user did or didn't do, rather than a fault in the code itself. New Linux users often find themselves online, trying to learn new things. While much of the advice you'll find online is at least well-intentioned, there are people who post things that could harm your system or expose it to risk. Table 19.1 recaps four ways to make sure you don't accidentally run a harmful command.

Table 19.1   Running commands safely

Does the command ...	Safe behavior
... require `sudo`?	Ask yourself if it makes sense that the command you're running requires `sudo`. If you just want to move a file and someone is recommending `sudo`, think about how that doesn't make sense because moving a file isn't an administrative task.
... make sense to you?	Figure out what a complex command does. If it uses pipes, research each part of the pipe. Make sure you can roughly understand what each part of the command you're using is doing and why you're doing it. And if you need a refresher on pipes, we discussed them in chapter 12. Back in the early days of Linux, certain people thought it was funny to advise new users to run the command `rm -rf` which would erase everything on their system. It's not funny but was possible because people would run commands without knowing what the command would do.
... remove or overwrite files?	Back up files being changed. Because unless you're 100% sure about the change, you could wind up breaking your system. It never hurts to make a backup of a file by copying it and saving the copy in a different location. If your command works successfully, you can delete the backup. And if it doesn't, you'll be glad you were careful.
... seem to be commonly used?	Before running a command you find online, do some research and see if other people recommend the same command for the same issue. There are lots of forums and lots of commands, but just because someone posted something doesn't mean it's correct. There's a nice list of sites you can visit for this sort of thing in chapter 23. If you can find other people using the same command for the same issue, there's a better probability the command is what you need.

19.6   *Wrapping up*

These are the bare-bone basics of security on Linux. If you want to delve deeper into security, there are a few places to explore:

- The ArchWiki (https://wiki.archlinux.org/), which I mentioned previously, has lots of great information on all of the tools discussed here. Although it's for users of the Arch distribution, everything on it will work across other distributions.
- The Ubuntu Wiki (https://wiki.ubuntu.com/) isn't as in-depth as the Arch one, but also has some useful security information.

- The man pages for many of these tools are great for getting a sense of what they can do. If nothing else, the man pages also give you a way to search the internet more precisely.

Having gone through this chapter, you now have a sense of how to keep your system secure, based upon your personal comfort level. Personally, I turn on ufw and never tweak it. And, as I mentioned before, I also don't run an antivirus. I encrypt the home drives of computers I travel with but don't bother with my desktop, which stays at home. And I *always* keep my system up-to-date.

Start small. Encrypt a directory and keep your important files there. See how that works for you before moving on to playing with the firewall. Even if you decide not to use all of the tools described here, at least you'll be making an informed choice.

GLOSSARY OF TERMS
In this chapter I explained:

Encryption—A way to keep data safe by requiring an electronic key to decipher it.
Firewall—Controls network traffic into and out of your computer.
Port—Numbered exits and entrances on your computer through which traffic travels. There are thousands of ports used for specific purposes.
Virus—Pieces of software that replicate themselves on a computer.

19.7 *Lab*

Now it's time see what you learned about Linux security.

1 Create an administrator account named tommy. Does this account have access to sudo? How do you know?

2 Delete the account using the command line. (If you get a message that the user is being used by a process, you can kill the process with sudo kill -9 and the process number.)

3 What happens when you try to save a file in the unmounted Private directory? Why does this happen?

4 Install Gufw (package name gufw) and create a rule (steps 1 and 2 in figure 19.4) denying traffic out from the application BitTorrent (see figures 19.4 and 19.5).

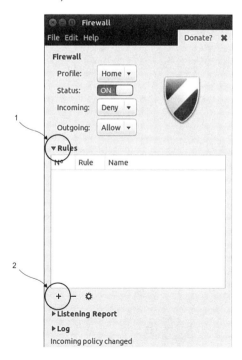

Figure 19.4   Gufw lets you create rules using a GUI

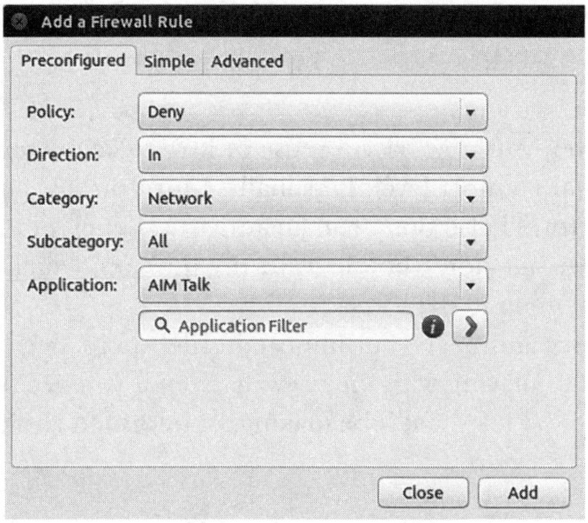

Figure 19.5   Gufw has preconfigured rules to make allowing and denying certain applications a matter of searching a box.

5   Turn off the firewall. We don't want it on for the next chapter.

Connecting to other computers

We've spent a lot of this book using the internet to do different things, from pulling in updates so we can upgrade packages to downloading software package files, to researching different distributions online. However, we haven't spent much time talking about *how* we're connecting to the internet. If you're using a virtual machine to explore Linux, then the virtual machine is using whatever internet connection your main operating system is using. If you're using a live version of Linux, you've already spent some time using NetworkManager, the tool used by Ubuntu to help you connect to the internet.

Like security, networking is a complex topic. System administrators use networking concepts to get machines in disparate places to communicate with each other quickly and efficiently. We're not going to get too deep into those concepts here. The goal of this chapter, like the security chapter, is to give you enough information to do what you need to do, which in this case is to configure your internet connections and connect to other computers.

In this chapter, we're going to cover:

- Connecting to wireless and wired networks using NetworkManager.
- Connecting to other computers using SSH, which we discussed briefly in the previous chapter.

By the end of this chapter, you'll be able to tweak your internet connection settings, changing how your computer looks up internet addresses. You'll also understand how to connect to a Linux computer using SSH, which is commonly used by systems administrators to connect to remote servers.

However, SSH has more pedestrian uses. As you'll see later in this chapter, it can be used to transfer files between two computers. There are other interesting uses. For instance, if a keyboard isn't working, you can SSH into a machine, using a machine with a working keyboard, to access files. SSH also comes in handy with something like a Raspberry Pi, which is essentially a server.

Now let's start by taking a look at NetworkManager.

20.1 *Connecting to the internet with NetworkManager*

NetworkManager is the tool used by Ubuntu and many other distributions to manage your internet connections. It does things like show you which wireless networks are available, and helps you to connect if they're hidden or require passwords. As I mentioned earlier, if you're using a virtual machine, you haven't had to think about these things because the virtual machine is using the connection set up by the computer where it's installed. If you're using a live CD/DVD/USB, or if you've already installed Linux on your computer, then you've probably already worked with it, too.

Unity has what's called the NetworkManager applet which appears at the top of the screen (see figure 20.1). An applet is a small program that lets you interact with a bigger one. In Linux, taskbar items are often applets, giving you fast and convenient access to certain programs.

Figure 20.1 The NetworkManager applet lets you interact with NetworkManager.

The NetworkManager applet is a way to interact with NetworkManager and easily see the status of your connection since it lives on your top navigation bar.

If you click the NetworkManager applet, you'll get more options. In a virtual session, you won't see much since NetworkManager thinks your computer is plugged into a wired connection and isn't using your system's wireless configurations (see figure 20.2). This makes sense. If your main operating system is using a wireless network, how could a virtual machine within that operating system use a different one? So instead, the virtual machine treats the connection as a wired one.

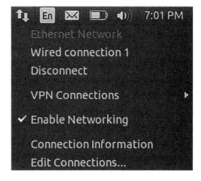

Figure 20.2　NetworkManager doesn't show much in virtual sessions because connectivity is being handled by the operating system into which the virtual machine is installed.

However, in a live session, or with Linux fully installed, NetworkManager is much more interesting, showing things like wireless networks and allowing you to connect to hidden wireless networks that are not broadcasting their names (see figure 20.3).

Using NetworkManager is fairly straightforward. If you're using a wired connection, connecting to the internet via an Ethernet cable, you're already set. If you wish to use a wireless connection, you click the applet. You'll see a list of all of the available wireless networks. Then, you click the network to which you want to connect. The process should be quite familiar to most computer users.

If the wireless network requires a password, you enter the password and that's it.

Because using NetworkManager to connect to a network is a matter of clicking a network name, I thought it might be more fun to show you how to change your Domain Name System (DNS) settings.

Figure 20.3　NetworkManager shows available wireless networks and gives you the option to connect to hidden ones.

20.1.1　*Customizing your Domain Name System*

When you type in a web address, you're directed to a DNS server that looks up the web address, like www.manning.com, and translates it to an Internet Protocol (IP) address, which is a unique number assigned to a device on a network.

In the case of a website, you're connecting to a server, or computer connected to the internet (and which is accepting incoming traffic!), which is then providing (or serving) you content.

Sometimes your ISP doesn't have a great DNS lookup service, which can slow down your computer. When you type in a web address, it might take a while for the address, like www.google.com, to be translated to an IP address, like 216.58.218.132. This address is IPv4, which means it can be as few as four digits and as many as 12.

IPv6, which is slowly being used for IP addresses, is a much longer number. Type 216.58.218.132 into your URL bar and you'll be taken straight to www.google.com.

One way around sluggish DNS lookups is to change the DNS settings for your connection. There are many DNS services you can choose from, like Google Public DNS or OpenDNS. To see what your current DNS settings are, we're going to use the `nm-tool` command. The `nm-tool` command is a command-line way to see information about NetworkManager and its networks and configurations—like which DNS servers it's using, what connection it's using (wired or wireless), and even which driver it's using.

At the end of its output, you'll see which DNS server it's using. It will look something like this:

```
DNS: IP address of DNS server
```

To change your DNS settings:

1 Click the NetworkManager applet.
2 Go to Edit Connections.
3 Click your connection. If you're using wireless, it'll be your wireless network name. If you're using a virtual machine, it'll be a wired connection.
4 Click the Edit button to change the DNS settings for that individual connection (see figure 20.4). If you're editing the DNS settings on your home wireless network, you're changing the DNS settings only for that connection and not any others you use on the same computer.

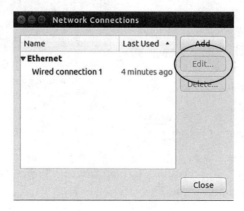

Figure 20.4   NetworkManager lets you change the DNS settings for an individual connection.

5 Go to the IPv4 Settings tab (see figure 20.5).

6 Go to Additional DNS servers and add 208.67.222.222, 208.67.220.220. Those are OpenDNS servers. Despite its name, OpenDNS is a company, not an open source project, that provides a free DNS lookup service. I find its servers to be fast and reliable, though.

7 Click the Save button and close out of NetworkManager.

Figure 20.5   IPv4 is the version of IP address most people are using right now.

You've updated the DNS settings! But run `nm-tool` again. What happens? The new servers aren't showing. Now we need to tell the computer to re-check them. We could reboot, but a quicker way is to use the `sudo service network-manager restart` command, which will restart NetworkManager for us. Run `nm-tool` now and you'll see the new servers. Hopefully, you'll notice your browsing is now a bit faster, although the improvement could be subtle.

Many distributions use NetworkManager as the default tool for handling internet connections. But it's not your only option. There are other tools.

One is Wicd, which you'll also find in the Ubuntu repositories. I've had some laptops, wireless cards, and networks that didn't work well with NetworkManager, which dropped a lot of wireless connections. Wicd was always a useful plan B. But to be fair to NetworkManager, it's run perfectly well for me across machines for quite a few years. However, if it's not working for you, be aware that you have options.

One of the nice things about Linux is that you're rarely locked into a single type of software. If there's something about NetworkManager you don't like, even if it's something as simple as its taskbar display, you can install Wicd.

Now that our connectivity is all set, let's talk about how to connect to our computer from another computer using SSH.

20.2   *Connect to your computer with Secure Shell (SSH)*

We talked about SSH briefly in the last chapter. It's a way to securely connect one computer to another. It's most commonly used to connect to servers, which are often not physically in the same space as the user. It could also be used to connect to a desktop computer. For instance, if you needed a file from your home computer, you could use SSH to access it from your office.

However, this case is rare, thanks to myriad cloud-based file-sharing services we have at our disposal nowadays. But if you work with servers, or want to work with servers, it's useful to know about SSH.

To show you SSH, we're going to need two computers. Luckily, I suspect many of you are using a virtualized Linux, which is a perfect way for me to show you SSH. If you've already installed Linux on your computer, you can create a virtual Linux machine. Chapter 3 will walk you through the steps. Live users might not have enough disk space to build a virtual machine. Around 8 GB of space is recommended.

I'm also assuming many of you are using Windows as your underlying operating system, with the virtual Linux machine within that. If you are using Windows to virtualize Linux, you need to download a tool called Putty, which is an SSH client for Windows. It can be found at www.putty.org/. If you're using OS X or Linux as your main operating system, you already have SSH installed.

You also need to install an OpenSSH server on the Linux computer to which you are connecting. The package is called `openssh-server`.

For the purposes of this chapter, the machine hosting the virtual machine is the *host* machine and the virtual Linux computer is the *remote* machine (see figure 20.6).

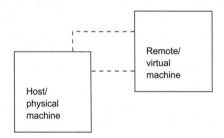

Figure 20.6   For this chapter, the host machine is your physical computer and the remote machine is your virtual Linux installation.

Once you've completed those tasks, you need to configure your virtual machine so we'll be able to SSH into it.

20.2.1 Configuring your virtual machine

Configuring your virtual machine is a simple process:

1 Shut down your virtual machine.
2 Go into your VirtualBox client, right-click your Linux image, and go into Settings (see figure 20.7).
3 Click Network and make sure you're attached to Bridged Adapter (see figure 20.8). This change will allow you to send data between both operating systems.
4 Restart your virtual Linux machine.
5 Make sure your firewall is off. The command for that is `sudo ufw disabl`.
6 Get the IP address of your virtual machine by using the `ip addr` command. The IP address of that machine will be the inet address next to the eth0 connection, which is the wired connection your virtual machine thinks it's using (see figure 20.9).

Figure 20.7   Before you can SSH into your virtual machine, you need to change some network settings.

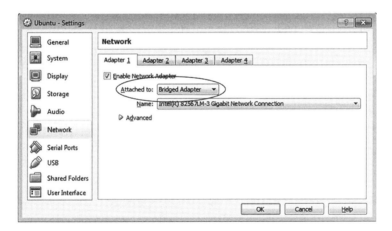

Figure 20.8   Make sure you're attached to Bridged Adapter in VirtualBox.

```
steven@steven-VirtualBox: ~
steven@steven-VirtualBox:~$ ip addr show
1: lo: <LOOPBACK,UP,LOWER_UP> mtu 65536 qdisc noqueue state UNKNOWN group defaul
t
    link/loopback 00:00:00:00:00:00 brd 00:00:00:00:00:00
    inet 127.0.0.1/8 scope host lo
       valid_lft forever preferred_lft forever
    inet6 ::1/128 scope host
       valid_lft forever preferred_lft forever
2: eth0: <BROADCAST,MULTICAST,UP,LOWER_UP> mtu 1500 qdisc pfifo_fast state UP gr
oup default qlen 1000
    link/ether 08:00:27:58:67:5c brd ff:ff:ff:ff:ff:ff
    inet 192.168.1.6/24 brd 192.168.1.255 scope global eth0
       valid_lft forever preferred_lft forever
    inet6 fe80::a00:27ff:fe58:675c/64 scope link
       valid_lft forever preferred_lft forever
steven@steven-VirtualBox:~$
```

Figure 20.9   The `ip addr` command tells you your virtual machine's IP address.

7   Copy the IP address into Putty's Host Name field (see figure 20.10) and click Open.

8   Putty will ask you to login as a name. Use the username for your Ubuntu account.

9   Use your Ubuntu password.

10 Putty will give you a security alert and ask if you trust the host. You can say Yes. Always be careful when connecting to foreign machines, though. Double-check the IP address so you know you're connecting to a secure machine.

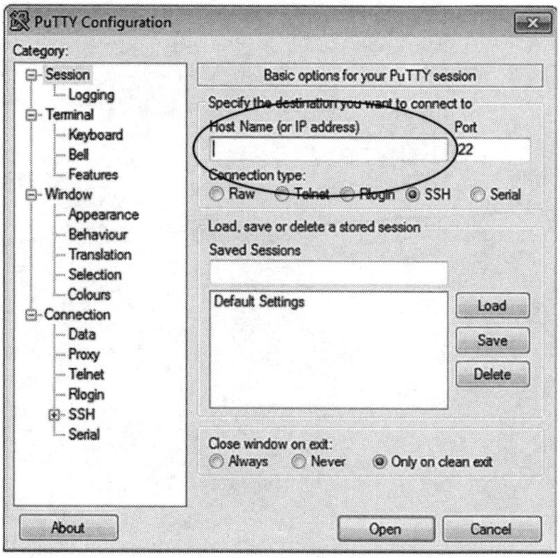

11 If you're using Linux or OS X,

Figure 20.10   Putty is an SSH client for Windows.

you can skip Putty and connect to the virtual Linux machine with the command ssh*username@IP address of virtual machine*.

12 Enter in your Ubuntu password.

You are now connected to your virtual Linux machine, but because SSH is terminal-based, you don't have access to the GUI. This is why we spent so much time using the terminal! You've been training for this! You remember how to see where you are, right? Type `ls`. You'll recognize the directories and realize you're in your virtual machine's home directory!

In terms of reading files, you're limited by what you can read in the terminal. You couldn't look at images or even word-processed files. However, you could create a file. Create one called *hi* using the `touch` command. Now go into your virtual Linux machine. You'll see the file on your desktop. Use the `exit` command to end the SSH session.

In our example, we used SSH to connect to a machine we had easy physical access to. However, as I mentioned before, all you need to SSH into a machine is its IP address, a username, and a password. So you could SSH into your home Linux machine from work, as long as the home machine was on and your firewall allowed that kind of access. And as you saw, because of the limited graphical tools available with SSH, you depend upon the command line to do things like open and move files on the remote machine. But what if you wanted to transfer files between two computers? Let's try it!

20.2.2 *Transferring files with SSH FTP*

If you've ever done any work with remote servers, you've probably used an FTP client to upload files. That same client can be used to transfer files between computers.

We're going to use the FileZilla FTP client on the operating system hosting the virtual Linux machine.

FileZilla (https://filezilla-project.org/) is free and available for Windows, OS X, and Linux, so I know it will work for everyone reading this. It's also my favorite FTP client on any operating system, but you can use any client that supports SSH File Transfer Protocol (SFTP). We're going to connect FileZilla using SFTP. This is a connection that uses SSH, but also allows you to transfer files between servers.

Once FileZilla is installed on the host machine, click Site Manager (see figure 20.11) and click New Site to create a new connection:

1 Enter the IP address of the virtual machine where it says Host (see figure 20.12).
2 Change the Protocol to SFTP - SSH File Transfer Protocol.

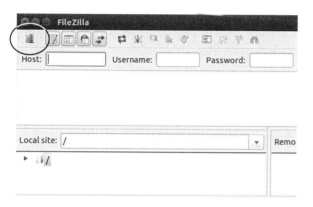

Figure 20.11   An FTP client, like FileZilla, can be used to move files between different physical (and virtual) machines.

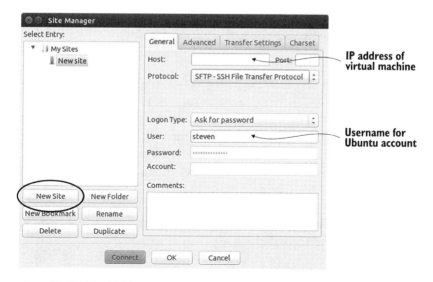

IP address of virtual machine

Username for Ubuntu account

Figure 20.12   The SFTP protocol allows you to securely move files using SSH.

3 Select Ask for Password in the Logon Type section so FileZilla will always ask you for the password before connecting.

4 Enter the username for the Ubuntu account.

5 Click Connect.

6 As with SSH before, FileZilla will ask if it can trust the machine to which you're connecting. Click OK.

You are now connected to your virtual Linux machine. If you look around the right FileZilla pane, which represents the files on the remote machine, you'll see that you're now back in the home directory of your virtual machine, just like with SSH. The left pane shows the files on the host computer. Navigate to the desktop of your virtual machine and drag the `hi` file to your local desktop. You have now copied the file so it exists on both machines.

There is also a command to do this. It's called `scp` on Linux and OS X. On Windows, the tool is called `PSCP`. It can be downloaded for Windows via the Putty site. Both `scp` and `PSCP` work the same, but when your run the command in Windows, it has to be from the same directory where you downloaded the `PSCP` file.

On a Windows system

```
pscp localfile user@ip :Desktop
```

sends a file from the directory from which you are executing the command (and from where you downloaded `PSCP`) to the Desktop directory of the remote server. On a Linux or OS X system

```
scp user@ip:file name Desktop
```

moves a file from the home directory of the remote machine to the Desktop of the local one. Both commands use similar syntax with the first variable as the file or directory to be moved and the second variable as the destination.

20.3   *Wrapping up*

We covered a few different aspects of home networking today. You now know how to connect to networks with NetworkManager. And we experimented with SSH to connect to a virtual Linux machine and transfer files between computers using SFTP.

Networking is a complex topic, but this overview will put you on a path to learning more, if it's a topic that interests you. However, even if you have no aspirations to manage and administer servers, understanding SSH and SFTP can still come in handy. As I mentioned earlier, Raspberry Pi often requires the use of SSH.

One last note. Tomorrow we're printing! It might not be practical to bring your printer to lunch with you (unless you're unusually close with your printer), but it might be helpful to have it nearby for tomorrow's chapter.

GLOSSARY OF TERMS

In this chapter I explained:

Applet—A small program that lets you interact with a bigger one.

DNS—The process by which domain names are translated to IP addresses.

FTP—Allows you to transfer files and directories between remote machines.

IP address—Internet Protocol address. A unique number assigned to a device on a network.

SFTP—SSH FTP. Allows you to transfer files and directories between remote machines using SSH.

20.4   Lab

Spend time connecting to your virtual machine. This is very similar to how you connect to remote servers so it's good practice.

1   Enable the firewall of your virtual machine and then SSH into it. Are you able to connect to the remote machine?

2   What happens if you block SSH in the virtual machine with `sudo ufw deny ssh/tcp`?

3   Use `PSCP` (or `scp` if your host machine is Linux or OS X) to move the hi file to your local machine.

4   Can you update and upgrade your virtual machine via SSH? If so, do it.

21 *Printing*

Printing is one of those things that's invisible when it's working, but incredibly annoying when it isn't. Printing issues, like getting your computer to recognize your printer, can be challenging across operating systems. For the most part, printing on Linux simply works. You plug in your printer, you configure it, and you're all set. But that doesn't make for a very long or exciting chapter. So the rest of this chapter is going to be about solving the challenges of printing that come up on Linux.

Why is printing a challenge across operating systems? Most of the challenge comes from printer drivers. Remember drivers from chapter 4? Drivers are the software that allow the operating system, or the Linux kernel, in our case, to talk to your hardware—in this case, the printer.

When the drivers aren't working, your computer can't talk to your printer. And that's where you run into problems. But the problems are fixable. It's not hard—it's mostly trial and error, as you'll see.

In this chapter, we're going to explore printing, learning about:

- Ubuntu's printer tool, which lets you add and configure a printer to your system. It's got a nice interface, so I usually start with this and only move to CUPS, which we'll talk about in just one moment, if I'm having trouble getting something to work with my printer, like double-sided printing.

- Common Unix Printing System (CUPS), another way to configure printers, is common across all Linux distributions, and not just Ubuntu. It's good to know how to use CUPS in case you're ever using a distribution without its own printing tool.

- Other ways to troubleshoot printer issues and avoid them before they become issues. Printers, like any device, don't all work equally well with

Linux, not so much because of the hardware, but because of the drivers that help Linux communicate with the hardware. We'll talk more about choosing a Linux-friendly printer later in this chapter.

One final note. We're going to do lots of hands-on stuff in this chapter, but it might be slightly more abstract than in previous ones, because I'm guessing some of you won't have a printer with you at lunch. However, I'm going to assume some of you are working on this chapter at home where you have access to a printer. But because I don't know what kind of printer you're using, the directions and exercises are going to be general. I'm hoping you're so relieved I don't know things about your personal life, like what kind of printer you have, that this won't detract from your enjoyment of the chapter. So let's start printing!

21.1 Installing a printer with Ubuntu's Printers tool

As I said before, Ubuntu's Printers tool has a user-friendly interface, so we're going to begin with that. The Printers tool works with CUPS. When we set up our printer using the tool, when we go into CUPS later in this chapter, everything will be configured.

I'm going to assume you're connecting to your printer via a USB cable. Even if you wish to print wirelessly, you usually begin the configuration with a USB connection. If you're using a virtual machine, you need to enable USB so the virtual machine will be able to access your printer. To do that, see the sidebar.

Try it now: Enabling USB in virtual machines

1 Plug your printer into your computer.
2 Launch VirtualBox, right-click your virtual Linux machine and click Settings.
3 Click USB and then click the icon to Add Filter from Device. If you have multiple USB devices plugged into your computer, you'll need to choose your printer.
4 Click OK and you'll have access to the printer in your virtual machine.
5 Now launch your virtual Ubuntu machine.

Virtual machine users will need to make their printer available via the Settings menu.

Once your printer is connected to your computer, launch Printers from the Dash.

To add your printer to your computer:

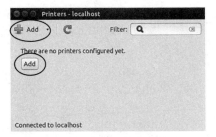

1   Click either Add button (see figure 21.1).

2   Your printer should show up as a device (see figure 21.2). Select it and click the Forward button. Don't worry if the information isn't quite right. For instance, it might not display your exact printer name or model. You'll have the chance to correct it.

Figure 21.1   The Ubuntu Printers tool allows you to add a new printer to your system.

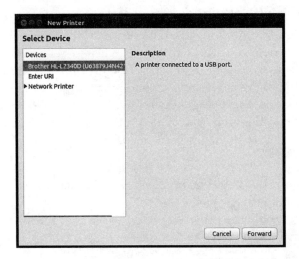

Figure 21.2   Ubuntu should detect your printer. Don't worry if the information isn't quite right.

3   Ubuntu will now look for drivers for your printer. This is where our paths will diverge a bit, depending upon your printer. Ubuntu will now give you options for installing your printer (see figure 21.3).

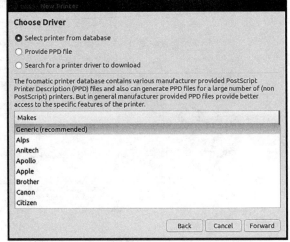

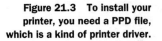

Figure 21.3   To install your printer, you need a PPD file, which is a kind of printer driver.

- Option 1 is Select printer from a database. You choose your manufacturer, then model, and Ubuntu will try to find a driver that matches it. Unfortunately, the database isn't that big and Ubuntu doesn't have access to proprietary drivers, so even if it does find a match, it's often not a good one, so you'll have problems printing.

  This option works well for HP printers, which tend to have open drivers, but doesn't work well for other manufacturers. You can always start with this option and see if it allows you to print.

  There's also you can use if your printer isn't in the database. If neither of these allows you to print, delete the printer and start over using option 2.

- Option 2 is Provide PPD file. A PPD file is a PostScript Printer Description. It's a type of printer driver that you usually download from your printer manufacturer's website.

  Unless it's an HP printer, I usually go for option 2 and download the PPD file. Just do an internet search for your printer make and model and PPD.

  Sadly, even this isn't always straightforward. For instance, my printer is a Brother HL-2340DW. Brother doesn't have the PPD file on its site, but instead has a package file (a .deb, like we learned about in chapter 17). To get the PPD, I downloaded the .deb, right-clicked, and opened it with the Ubuntu Archive Manager. (I'll show you how to do this later in this chapter.) Then I looked around the package files until I found a PPD file in the opt folder.

  Finally, I moved the PPD to the Desktop and pointed the Ubuntu Printer tool to it. After that, Ubuntu installed my printer and I was able to print.

Once you upload the PPD to the Printers tool, it will configure your printer settings for you, allowing you to print a test page (see figure 21.4).

Print the test page to make sure everything works okay. If it doesn't, delete the printer (I'll show you how in a moment) and start over, choosing a different option this time.

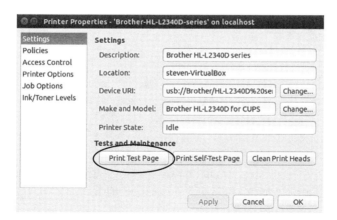

**Figure 21.4   Print a test page
to make sure your printer works.**

If you used the printer database and it didn't work, try finding the PPD online. Sometimes you have to do a little research to get a printer to work. Configuring the printer isn't hard, but it does take trial and error.

Once your printer is installed and printing, close out of the Printers tool. In the next section, I'm going to show you how to delete a printer and how to configure one.

21.1.1 Deleting and configuring printers with the Ubuntu Printers tool

The next time you open the Printers tool, you should see your printer there with a green check, meaning it's the default printer. If you right-click your printer, you'll see some options (see figure 21.5).

Let's enable double-sided printing. Right-click your printer and click the Properties link.

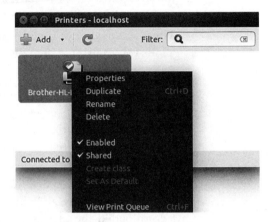

- Click the Printer Options link to do things like change your paper size and configure double-sided printing, which is controlled by the Duplex option (see figure 21.6).
- Change it to DuplexNoTumble. We'll talk more about this later in the chapter.

Figure 21.5 Right-clicking on your printer from the Printers tool lets you delete and configure your printer.

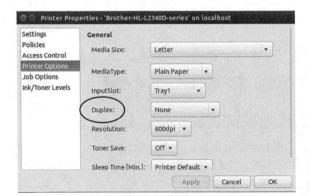

Figure 21.6 The Duplex option controls two-sided printing.

You can also use the Properties area to change other things about your printer. For instance, in the Settings area, you can change your printer URI, which will allow you to print to a WiFi printer (see figure 21.7) based upon your printer's settings.

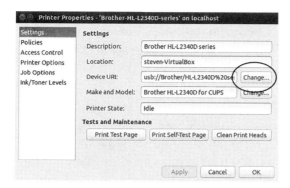

Figure 21.7 Changing your device URI will allow you to print to a Wifi printer.

To delete a printer, right-click your printer and click Delete. To see what jobs are printing, right-click your printer and use the View Print Queue link.

Now that your printer is up and running, let's take a look at CUPS. CUPS is another tool you can use to configure your printer. It's helpful to be familiar with it in case you're on a system without a user-friendly printing tool. It's also useful to know if the Ubuntu Printers tool isn't working for you.

21.2 CUPS

CUPS gives you more granular control of your printer than the Ubuntu Printers tool. Administrators often use it to configure network printers, but since most people reading this aren't running intricate network printing environments requiring policies, you probably won't use it very often at home.

It's a useful tool to explore, though, because not all Linux systems have a pretty CUPS interface like the Ubuntu Printers tool.

To access CUPS (which is standard across most distributions), you're going to use your web browser, which is kind of an odd way to interact with your local computer (although you might recall from chapter 5 that the GNOME desktop can be customized using a web interface). To see CUPS, open any web browser and go to http://localhost:631/. It should look something like figure 21.8.

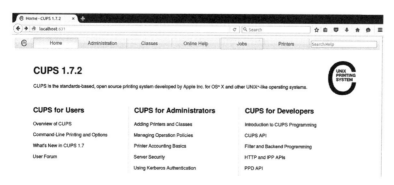

Figure 21.8 CUPS lets you control your printers through a web interface.

You'll see much of the same functionality we saw in the Ubuntu Printers tool along the top menu of CUPS, because the Ubuntu Printers tool is essentially a user-friendly CUPS interface. When you use the Ubuntu Printers tool, you're actually using CUPS:

- *Jobs* lets you see your print queue.
- *Printers* lets you see your printers.
- *Administration* lets you add more printers. It also gives you the ability to group printers into classes. Classes allow you to centrally set permissions for who can print to which printer. They also allow you to do things like set page limits on printers. These are things you'd want to do in an office environment, but most people are unlikely to need these options at home.

Click the Printers link at the top and you'll see your printer listed. If we hadn't used the Ubuntu Printers tool, we could've installed our printer via CUPS. Click on your printer and you'll see how it's configured (see figure 21.9).

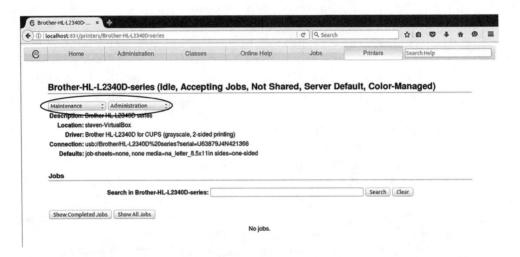

Figure 21.9   CUPS is another way to change printer settings.

If you click the Maintenance pull-down, you get options like the ability to print a test page and cancel all jobs. If you click the Modify Printer pull-down, you can do things like only allow certain users access to the printer (again, something you probably don't need at home but is helpful to a network administrator) and modify the printer.

Toggle to the Modify Printer option. You're asked for a login and password. You need to provide the credentials of someone with printer access. Remember when we looked at groups in chapter 19? Our default Ubuntu accounts are members of a group called lpadmin. That group has access to CUPS. Anyone who is part of that group can configure it and anyone who isn't a part of that group won't be able to make changes. If you want to see for yourself, go into the terminal and type `groups` to see that you're a part of that `lpadmin` group.

Once you've entered your Ubuntu username and password, you can see how your printer is connected to your computer. Click Continue to go to the next screen, where you can change your printer description and location, (which is helpful in a network situation), and set up multiple printers in a network. This lets you label where the printers are physically located instead of having a bunch of printer models in a list.

Click Continue again and you have the option to change drivers and upload new PPD files. This screen (see figure 21.10) is helpful if you're trying to get a printer installed. It's easy to try different drivers and PPD files from this screen—perhaps even easier than from the Ubuntu Printers tool.

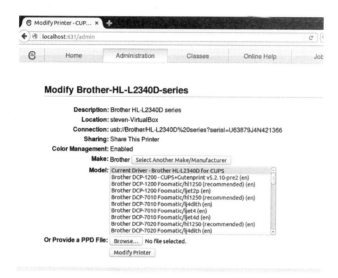

Figure 21.10   **CUPS makes it easy to tweak drivers and try new PPD files.**

If you're having trouble getting a printer installed with Linux, you might consider moving to CUPS and navigating to this screen to quickly test different configurations.

Speaking of troubleshooting printing, in the next section I'm going to give you some tips to help you troubleshoot printer issues, but even better, to help you avoid them.

21.3   *Tips for printing with Linux*

Getting a printer installed in Linux is sometimes easy, but sometimes takes work. I'm hoping things were on the easier end of the scale for you. But if they weren't, or just for future reference, here are some general tips to help you with printing on Linux:

    1   *Choose a printer carefully.* My best tip in terms of troubleshooting printer issues is to prevent them in the first place. How? By choosing a printer known to work well with Linux.

I'd love to list printers you should buy, but printers go out of production fairly quickly. The internet is the perfect format for keeping up with quickly changing hardware. Ubuntu keeps a nice list of resources here: https://help.ubuntu .com/community/Printers. Unfortunately, not every printer will work with Linux. Sometimes there are simply no drivers that will allow Linux to communicate with a printer.

In addition to manufacturer driver pages, it also links to printer manufacturers who use open drivers. As we discussed back in chapter 4, open drivers make a printer easier to install since the operating system can see everything it needs to connect to the printer. With proprietary drivers, the operating system sometimes doesn't get enough information. When that happens, your system can't talk to your printer, and you can't print.

2 *Find the PPD file.* If the internal Ubuntu database isn't working for you, find the PPD file for your printer online. Hopefully, it's on the manufacturer's website and is easy to find. But as we saw with my Brother printer, sometimes it's hidden. If there's no PPD file, but some kind of .deb or .rpm (another software package format), you can download it, open it as an archive (see figure 21.11), and poke around until you find the PPD. It's not easy but it's effective.

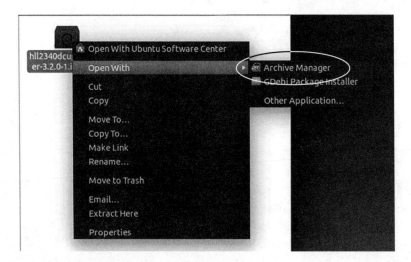

Figure 21.11 Sometimes PPD files are hidden in packages. Don't be afraid to look around.

3 *Double-Sided Printing.* We're all green. We like to save paper. So we print double-sided (assuming our printers have that ability). For whatever reason, Linux printer utilities often don't use the term double-sided. They use the term *duplex.*

- *DuplexTumble* is when you want a document whose width is greater than its length (see figure 21.12). It's also known as landscape.
- *DuplexNoTumble* is when you want a document whose length is greater than its width. This is the setting used most people probably want, since it's how we print things like reports and letters. This is also known as portrait.

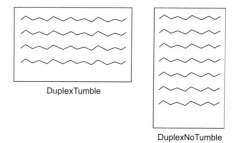

DuplexTumble

DuplexNoTumble

Figure 21.12   Linux printing systems use the terms DuplexTumble and DuplexNoTumble to indicate how a page is being flipped when printing on two sides.

4 *Leverage the challenges.* Getting a printer to work can sometimes be frustrating, but because it's not always easy, that means other people are going through the same thing, so there's usually an answer online. I mentioned some sites to look for help in chapter 4, like Unix and Linux Stack Exchange and Ask Ubuntu, but it's also helpful to search for your printer model and the word Linux or Ubuntu. If you're having trouble, someone else has, too. And they've most likely posted an answer somewhere, because Linux people are helpful like that.

5 *Print to PDF.* One of the neat things about Linux is that the printing dialog can make any document into a PDF. This doesn't help with printing to paper, but it's a neat trick to quickly made PDFs out of anything, without having to install any special software.

To make something into a PDF:

- Open a Print dialog.
- For the printer, choose Print to File (see figure 21.13).
- Name the file and choose PDF as the output format.

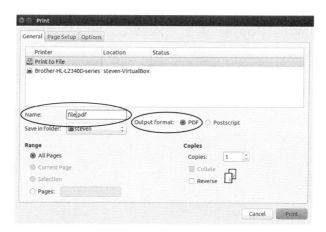

Figure 21.13   The Print dialog can be used to generate PDFs from any program.

21.4 *Wrapping up*

We learned two ways to install printers today, one using the Ubuntu Printers tool and the other using CUPS. For most users, the Ubuntu tool is fine, but it's good to be familiar with CUPS if you're planning on being a print server administrator, or just in case you're ever using a system without a more user-friendly printing utility. We also gave some tips to help you get your printer running, shown in table 21.1.

Table 21.1 **Tips for printing with Linux**

Tip	Explanation
Choose carefully	If you're using Linux and about to buy a printer, find one that works well with it.
Find the PPD	If you can find the PPD file, it's much easier to get your printer working in Linux.
Remember duplex	Duplex means double-sided.
Look for help	If you're having trouble, so has someone else. Learn from their pain.
"Print" PDFs	Printing in Linux doesn't just mean printing to paper. The print utility can also be used to make a PDF out of anything.

GLOSSARY OF TERMS

In this chapter I explained:

DuplexTumble—Landscape orientation for printing
DuplexNoTumble—Portrait orientation for printing
PostScript Printer Description (PPD)—A type of printer driver usually found on your printer manufacturer's website

21.5 *Lab*

In this chapter we discussed printing and why it can be a challenge across operating systems.

1 Is your printer working? Print a test page using the Ubuntu Printing tool. If your printer isn't working, figure out what the problem is and try to fix it. HINT: Start by reviewing the parts of the chapter about PPD files.
2 Once it's working, delete your printer and reinstall it, this time using CUPS.
3 Open Firefox and print a webpage as a PPD file.

Version control for non-programmers

You probably have a folder full of documents that say things like importantpresentation.final.odp, importantpresentation.real.final.odp, and importantpresentation.final.changesfromjen.odp. The dates the files were created might help you figure out which one is the latest version, but it can get confusing easily. Version control solves that problem by tracking document versions for you.

Version control is a process that lets you keep track of changes to electronic items. It's used by coders who might make a change that breaks things. Version controls allows them to go back to the last working version. But it's also a useful workflow for collaborating on documents. Because you now understand a lot about Linux, from installing software, to the using the command line, to printing, I thought we could end with the advanced concept of version control.

In this chapter, you're going to learn how to use version control to collaborate on a document. We're going to use a program called Git to track our files and a site called GitLab to host them. Git is the perfect tool because it's a command-line tool that you can use with graphical tools, like text editors. In other words, it uses a lot of the concepts you've spent the past month studying. Git works well with Linux and is a popular technology that you've probably heard about. It's a great next step for a brand new Linux user like you.

By the end of this chapter, you'll have your own repository set up so that you can track versions of files. This is helpful when you're collaborating, but also when you're working alone. Let's get started by learning a bit more about version control.

22.1 What is version control?

Version control allows you to track different version of files, be they code files, word processing documents, images, or sound files. As long as the file is electronic, version control can track how it is changing and remembering different versions. One of the easiest ways to understand version control, and how it can help you, is for you to understand how I'm writing this book and collaborating with my editors.

As you've probably figured out by now, I wrote a book about learning Linux in a month. I wrote it alone but with the help of my editor, Frances, and my technical editor, Gary. They read everything I write and made it better by making changes and suggestions and asking me questions within my manuscript. So we've got three people looking at and working on the same document. How do we keep everything straight without someone editing the wrong version of a file? We use version control. Our workflow looks like this:

1   I finish writing my chapter and upload my file to a central repository that only the three of us can access.
2   Gary and Frances then run a command on their computers to download the files to their computers.
3   They make their edits and upload the file when they're done. Sometimes one of them makes their changes first, and then the other downloads the more recent version of the file. But even if they both make changes at the same time, our version control system reconciles the changes for us. The result is a single document with both sets of changes.

We're all able to make changes and easily upload and download the most recent version of the file. So rather than emailing around different drafts, the most recent version is always immediately available to us. However, if there's a problem with a change, like someone accidentally deletes something we decide we want to keep, our version control system tracks the different versions of the document, so nothing is ever truly gone.

As I mentioned earlier, version control is wonderful when you're collaborating, but it's also helpful when you're working alone. It provides a history of your document without your needing to save different versions.

In the case of this book, our version control tool is Git. There are other version control tools, though. Subversion, Mercurial, and Bazaar are three examples. In terms of choosing one, you'll choose one that makes sense for you and for your collaborators. If everyone you work with likes to use Subversion, it doesn't make much sense for you to use Mercurial. But for now, let's work with Git, since it's popular and likely to be used in different workplaces and across all operating systems.

22.2   *A quick introduction to Git*

We've talked about the person who developed Git. It's Linus Torvalds, the same person who developed Linux! He created it to help with our friend, the Linux kernel, which accepts code from people around the world. Git allows multiple people to work on the kernel, letting Torvalds accept code that enhances the kernel and reject code that's faulty. Git also keeps a complete history of the kernel code, so previous versions are always available, in case something is changed that shouldn't have been.

One confusing thing about Git is that it has two components:

1 *Git, the software*, which you use from the command line of your computer
2 *Git repositories*, which are web-based and hold the content being tracked.

So while every person using the Git software is using the same program, the repositories where the content is synced and tracked can vary. If you stop to think about this, this setup makes sense. You have Git, a program on your local machine, tracking files. But you need someplace that collaborators can see and access the files, which is where the web-based repository comes in.

The most popular repository is probably GitHub, which holds the code from lots of different projects and has become a sort of living resume for people who program. But there are other repositories with which Git can be used. We're going to use the GitLab repository, which I'll discuss in the next section.

There are a few Git concepts you'll need to understand before you start using it for a project.

I'm going to show you everything you need to get started using it for a very simple project, but if you really want to know what Git can do, I *highly* recommend *Learn Git in a Month of Lunches*, by Rick Umali (Manning 2015). I know for a fact you're almost done with this book, and you're probably looking for something to do with your lunch hours.

Here are some basic commands you'll use regularly.

- `git add` adds files to Git so they're tracked.
- `git commit` is used to signal your intent to submit a file into the repository. It also allows you add a message to your changes so collaborators have a sense of what changed. In my case, a commit message might be something like "2Fixed chart with Git commands."
- `git push origin master` submits your changes to the repository. (Origin is our online repository and master is the name of the part of repository we're using; Git chooses these names for us.)
- `git pull` downloads the most recent versions of files from your repository. This is how you make sure you're working with the most recent versions of files.

We're going to work through these commands later in the chapter.

In order to collaborate with someone, you need a Git repository. In the next section, you're going to learn about repositories, using the example of GitLab.

22.3 Using GitLab as a repository

As I mentioned, there are lots of web-based repositories. Some are hosted, but you can also host your own repository on your own server. We're going to use GitLab because it allows you to create free private repositories, meaning the whole world won't be able to see your files—only your collaborators. GitHub, which is probably more popular, charges for private repositories, which is why we're not using it. However, for some projects you might want a public repository.

Open source projects tend to have public repositories, because the code needs to be publicly available, and contributors can be everyone and not necessarily anyone known to the people running the project. But even people creating non-code-based projects might want a public repository. If you're creating open education resources, which are shareable lessons, syllabi, and assignments, you probably want as many people as possible to have access, so you'd host them using a public repository. Anyone wishing to use your materials could easily download them, but they could also offer their modified versions of your work. In essence, you could begin to collaborate with people you've never met!

For the purposes of this chapter, though, we're going to create a private repository in GitLab.

Try it now: creating a private Git repository

1 Go to GitLab (www.gitlab.com) and create an account.
2 Once you have confirmed your email address, you'll be able to log in.
3 Click New Project.

We're going to configure our repository in GitLab.

4 Make the project path end in `linuxlunches` and keep the visibility level private so that no one can see your repository without your permission.

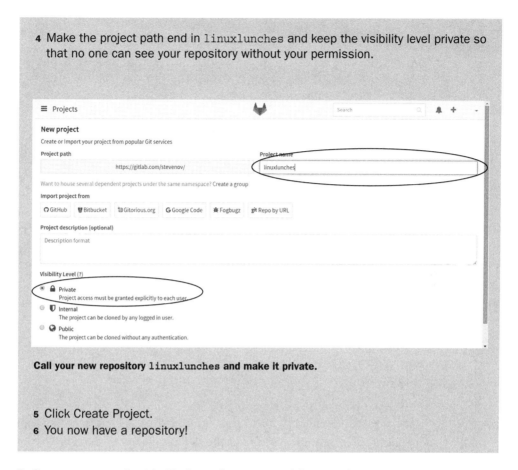

Call your new repository `linuxlunches` and make it private.

5 Click Create Project.
6 You now have a repository!

Before you can work with Git from the command line, you're going to need to add an SSH key to your profile. Remember SSH from chapter 20? SSH is a way to securely connect one computer to another.

This key will help GitLab authorize you to use the repository. It's an added measure of security used by Git and repositories. It allows you to authenticate with the repository without using a password. Instead, your SSH server will use the key you create to verify your identity.

SSH keys have two parts: a private key that only you can access and a public key that you can share widely. The two are used together to verify your identity. To add a key, either click the link at the top of the page (see figure 22.1) or visit https://gitlab.com/profile/keys/new.

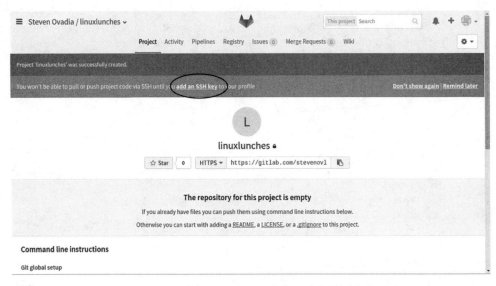

Figure 22.1   GitLab has you add an SSH key to your account to help keep it secure.

22.3.1 Generating an SSH key for GitLab

To generate an SSH key, we're going to go back to Linux on our own computer and open the terminal:

1   Use the command `ssh-keygen -t rsa -C "email address you used for your GitLab account"`. Make sure your email address is in quotation marks.
2   Click enter to save the SSH file in the default location, which is what we want in this case.
3   Create a password for your key and write it down in a secure place.
4   You now have an SSH key to help GitLab see you are who you say you are.
5   To generate the public key, which is safe to share, use the command `cat ~/.ssh/id_rsa.pub`.
6   You'll see a long string of text beginning with `ssh-rsa` and ending with your email address. Copy and paste this into the GitLab key page and click Add key.

You have your GitLab repository configured. Now it's time to work with Git.

22.4   Connecting to your repository with Git

The first thing you need to do is install the Git package on your computer. Conveniently enough, the package is called `git`.

22.4.1 Creating your Git identity

Once `git` installed, you need to tell Git who you are. You'll do that with two commands. The first one will set up your email and the second will set up your name. This will let your collaborators know who's doing what in the repository:

```
1  git config --global user.email "your email address"
2  git config --global user.name "your name"
```

Once you've done that, create a folder called repo in your Documents directory and navigate into it via the command line. This folder is where we'll add the repository we just created in GitLab. To get the address for your repository, go into GitLab and click the link for your project. You should see an SSH link for your repository that begins git@gitlab.com: (see figure 22.2). Copy the link.

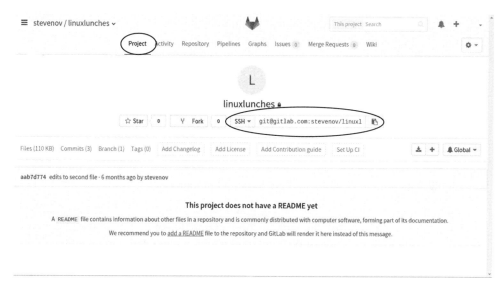

Figure 22.2   GitLab will tell you the address for your repository, which you'll need to tell Git.

22.4.2 Cloning a repository

Now that we have the address for our repository, we can tell Git to clone it, or copy it into that repo directory on our local computer.

1 The command to copy the repository is git clone and the full git@gitlab.com link you just copied.
2 You'll be asked for the password for your key. It's a good thing you wrote it down someplace secure! You should now see a linuxlunches directory in your repo folder.

22.4.3 Adding files to your web-based repository

While you were cloning the repository, you probably saw a message that it's empty. That's fine. Let's add a file now. Go into the linuxlunches directory within the repo folder. Create a file called firstfile.txt. To upload it to your repository:

1 git add firstfile.txt. Git is now tracking this file.

2   To prepare the file for upload, use `git commit -m "My first file"` (see fig-
    ure 22.3). The file is ready to be uploaded to the repository.

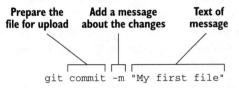

Prepare the   **Add a message**   **Text of**
file for upload **about the changes** **message**

`git commit -m "My first file"`

**Figure 22.3   When committing a file
with Git, it's good to add a descriptive
message about your changes.**

3   To finish the job, use the command `git push origin master`. This will push
    the committed file, or files, to the repository.

Go into your GitLab repository via the web interface and click Files. You'll see your
empty file in the repository. You just uploaded your first file via Git! Now, let's see how
we would pull down files someone else added to the repository.

22.4.4 *Pulling files from your web-based repository*

Since we're not collaborating with anyone yet, we probably shouldn't wait for someone to add a file to your repository. We can do it ourselves, this time using the web
interface:

1   Click the + sign on the right side of your screen and add a new file (see figure
    22.4). Call the file mysecondfile.txt, write some text in the text box, and scroll
    down to add a commit message, which is required.

2   Then, click Commit Changes.

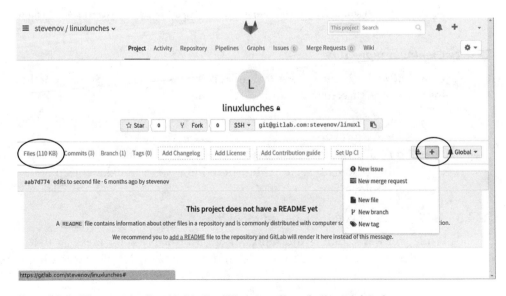

Figure 22.4   Files can also be added to the GitLab repository via the web interface.

Go back to your Linux system. To get the latest versions of files, use the `git pull` command. The new file will be downloaded, or pulled, into your linuxlunches folder. This command is how you know you're working with the latest versions of files on your local computer.

22.4.5 *Viewing the history of files*

As I mentioned earlier, version control lets you track how your files are changing. Let's change a file and look at the changes. Back on your Linux system, open mysecondfile.txt and add text to it. We're going to upload it back into our repository. To do so, use the same commands as before:

1 `git add mysecondfile.txt` tells Git to begin tracking the file.
2 `git commit -m "edits to second file"` prepares the file to be loaded with a message about our changes.
3 `git push origin master` uploads the file into the repository.

Now we can see the history of the file in GitLab:

1 Toggle back to GitLab and click Files.
2 Click mysecondfile.txt.
3 You'll see the file in your browser. Click History (see figure 22.5)
4 Click the latest version of the file, which will be at the top of the list.

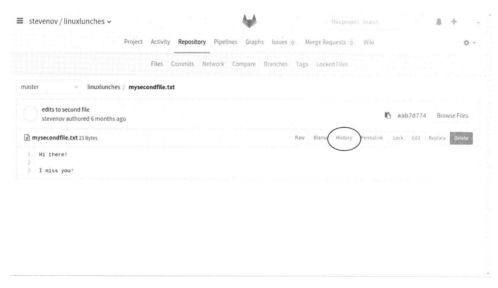

Figure 22.5   You can track the history of a file via GitLab's web interface.

5   You can see how the file has changed: deletions are red and begin with a - sign; additions are green and begin with a + sign (see figure 22.6).

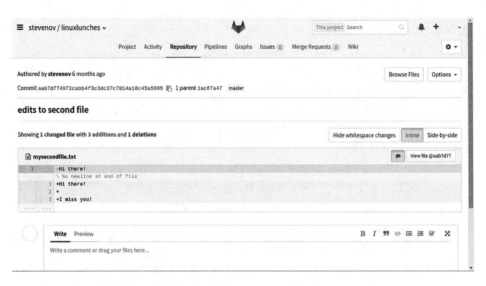

Figure 22.6   GitLab shows you additions and deletions to your file.

You can probably see how this is helpful. For instance, let's say you had an earlier draft with a great paragraph in it. Let's also say you deleted that paragraph because you thought you didn't need it. But now you do! Having the whole history of the document in your repository lets you go back and grab the text you need—assuming you've been diligently pushing your changes to the repository. It's a great safety net that lets you see how code and text evolve as you create it.

This also shows you why descriptive commit messages are so important! They allow you to see what you changed without reading through lots of files. But what about situations where it's not only you creating text?

22.4.6   *Sharing your repository*

The workflow so far is good for us, but what if you're like me and want to share your repository? For instance, let's say you work on a podcast with three different people around the world and you want everyone to be able to contribute to the show notes. In that situation, you might use Git to collaboratively track the script.

You can add members to your project through the GitLab interface:

1   Go into your project, click the gear icon on the right, and select Members (see figure 22.7).

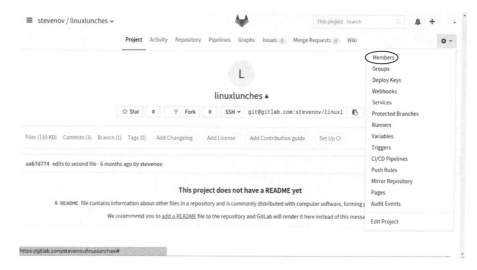

Figure 22.7   The GitLab web interface lets you add collaborators.

2   Search for your collaborators by name or by email (see figure 22.8). If they have
    GitLab accounts, they'll turn up. Otherwise, you'll be given the option to invite
    them into the project. They'll need to create GitLab accounts to have access to
    your repository.

3   You can also choose the level of project access your collaborators will have to
    the repository. If you want them to be able to pull down your project, you'll
    need to give them access higher than guest.

4   When you're done adding collaborators, click Add Users to Project and your
    collaborators are all set.

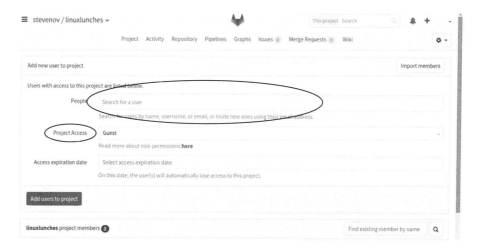

Figure 22.8   You can search for collaborators by name or email address.

22.5   *Wrapping up*

That was a *very* quick and limited look at using Git to collaborate on projects. However, it's more than enough to allow you to start using Git and a repository for revision control purposes, alone or working with others. While tools like Git are closely associated with code, as you just saw, you can use it with anything. I encourage you to play with Git because it's an amazing tool. It's great to use it to track your own documents, but it's even better if you're collaborating on a project with someone else.

It lets you track the history of your files and is a fantastic way to easily collaborate on a document without sending a million emails or using a web-based editor, like Google Docs. And if you want a job in a technology-related field, it's a great skill to have on your resume.

Table 22.1 is a table of the Git commands I covered today.

Table 22.1   Git commands

Command	Explanation
`git config --global user.email` `"your email address"`	Configures your email address in Git
`git config --global` `user.name "your name"`	Configures your display name in Git
`git clone address of respository`	Copies a new repository to your local computer. You use this the first time you're working with a new repository.
`git add`	Adds files to Git so that they're being tracked.
`git commit`	Signals your intent to submit a file into the repository and allows you to add a message to summarize your changes.
`git push origin master`	Submits your changes to the repository
`git pull`	Downloads the most recent versions of files from your repository

GLOSSARY OF TERMS

In this chapter I explained:

SSH key—A method of verifying your identity. It's made up of a private key, which only you have access to, and a public key you can share.

Version control—The process of tracking changes to electronic items.

22.6   *Lab*

In this chapter we learned about tracking our files with Git and hosting them on Git-Lab. Your assignment is to:

1 Create a new public project from scratch in GitLab.
2 Push a file to the project from the terminal.
3 Add a file to the project via the web interface.
4 Pull in the file using Git.

Bonus

Make your project private using the web interface.

Never the end 23

Congratulations! You made it through the book! You now know Linux. But the journey of learning doesn't end here. What happens next? That's up to you.

You have a whole world of software, distributions, desktop environments, and commands to explore. But having a whole world in front of you can sometimes feel intimidating. So in this final chapter, I'll point you to some places to take your new-found knowledge. But in general, I encourage you to:

- Take the plunge into Linux by installing it on hardware, if you haven't done that yet. Virtualization and live sessions are a wonderful way to begin to learn Linux, but you'll be amazed how much more you learn when you're using it regularly on its own hardware. Yes, there will be occasional issues to trouble-shoot, but that's how you learn. But if you're anything like me, once you're using Linux full-time, you'll find you work much more efficiently, since you have much more control over your system.
- Play with different distributions and desktop environments. We used Ubuntu and Unity, but as I've mentioned, there are many other distributions and desktops. There's always a learning curve when you try a new distribution, and an even greater one if you try one that isn't Debian-based, like Ubuntu—but I always walk away from a new distribution having learned something, whether it's a preferred way to install software or a slightly different desktop environment configuration.

  I learn just as much from new desktop environments. Exploring new distributions and desktops keeps your mind open and flexible to new computing ideas. Plus, it's like a fun little vacation from your usual computer setup, whatever it is.

Of course, installing Linux directly on hardware and trying new distributions might create some challenges. Let's recap where to go for help.

23.1 *Finding help with Linux*

We talked about where to go for help in chapter 4 and at various other points in this book. I want to recap them here, so you have them all in one place, but also to remind you that there's always a lot of help and support available to you:

- My go-to troubleshooting tool is an internet search. I go to my preferred search engine, DuckDuckGo (www.duckduckgo.com), and search for the issue. Usually, there's an error message or something in the log file to help narrow the search. But I've even done searches like "sound stuck Ubuntu" to see what comes back.

  The reality is, as you get to know your hardware and distribution, you'll learn which aspects tend to be the troublemakers. You'll also have better vocabulary to describe your particular problems.

- UNIX and Linux Stack Exchange (http://unix.stackexchange.com/) is the site where users can vote on answers. Answers from here tend to turn up in my search results, so there's often no need to search here directly. However, if I have a very technical issue, I'll often cut out the middle person of an internet search and come here directly for an answer. +Ask Ubuntu_ (http://askubuntu.com/) is the Ubuntu-centric version of this site, although the answers often apply to other distributions.

- The ArchWiki (https://wiki.archlinux.org/) is an amazingly comprehensive resource, with information on configuring and installing software, as well as great explanations of how certain processes work with Linux. While it's a product of the Arch Linux community and has an Arch Linux bent, much of the information is useful for *any* distribution.

- The Ubuntu Wiki (https://wiki.ubuntu.com/), though not as complete and a bit more narrow in its scope, is also helpful in a similar way—especially if you're an Ubuntu user. But less so if you're not. Ubuntu also has its own forums (http://ubuntuforums.org/). The information there can be a bit more hit-or-miss. It tends to be a last resort for me since it lacks the voting seen in UNIX and Linux Stack Exchange and Ask Ubuntu. However, the Ubuntu forums have gotten me out of a few odd Ubuntu-centric issues, so it's worth considering.

- Most distributions also have their own forums and help areas. None are as good as the ArchWiki, but they're a great place to search for distribution-specific help.

- The Manning Forums (https://forums.manning.com/) are another place to get help, especially if you need help with something pertaining to this book!

Now that you're done with the book, you might find yourself wondering how you find out about new, cool Linux things. Don't worry! I've got that covered.

23.2 *Finding Linux news*

How do you find out about all of the neat things you can do with Linux? How do you stay on top of changes, enhancements, and new projects? There are a few sites I visit regularly:

- Like many people, I get a lot of my news from Linux people on Twitter. If you're a Twitter person, you can follow me @steven_ovadia. I also have a Twitter list of Linux-y people here: https://twitter.com/steven_ovadia/lists/linux.
- LXer (http://lxer.com/) is a Linux news aggregator with news from lots of different Linux sites. It's comprehensive, but overwhelming. If you only have time to check one site each day, this is probably the one you're going to check.
- The Linux Foundation's news page (https://www.linux.com/news), in addition to news, has nice tutorials and software and distribution reviews. The Linux Foundation is a non-profit that supports Linux (actually paying Linus Torvalds to work on it) and promotes Linux.
- Whatever you think of reddit, the Linux subreddit (www.reddit.com/r/linux/) always has interesting links and news. There are also distribution-specific subreddits. Some are better than others. For instance, the subreddits for the less popular distributions tend to be quiet. I spend most of my time in the Linux subreddit and I don't feel like I miss much.
- Opensource.com (https://opensource.com/) is supported by Red Hat, a company that creates and supports Linux distributions for companies. It's also the company behind Fedora, one of the Linux distributions we discussed in chapter 2. Opensource.com isn't purely Linux news. However, since it focuses on free and open source software, a lot of the content relates to Linux in some way.
- My Linux Rig (http://mylinuxrig.com/) is my Linux blog. There's Linux news but I also interview Linux users about their Linux setups, so you get to learn what tools people are using with their Linux systems. I started this site because I'm always curious about how people configure their Linux systems. If you've ever creepily stared at someone's laptop setup in a coffee shop, trying to figure out what they're using, you might enjoy this site.

Linux is more than just a fun hobby, though. You can also make a career out of it. We're going to discuss some paths to doing that in the next section.

23.3 *Using Linux professionally*

System administration is a common career path for people wishing to use Linux professionally. System administrators, or SysAdmins, are responsible for keeping servers running. They work everywhere, from banks to hospitals to stock exchanges. While we covered a lot this month, you probably don't know quite enough to jump right into this field. Yet. You now know more than enough to begin to study for one of the certifications.

23.3.1   *Do you need a certification?*

I don't work in IT nor do I work as a SysAdmin, so I asked a bunch of my friends who are SysAdmins. They said that a certification isn't always necessary, but they're usually required for large corporations. Smaller companies, like startups, might be more interested in your skills and experience. So if you go from this book to teaching yourself system administration, you might qualify for certain jobs.

23.3.2   *Which certification?*

Some of the major Linux certifications include:

- Red Hat (www.redhat.com/en/services/certification)
- Linux Professional Institute (www.lpi.org/our-certifications/summary-of-certifications)
- Linux+ (https://certification.comptia.org/certifications/linux)
- Oracle Linux (http://education.oracle.com/)
- Linux Foundation (https://training.linuxfoundation.org/certification).

Most of my friends recommended the various Red Hat certifications, as they're widely known and respected and require hands-on knowledge and not just an exam. However, if you're just getting started, the Red Hat certification might be a bit advanced.

In that case, they recommend the Linux+ certification, which is more general than the Red Hat certification. The Linux+ is three certifications in one, so if you pass, you also have the LPIC-1 certification from the Linux Professional Institute and the SUSE Certified Linux Administrator. After the Linux+, you're in a better position to move forward with the Red Hat certifications, if that's something you want. But you also might be able to use the Linux+ certification to get a job at a smaller company, where you could grow your SysAdmin skills on the job.

After figuring out which certification is right for you, it's a matter of studying for the test, taking advantage of training materials, and perhaps even taking a class, online or face-to-face. Each of the certification sites has links to connect you with the kind of training you want, although the training isn't free.

For many people looking into becoming a SysAdmin, the challenge is getting used to Linux. Your advantage is that you're already used to it! You spent a month working with it! So you're already well-positioned to take the next step in your career, should you want to.

I encourage you talk to SysAdmins in your city. Ask them about the market where you live and ask them what kind of certifications *they* think are important. Not only will you get great information about your local job market, but you'll also meet a bunch of people who might wind up hiring you!

23.4   *Wrapping up*

And now for my final note. I want to remind you that you can use Linux professionally without being a SysAdmin. I'm an academic librarian who uses Linux for all of his research and writing (including the writing of this book). There are lots of non-technical people who use Linux for their professional work:

- There are journalists who use it for writing.
- There are musicians who use Linux to write and record.
- There are artists who use Linux for everything from creating logos to editing photos.

They use it for many reasons. For some, Linux represents a way to save money, because it's cost-free and it runs well on older hardware. Other people choose Linux because it's customizable, allowing you to choose and tweak your computing experience. And others use Linux because they relate to the free and open software aesthetic.

My hope is you now see the potential of Linux and make it a part of your daily life. Maybe it will be a part of your daily life as a SysAdmin, but as you can now see, it can also be a part of your daily life as a teacher or small business owner or property manager. If you use a computer for your work, Linux can move that work forward!

Answer key

Chapter 4

1 How would you find out what kind of wireless card you have on your computer?
   Answer: `lspci -v`
2 Where do you find your computer's log files?
   Answer: /var/log directory or System Log.

Chapter 6

1 What happens when you go to the homework bookmark? Did homeworkfile move with it?
   Answer: The file moved with it.

Extra credit

1 How would you see the properties of a file?
   Answer: Right-click and then Properties.
2 How would you see the properties of a folder?
   Answer: Right-click and then Properties.
3 How do you make a shortcut to a file or folder?
   Answer: Right-click and then Make Link.

Chapter 7

1 How do you initiate a search in Synaptic?
   Answer: Use the search box in the middle of the screen.
2 How do you initiate a search in the Ubuntu Software Center?
   Answer: Use the search box on the right side of the screen.

Chapter 8

1 Use LibreOffice Calc to compute the average of 10, 15, 19, and 18.
   Answer: Use the formula `=AVERAGE(10, 15, 19, 18)`.

2   Download GIMP and try to scale an image from archive.org, this time making it bigger.

    Answer: Image → Scale image.

3   Use Rhythmbox to install the song lyric plugin. HINT: It's under Tools.

    Answer: Tools → Plugins → Song lyrics → Close.

Chapter 9

1   Install Emacs using the terminal.

    Answer: `sudo apt-get install emacs`

Advanced lab

1   Open the file in Vim and copy and paste each line so each one appears twice in the file.

    Answer: Use `:y` and `p`.

Chapter 10

1   Create a folder within your Documents folder and call it command_line _homework.

    Answer: `mkdir command_line_homework`

2   In the command_line_homework folder, create a document called homework-file.

    Answer:

```
cd command_line_homework
touch homeworkfile
```

3   Move homeworkfile into linux.lunches

    Answer: `mv homeworkfile ../linux.lunches`

4   Go into linux.lunches and make another file called homework2

    Answer:

```
cd ..
cd linux.lunches/
touch homework2
```

5   Copy homeworkfile into Documents

    Answer: `cp homeworkfile ..`

6   Delete *homework2* from *linux.lunches*

    Answer: `rm homework2`

7   Delete *command_line_homework*

    Answer:

```
cd ..
cd command_line_homework
rm homeworkfile
```

```
cd ..
rmdir command_line_homework
```

Advanced lab

1 Create three .txt files in a single directory called recursive

Answer:

```
mkdir recursive
cd recursive
touch 1.txt
touch 2.txt
touch 3.txt
```

2 Copy recursive to your desktop.

Answer:

```
cd ..
cp -R recursive ../Desktop
```

3 Use a single wildcard command to delete all three recursive .txt files at once.

Answer:

```
cd ..
cd Desktop
cd recursive
rm *.txt
```

Chapter 11

1 What command would you use to shut down all instances of Firefox? Open Firefox and use that command to force it closed.

Answer: `killall firefox`

2 What command would you use to find audio information in your hardware configuration? Run that command to locate yours.

Answer: `lspci -v | grep Audio`

3 What command would you use to download a PDF of the U.S. Constitution from http://mng.bz/o25h. Use `wget` to download it.

Answer: `wget http://constitutioncenter.org/media/files/constitution .pdf`

4 Which command requires the PID of the process to shut it down? Open Firefox and use that command to shut it down.

Answer: `top`

Advanced lab

1 Use the `wget` command to download the plain-text version of *Debian GNU/ Linux : Guide to Installation and Usage* from Project Gutenberg (http://www .gutenberg .org/ebooks/6527.txt.utf-8).

Answer: `wget http://www.gutenberg.org/ebooks/6527.txt.utf-8`

2 Use `grep` to search the file for the word linux, but make the search case insenstive.

Answer: `grep 'linux\|Linux' 6527.txt.utf-8`

Chapter 12

1 Install the Midori web browser on your computer using the command line.

Answer: `sudo apt-get install midori`

2 Remove it using the command line.

Answer: `sudo apt-get remove midori`

3 Find all of the mentions of root in the manual for sudo.

Answer:

```
man sudo
/root
```

4 Use a single-line command to copy the sudo manual text file called sudo.txt.

Answer: `man sudo > sudo.txt`

Advanced lab

1 Pipe the output of your `grep` search from the previous lab (a search for Linux or linux) into a text file called linux.txt.

Answer: `grep 'linux\|Linux' 6527.txt.utf-8 > linux.txt`

Chapter 13

1 Install Guake and Terminator using the command line, if you haven't already done so.

Answer:

```
sudo apt-get install guake
sudo apt-get install terminator
```

2 Use autocomplete to move into your Documents directory

Answer: `cd Doc <Tab>`

3 Now, pipe the output of history into a text file.

Answer: `history > history.txt`

4 Go into Guake and look at your history. How does it compare to the output from the default terminal?

Answer: The history is the same.

5 Configure Guake to launch with the F11 command.

Answer: Guake preferences → Keyboard shortcuts

6 Split Terminator into four windows in a grid of 2 x 2.

Answer: Ctrl-Shift-E, Ctrl-Shift-O in each vertical terminal

7 Type apt and then Tab twice. What happens? What does that output mean?

Answer: These are the commands beginning with apt

Chapter 14

1 Return your terminal prompt to its original state.

   Answer: Remove `export PS1="\u@\h:\w \d\\$ \[$(tput sgr0)\]"` from .bashrc.

2 Return your GRUB to its original state so it boots and closes without any messages.

   Answer: Return `GRUB_CMDLINE_LINUX_DEFAULT="quiet splash"` to the GRUB file (/etc/default/grub), replacing `GRUB_CMDLINE_LINUX_DEFAULT=""`. Don't forget you need to do this as root and run `sudo update-grub` after making the change.

3 Use the terminal to delete your hidden file (mynewhiddenfile).

   Answer: `rm .mynewhiddenfile`

4 Pipe a list of all of the files and directories in your home directory, including the hidden ones, into a hidden file.

   Answer: `ls -A > .hiddendirectories.txt`

5 Save a file called important.txt in your tmp directory and restart your computer. What happens to the file? Why does it happen?

   Answer: It disappears because the tmp directory isn't persistent storage—it's just for temporary files.

Chapter 15

1 Use Wine to uninstall the Savings Bond Wizard.

   Answer: Uninstall Wine Software → Savings Bond Wizard → Remove.

2 Use Wine to create a D: drive on a USB, as you might do if you want to keep your Wine programs off your main hard drive.

   Answer: Configure Wine → Add Drive → D: → Browse path to USB drive.

3 Play only one game of Solitaire. If anyone asks what you're doing, tell them it's homework for this book.

   Answer: "I'm not playing. I'm learning Linux! Sheesh!"

Chapter 16

1 Use GNOME Do to create a folder on your Desktop called testfolder.

   Answer: GNOME Do → type `testfolder` → Tab → Create New Folder.

2 Use Kupfer to move that folder into Documents.

   Answer: Kupfer → type `testfolder` → Tab → Move To... → Tab → Documents.

3 Use GNOME Do to create a file on your Desktop called linuxlunches.doc.

   Answer: GNOME Do → type `linuxlunches.doc` → Tab → Create New File.

4 Use Kupfer to open the linuxlunches.doc file with gedit.

   Answer: Kupfer → type `linuxlunches.doc` → Tab → Open With... → Tab → gedit

5 Map gedit to Ctrl-Shift-G.

Answer: Keyboard → Shortcuts → + → Name: gedit; Command: gedit → Click on Disabled to map.

Advanced lab

Assign a key combination to the `xkill` command we used in chapter 11. Use that shortcut to kill an open program.

Answer: Keyboard → Shortcuts → + → Name: xkill; Command: xkill → Click on Disabled to map to shortcut.

Chapter 17

1 Use only commands to install the Atom text editor. Its PPA is ppa:webupd8team/atom and details can be found on the project page at https://launchpad.net/~webupd8team/+archive/ubuntu/atom

Answer:

```
sudo add-apt-repository ppa:webupd8team/atom
sudo apt-get update
sudo apt-get install atom
```

2 What dependencies does Atom have?

Answer: gconf2, gconf-service, libgtk2.0-0, libudev0, libudev1, libgcrypt11, libgcrypt20, libgnome-keyring0, gir1.2-gnomekeyring-1.0, libnotify4, libxtst6, libnss3, python, gvfs-bin, xdg-utils, libdbus-1-3, libcap2.

3 Remove Kupfer and its dependencies.

Answer: `sudo apt-get --purge remove kupfer`

Chapter 18

1 What version of Firefox is on your system? What version is in the Arch repositories? What does this tell you about how frequently Firefox is updated for Ubuntu?

Answer: In Ubuntu, Firefox is 45.0.1, as of this writing. In Arch, Firefox is 45.0.1-5, as of this writing. Firefox is updated more frequently in Arch because it's a rolling release, although the two versions are close, as you can see by the version numbers.

2 What is the difference between the `update` command and the `upgrade` command?

Answer: `update` downloads the updates, but `upgrade` installs them.

3 Configure the Ubuntu Software Updater to automatically download security updates.

Answer: Software & Updates → Updates → When there are security updates: → Download and install automatically.

4   Configure the Ubuntu Software Updater to immediately show non-security related updates.

    Answer: Software & Updates → Updates → When there are other updates: → Display immediately.

5   Go to the Gentoo repository at https://packages.gentoo.org/. How do its Firefox and LibreOffice holdings compare to Arch and Ubuntu? Are they older or newer? By how much?

    Answer: Gentoo's Firefox is at 45.0.1, as of this writing, which is slightly older than Arch but the same as Ubuntu. Gentoo's LibreOffice is at 5.1.2.2, as of this writing. Arch is at 5.1.1-4, as of this writing, which is slightly older. Ubuntu's LibreOffice is 4.2.8.2, which is much older than both.

Chapter 19

1   Create an administrator account named tommy. Does this account have access to sudo? How do you know?

    Answer: User Accounts → Unlock → + → Account Type: Administrator → tommy; tommy

    If you use groups tommy you'll see the account is in the sudo group.

2   Delete the account using the command line. (If you get a message that the user is being used by a process, you can kill the process with the sudo kill -9 and the process number.)

    Answer: sudo userdel -r tommy

3   What happens when you try to save a file in the unmounted Private directory? Why does this happen?

    Answer: You get a message you don't have permission. You can't access an encrypted directory without first unlocking it.

4   Install Gufw (package name gufw) and create a rule denying traffic out from the application BitTorrent (figures 19.9 and 19.10).

    Answer: + → Policy: Deny → Direction: Out → Application: BitTorrent.

5   Turn off the firewall.

    Answer: sudo ufw disable

Chapter 20

1   Enable the firewall of your virtual machine and then SSH into it. Are you able to connect to the remote machine?

    Answer: Yes.

2   What happens if you block SSH in the virtual machine with sudo ufw deny ssh/tcp?

    Answer: You can't connect.

3   Use `PSCP` (or `scp` if your host machine is Linux or OS X) to move the hi file to
    your local machine.
    Answer: `scp  user@ip:Desktop/hi  Desktop` (Linux/OS) or `pscp  user@ip`
    `:Desktop/hi Desktop` (Windows)

4   Can you update and upgrade your virtual machine via SSH? If so, do it.
    Answer: Yes.

Chapter 22

1   Create a new public project from scratch in GitLab.
    Answer: New Project → Public → Create Project

2   Push a file to the project from the terminal.
    Answer:

```
git add your file
git commit -m "your commmit message"
git push origin master
```

3   Add a file to the project via the web interface.
    Answer: Files → + → New file → Commit Changes

4   Pull in the file using Git.
    Answer: `git pull`

Bonus question

Make your project private using the web interface.
    Answer: Gear icon → Edit project → Visibility Level → Private

index

q! command 118, 148
y command 118
Vim text editor 93–95, 116–118
VirtualBox 29, 172, 210
virtualization 20, 29, 172–174,
    179
viruses 220–222, 227
    antiviruses 220–222
    whether Linux is immune
        to 220
VLC Video Player 109–110
VM (virtual machine) 20

W

web-based repositories
    adding files to 257–258
    pulling files from 258–259
wget command-line
    application 139–140
Wicd 233

Wikipedia 155, 222
wildcards 131
Windows image 172
Windows programs
    lab 179
    terminology related to 179
    virtualization and 172–174
    Wine application 175–178
Wine application 175–178
WinMD5Free 28
wired connection 231
wireless card 32
wireless connection 231
workflow
    file/application
        launchers 181–188
        GNOME Do 181–185
        Kupfer 185–188
    keyboard shortcuts 188–191
        KDE 190–191
        Unity/GNOME 189–190

Xfce 191
    lab 192
    terminology related to 192
writing with text editors 120–121

X

Xfce 53–55, 191
    customizing 54
    interface 53–54
    keyboard shortcuts 191
    software 54–55
xkcd comic 145
xkill command 137–138
Xubuntu 54, 57

Y

y command, Vim 118
YaST (Yet Another Setup Tool)
    Control Center 84